STUDY ABROAD

PERSPECTIVES AND EXPERIENCES FROM BUSINESS SCHOOLS

ADVANCES IN INTERNATIONAL MARKETING

Series Editor: S. Tamer Cavusgil

ADVANCES IN INTERNATIONAL MARKETING   VOLUME 13

STUDY ABROAD

PERSPECTIVES AND EXPERIENCES FROM BUSINESS SCHOOLS

EDITED BY

G. TOMAS M. HULT

Michigan State University, USA

and

ELVIN C. LASHBROOKE

Michigan State University, USA

2003

JAI
An imprint of Elsevier Science

Amsterdam – Boston – London – New York – Oxford – Paris
San Diego – San Francisco – Singapore – Sydney – Tokyo

ELSEVIER SCIENCE Ltd
The Boulevard, Langford Lane
Kidlington, Oxford OX5 1GB, UK

First edition 2003

Library of Congress Cataloging-in-Publication Data

Roundtable on Study Abroad Programs in Business Schools (2001 : East Lansing, Mich.)
Study abroad : perspectives and experiences from business schools / edited by G. Tomas
M. Hult and Elvin C. Lashbrooke.
p. cm. – (Advances in international marketing; v. 13)
Selected papers from the Roundtable on Study Abroad Programs in Business Schools,
held Sept. 2001 at East Lansing, Mich.
Includes bibliographical references.
ISBN 0-7623-0989-X
1. Business education – Congresses. 2. Business schools – Congresses. 3. Foreign study – Congresses.
4. American students – Foreign countries – Congresses. I. Hult, G. Tomas M. II. Lashbrooke, E. C.
III. Title. IV. Series.

HF1009.5.A39 vol. 13
[HF1111]
658.8′48 s–dc21
[650′.071′1]   2002192741

ISBN: 0-7623-0989-X
ISSN: 1474-7979 (Series)

CONTENTS

vi

LIST OF CONTRIBUTORS

Cindy Felbeck Chalou	Michigan State University, USA
Janice E. Clark	University of Connecticut, USA
Marc Dollinger	Indiana University, USA
Sharon Doyle	Indiana University, USA
David P. Earwicker	San Diego State University, USA
James R. Emore	University of Akron, USA
Marion Festing	ESCP-EAP European School of Management, Germany
Kenneth M. Holland	University of Memphis, USA
G. Tomas M. Hult	Michigan State University, USA
Edward C. Ingraham	Michigan State University, USA
Ben L. Kedia	University of Memphis, USA
Bruce D. Keillor	University of Akron, USA
Orlando R. Kelm	University of Texas at Austin, USA
Sally Innis-Klitz	University of Connecticut, USA
Elvin C. Lashbrooke, Jr.	Michigan State University, USA
Steven J. Loughrin-Sacco	San Diego State University, USA
Ivy McQuiddy	University of Texas at Austin, USA

R. D. Nair	University of Wisconsin-Madison, USA
Andrea Poehling	University of Wisconsin-Madison, USA
Kathleen Sideli	Indiana University, USA
Joan D. Solaun	University of Illinois, Urbana-Champaign, USA
Inge Ellen Steglitz	Michigan State University, USA
Michael Vande Berg	Georgetown University, USA
Jerry Wilcox	University of Texas at Austin, USA
Annagene Yucas	University of Pittsburgh, USA

PREFACE

This special volume of *Advances in International Marketing* is guest-edited by Professors G. Tomas M. Hult and Elvin C. Lashbrooke, Jr. of Michigan State University. The entire volume addresses a variety of topics relating to study abroad programs in business schools. This volume grew out of the Third Roundtable on Internationalizing Business Education hosted by the Center for International Business Education and Research at Michigan State University (MSU-CIBER). Serving as co-sponsors for this event were CIBERs at Duke University, Purdue University, San Diego State University, Texas A&M University, University of Memphis, University of Connecticut, University of Kansas, University of Illinois, University of Pittsburgh, University of South Carolina, University of Texas at Austin, and the University of Wisconsin. The contributions selected for this volume represent some of the best thinking and empirical findings on business-focused study abroad concepts.

We are grateful to the authors of these selections for making their work available to a larger audience of scholars and practitioners around the world. Professors Hult and Lashbrooke are owed full credit for selecting the contributions and guiding the authors in the revision process. It has been a pleasure to work with them.

At Michigan State University, Irem Kiyak, Beverly Wilkins, and Kathy Waldie of the MSU-CIBER performed final editing and prepared the volume for publication. Finally, I appreciate the able assistance of Debbie Raven at Elsevier Science for producing this volume.

S. Tamer Cavusgil

Series Editor

FOREWORD

The International Education and Graduate Programs Office of the U.S. Department of Education (IEGPS) is pleased to bring you this publication produced from the Roundtable on Study Abroad Programs in Business Schools that took place in East Lansing, Michigan, September 2001. This publication reports on the results of a three-day, invitational conference of national and international experts on study abroad. The conference was hosted by the Center for International Business Education and Research in The Eli Broad Graduate School of Management at Michigan State University (MSU-CIBER), which is funded under Title VI of the Higher Education Act.

The conference was the result of collaborative efforts of a number of the Title VI CIBERs as well as many other scholars in the U.S. and abroad. We at IEGPS are always pleased to see such collaboration with a number of federally funded projects pooling their resources and talents. Serving as co-sponsors for this event were CIBERs at Duke University, Purdue University, San Diego State University, Texas A&M University, University of Memphis, University of Connecticut, University of Kansas, University of Illinois, University of Pittsburgh, University of South Carolina, University of Texas at Austin, and the University of Wisconsin.

While liberal arts programs at our nation's colleges and universities have a long tradition of fostering study abroad programs, such programs are relative newcomers to our schools of businesses. We were therefore particularly gratified to learn that a network of Study Abroad Administrators in Business Schools has been established and will hold annual meetings in conjunction with one of the major national associations that focus on study abroad. This network should serve to focus discussions on issues of particular relevance to business schools and their students.

The conference at Michigan State University focused on fourteen thematic topics relating to curricular as well as administrative aspects of study abroad. The papers commissioned in preparation for the conference and the resulting peer review comments are presented in this publication. We look forward to further discussions and presentations by CIBERs as well as other business schools on this timely and important topic.

Sarah Beaton
Branch Chief

Susanna Easton
Senior Program Specialist
IEGPS, U.S. Department of Education, Washington, D.C.

INTRODUCTION

With the advent of the global economy and marketplace, cultural sensitivity and language proficiency have assumed new, higher levels of importance in business education. Consequently, business schools need to acclimate both faculty and students to the global environment. Study abroad is an effective way to accomplish internationalization of faculty and students; however, there are many challenges relating to study abroad that need to be resolved. The underlying rationale for study abroad is evolving, as are the anticipated outcomes for students studying abroad. Moreover, there is no single source of information about study abroad and best practices relating to study abroad. Formal assessment of study abroad programs is rarely undertaken in the belief that the value of study abroad is self-evident; therefore, assessment is not critical. Consequently, study abroad is a topic on which much more research is needed. There are great opportunities for scholars and practitioners in the field of study abroad to do research in the different aspects of study abroad and disseminate and publish the results. The educational opportunities are virtually unlimited, as the importance of study abroad as a response to training business and other students to be able to function effectively in the global economy increases.

As a response to these challenges, the Center for International Business Education and Research (CIBER) in The Eli Broad Graduate School of Management at Michigan State University in East Lansing, Michigan, USA hosted a three-day conference of national and international experts on study abroad activities from the United States, Europe, and Asia. This Roundtable of Study Abroad Programs in Business Schools, held September 22–24, 2001, was cosponsored by AACSB – The Association for International Education and the CIBERs at Duke University, Purdue University, San Diego State University, Texas A&M University, University of Connecticut, University of Illinois, University of Kansas, University of Memphis, University of Pittsburgh, University of South Carolina, The University of Texas at Austin, and the University of Wisconsin. More than sixty faculty and administrators from business and other disciplines gathered in East Lansing to share their perspectives and experiences and brainstorm for solutions to issues surrounding study abroad. These eminently qualified educators served as resource persons. Each brought a unique perspective to study abroad issues from their leadership positions in business schools, other disciplines, and the U.S. national resource centers for international business education and research (CIBERs).

The roundtable experts met in small discussion groups organized into 14 thematic topics that correspond to challenges surrounding study abroad. Authors prepared and submitted papers that served as the focus of the discussions in most of the small groups. These papers served to focus the discussions and form the text of this book.

There are many kinds of study abroad programs, each with different anticipated outcomes. So there is no best study abroad program for any individual student. Each business school should have an array of different kinds of study abroad programs in a diverse set of locations to satisfy student needs and demands. What is that optimal mix? Study abroad programs also must deliver the anticipated outcomes to be meaningful. Assessment is a necessary part of the program; however, at present, there is no accepted standard for evaluating study abroad program.

Study abroad requires faculty participation in curricular issues and in study abroad itself. Faculty are important in all aspects of study abroad, from being the champion of a particular program to recruiting students. There are impediments to faculty participation in study abroad, particularly participation by junior faculty. The promotion and tenure process and the annual review and salary processes do not place much value on study abroad in many business schools. Faculty incentives must be put in place to insure participation, but what are the most effective incentives?

Student recruitment is imperative. Faculty and study abroad administrators need to stress the importance of study abroad and tout the benefits of study abroad to students. Students are best recruited by their peers who have studied abroad. Parents need to be informed about the benefits of study abroad. Efforts need to be made to recruit minority students. We need marketing research to be able to identify the most efficient and cost effective ways of recruiting. Costs of study abroad may be a detriment to study abroad for many students with limited financial resources. Research needs to be undertaken to determine the effects of costs on student enrollment. Where is the breaking point? Efforts must be made to keep the costs down while still maintaining quality programs. More scholarship funds are needed. Fundraising efforts need to be planned and implemented to create endowments for study abroad scholarships.

All of these issues and others need further discussion and research. The Michigan State University Center for International Business Education and Research 2001 Roundtable on Study Abroad Programs in Business Schools was an important step in bringing participants together to share research and discuss the major issues surrounding study abroad. The undertaking and planning of this roundtable was a formidable undertaking, particularly in the light of the events of September 11, 2001, which occurred just prior to the roundtable on September 22–24, 2001. Most importantly are the outcomes of the roundtable that will carry the discussions and research further. The Network of Study Abroad Administrators in Business Schools has been established. Its organizational meeting was held in San Antonio, Texas, in May 2002. Subsequent meetings have been planned and an organizational structure created. The network's mission is to provide a forum for the continuation of the roundtable discussions and for the sharing of best practices and research on study abroad in business schools. This book is another outcome of the roundtable that will stimulate discussion and further research on study abroad. The seeds planted at the Roundtable indeed have begun to sprout.

G. Tomas M. Hult
Elvin C. Lashbrooke, Jr.

Michigan State University
East Lansing, Michigan

DOCUMENTATION AND ASSESSMENT OF THE IMPACT OF STUDY ABROAD

Edward C. Ingraham

INTRODUCTION

The purpose of this paper is to describe the study abroad impact assessment project that has been undertaken during the past year by Michigan State University and to present some preliminary (and tentative) conclusions. It should be emphasized that this is a progress report, vulnerable to the uncertainties that time will remove as the project matures.

Peter McPherson, President of Michigan State University, is deeply committed to the idea that study abroad is beneficial for undergraduates. Recognizing however that systematically gathered qualitative and quantitative information which assesses the impact of study abroad is scarce if existent at all, he instructed the Dean of International Studies and Programs, John Hudzik, in the late summer of 2000 to design and put in place mechanisms for continuously assessing the impact of study abroad on students, on faculty, and on MSU as a whole.[1] A high-level assessment committee was established, chaired by the Dean of International Studies and Programs, with representatives from the Office of the Provost, the Office of Study Abroad, the Office of Planning and Budgets, the Placement Institute, and International Studies and Programs. After a few meetings of the group, it became apparent that the level of work involved to get the project going was so substantial as to require temporarily a project director. The group was fortunate in being able to persuade a recently retired faculty member with extensive administrative experience to take on this task for six months, during which time the basic form of

Study Abroad: Perspectives and Experiences from Business Schools
Advances in International Marketing, Volume 13, 1–21.
© 2003 Published by Elsevier Science Ltd.
ISSN: 1474-7979/PII: S147479790213002X

the study took shape. This initial period of intense planning and study now being completed, there will be a transition during this coming year that will establish these assessment activities as an integral part of the continuing responsibilities of the various units on campus involved in study abroad.

As most of the components of the study did not focus on the distinct disciplines within the University, few of the results below are specific to colleges of business. However, we believe that the approach we have taken and the general results we have obtained will be of interest to the participants in this roundtable.

Sources of Information

So far our sources of information have been:

(1) student participants before, during, upon return, and sometime after their study abroad experiences;
(2) the central MSU student database;
(3) a bibliography of publications related to assessment of the impact of study abroad.

How We Are Gathering Information

1. From Students
   The heart of our project thus far has been the information gathered directly from students and therefore focuses on student satisfaction.[2] We will address issues of student learning later.
   (a) Student questionnaires:
       (i) Because there has been some urgency in this project, we decided to get reactions from students who had studied abroad recently ("post-only"), even though we could not compare their attitudes to those they had prior to departure. This involved sending out questionnaires to many participants who had recently returned from study abroad experiences, as well as conducting focus groups with such students.
       (ii) We also undertook to design and to administer paired questionnaires ("pre-post") designed to sample pre-departure and post-return opinion from students, allowing us to see what they felt were the changes in attitudes and expectations their study abroad experiences had produced.

(b) Student journals: We have requested submission of journals that students have written while studying abroad.

(c) In-depth studies: Two faculty leaders of study abroad programs (in Nepal and Brazil) have volunteered to provide the committee with in-depth studies of their programs, which involve case studies and on-site observation. The committee also is undertaking program studies that involve on-site staff visits to programs that are in progress, with the opportunity to interview *all* participants of a program. (One of the methodological difficulties in the approach in (a) and (b) above is that one gets responses only from those students who choose to turn in the questionnaire or attend the focus group, which may tend to attract only those students who feel strongly either positively or negatively about the experience, leaving out those for which it was a ho-hum happening.)

(d) Alumni studies: One of the committee members has designed, and is administering a general questionnaire to be given to a group of alumni of the Broad College of Business which contains study abroad impact questions.

2. The Central MSU Database

We were able to have access to much data concerning MSU's student body through the committee's representative from the Office of Planning and Budgets.

3. Bibliography

Two of the members of the committee have extensive experience with the literature in the field of study abroad and they have compiled an extensive bibliography for committee use.

Categories of Study Abroad Impact on Individual Students

For the purposes of its study, the group has identified five general categories of impact:

(1) academic progress and intellectual development;

(2) attitudes, e.g. tolerance towards others, self-confidence, cultural attitudes;

(3) skills, e.g. foreign language proficiency, coping with ambiguity, critical thinking;

(4) understanding and appreciation of the world and one's place in it, e.g. reflection on other and one's own cultures, perspectives on the role played by politics and the arts in the human condition;

(5) effect on one's place in society, e.g. employment opportunities, ability to do job.

In addition, such items as effect on health, finances, and family were grouped under the ubiquitous designation of "miscellaneous." By defining these categories, we have constructed a framework into which to place the various data and comments we receive.

QUANTITATIVE RESULTS

Student Opinion

As the first step in our gathering of student opinion, we sent a survey containing 33 statements to 1,475 students who had studied abroad during some portion of the 1999–2000 academic year ("post-only"). Students were given five responses from which to choose:

1 = not at all;
2 = very little;
3 = some;
4 = quite a bit;
5 = very much.

Four hundred and thirty-seven surveys were returned and analyzed, with the results grouped according to the five general categories listed above. Some of the statements had a positive slant ("Studying abroad has contributed to my understanding of my host country"), others a negative cast ("Studying abroad has delayed my graduation").

The responses held very few surprises for those of us convinced of the benefits of study abroad. Certainly the biggest (and perhaps the only) one was the fact that *of the 437 respondents, 84% had traveled abroad (not counting trips to Canada) for some reason other than study abroad*. The statement with the highest mean score (4.68) was "I will recommend (have recommended) study abroad to my friends" and the statement with the lowest mean (1.08) was "Studying abroad was a waste of time for me." Of the statements with a positive slant, the one with the lowest mean (2.46) was "As a result of my study abroad experience my ability to speak a foreign language has improved" and of those with a negative tone, "I could have accomplished a lot more academically if I had stayed on campus rather than studying abroad" had a mean of 1.42. For the full results, see Appendix A.

We also designed paired surveys ("pre-post") to be given first as a pilot to students who studied abroad during Winter Break 2000–2001 and then subsequently to the Spring 2001 and Summer 2001 programs. Once the results of these questionnaires have been analyzed, we will decide how often, and to which programs we will give them in the future. (There is a potential here for amassing daunting amounts of data that provide little in the way of new insight). With the same response options as the "post-only" survey, students are asked to consider 31 statements before they leave and the same 31 after they return. They are also provided with three pairs of "open-ended" questions both before and after their experience:

35. Pre: What are TWO THINGS that YOU MOST LOOK FORWARD TO/ARE EXCITED ABOUT when you think about your upcoming study abroad program? Post: What were the TWO THINGS that happened during your study abroad program that were the MOST EXCITING for you?

36. Pre: What are TWO THINGS that YOU ARE MOST CONCERNED ABOUT when you think about your upcoming study abroad program? Post: What TWO THINGS happened during your program that caused you the MOST CONCERN?

37. Pre: What are the THREE BIGGEST DIFFERENCES YOU EXPECT TO FIND between the host country and the USA? Post: What are the THREE BIGGEST DIFFERENCES YOU FOUND between the host country and the USA?

As only 16 students were involved in the pilot during Winter Break 2000–2001 and as the results from Summer 2001 are not yet available, it is premature to speculate on what significance will arise. (However, the writer can't resist mentioning that of the participants in these programs (which took place in Mexico and in the Caribbean), three anticipated (in answering #35) that the weather would be one of the exciting things about their experience, whereas none said so in retrospect. No "fun in the sun" on MSU programs!)

For the pilot version of the "post" part of the "pre-post" questionnaires, see Appendix B.

Centrally Provided Data: The 1994 Cohort

Much useful and interesting data is available from the central MSU database if one can figure out how to extract it, and the committee is fortunate in having Dr. William Sperber, a gifted data dentist, as one of its members. He suggested that it made sense to look carefully at a cohort of entering students and follow them through a six-year period. The committee agreeing, he selected those who entered MSU in the fall of 1994 because it was the most recent entering class for which we could get a full six-year profile. It is our expectation that similar studies will be done annually for each subsequent cohort.

Most of the results from this group reinforced popularly held views about study abroad, e.g. *women study abroad in greater proportion than do men, African-Americans in smaller proportion than whites*. (For this cohort as a whole, 11.9%[3] studied abroad as an MSU student prior to Fall 2000. However, 14.1% of the women studied abroad while only 9.1% of the men did so. And only 7.2% of African-Americans in the cohort studied abroad.) It also reinforced the belief that most students first study abroad in their third or fourth years of enrollment, although the percentage (59.0%) is lower than I would have predicted.

One recurring topic of concern for students and their parents is whether studying abroad delays time to graduation. One way to check this is to monitor graduation rates. First evidence is quite persuasive that on the whole it does not. To quote Bill Sperber: "From the limited data so far available, attending overseas study does not negatively impact a student's graduation rate or time to degree." To back this up, he provided us many tables and comparisons of which I will describe only one: If one looks at all the students in the Fall 1994 entering cohort who attended MSU during Fall Semester 1997 with a GPA of 2.0 or higher, *the graduation rate was about 5% higher for those who studied abroad than for those who didn't for each of the groups of students who graduates after four years, after five years, and after six years*. See Appendix C for the relevant chart.

Many involved in study abroad have speculated as to whether studying abroad tends to have *a beneficial effect on a student's cumulative grade point average* after the student has returned. (This is distinct from the question of whether grades earned during study abroad experiences are higher than those earned in the same courses on the home campus.) This is a hard question to answer in large part because students more often than not study abroad late in their undergraduate careers[4] and therefore the cumulative GPAs don't change much after they return. However, any detectable differences seem to be more positive for students who studied abroad.

While not strictly related to the impact of study abroad, the question of *which majors tend to study abroad* is an interesting one. The traditional view is that students who study abroad come primarily from the humanities and social sciences. More recently, as the economies of the world have become increasingly inter-dependent, and as business has become global in its nature, one would expect the rate of participation by business students to be high relative to most other majors. The 1994 cohort study bears out most of this with the exception that MSU's College of Agriculture and Natural Resources has an active study abroad program that involved 13.7% of all those of the cohort who studied abroad, which is tops in the University. More precisely, the following table shows the percentages by college of all those in the 1994 cohort who studied abroad, based on the students' preferred college as of Fall 1997:

Agriculture and Natural Resources	13.7
Social Science	13.6
Business	12.8
Arts and Letter	11.2
James Madison (Int'l Rels and Public Policy)	10.9
Communication	9.9
Engineering	8.8
Natural Science	7.2
Education	4.6
Human Ecology	2.9
Previously graduated	2.4
Nursing	2.1

QUALITATIVE RESULTS

Up to this point we have relied on the students themselves for qualitative information concerning the impact of study abroad on the individual student. By combining these individual responses (from questionnaires, focus groups, interviews, etc.), we are beginning to get a picture of the impact of study abroad from the students' points of view.

Our study has collected much in the way of subjective, discursive statements from students about their study abroad experiences. Often through journals, sometimes through focus groups and interviews, we have received many deeply felt and revealing statements. While these do not lend themselves easily to summary, I would like to include a few to show the insight and eloquence, often inadvertent, that such comments provide.

Written Comments

"I decided I really don't like [a particular city]. I can't stand the pollution, and the poverty depresses me. The street vendors won't leave you alone, I saw cripples, beggars, and bums today. It's [sic] awful to think there are so many people [who] live like that. They must think we live like royalty; we do compared to them. I know its bad to ignore it by saying I never want to go back there, but I don't."

A week later the same person wrote after visiting a village of mud huts: "It's so hard to imagine people living like that day in and day out. It was a very humbling experience. I hope that whenever I complain, I remember what these people have.

It's undescribable [sic]; the difference in lifestyles. We have so much, and there are people living like that. I know it is their way of life, a tradition that they continue. Some of them may not realize what the rest of the world is like, but [the host] is going to a university. I don't understand how or why you would want to live like that when you have the opportunity to have a decent home, medicine, food, etc. I would really like to hear things from their point of view to gain some insight on how they view the world. Obviously, they have a very different perspective on everything, and who knows – maybe they wouldn't want to live like us."

The following describes the difficulty a student had in dealing with his/her fellow participants in the program: "My whole life, I have been raised to love anything different, and never once swallow this idea of race, of one right sexuality, or plainly someone being better than someone else. The challenge for me on this trip is to swallow my anger and sadness when I hear these [racist] comments and try to voice civilly my disagreement. It is impossible here, on this trip, to be angry at someone for long since there's no escape. I have never been in this situation before where I couldn't walk away. The challenge that I have before me, for the rest of the trip is to take each comment out of citizens of both countries mouths not to heart, and try not to become so angry and sad, but instead show them the other side of view if possible and know that at least I have possibly helped one person see different people in a much brighter light."

Coping by three students on the same program:

"I find the bugs to be bothering me more than I expected. The idea that they could be carrying a disease kind of *bugs* me. I think I just have to get use to the idea and I won't be as worried. For piece of mind I just put and tuck my mosquito net all around my bed and fall asleep, if those dogs would just stop barking."

"Last night was exciting. I was sitting in the room with [another student], and we heard hyenas. She thought she heard a lion, but I reassured her it was just the hyenas. We soon learned it was a lion, it was a little scary. It was said it was across the river, and the guards said one has never been on the grounds. I bet. I was able to go to sleep with my headphones on, but [the other student] had trouble falling asleep."

"Our tents are . . . tents. The bathroom is large, but the shower could be better. No mosquito nets or locks, I guess we have to trust everyone. The bugs are a problem, and there's always the fear of monkeys."

On the Role the Arts Play in the Students' Perceptions
of the Host Countries and Culture
"At the point in the program when the woman and warrior did the duet, I nearly cried. The tone of the song and the apparent meaning behind it gave me a familiar

absolute feeling of safety I haven't felt since I attended church choir camp throughout middle school and we would sing around a campfire with all our friends."

"At the museum I was amazed at the [host people's] culture. I actually never made it off the first floor. I just could not believe the detail and intricate designs of their artifacts. The amount of patience and raw talent that was needed to make the pieces is mind boggling. I don't remember ever seeing anything in Native American artifacts that could compare to what I saw today. It got me really fired up to learn more about the [particular] culture! It also sparked questions about what types of people were/are they? Are there any tribes that exist today? If so, do they still practice traditional beliefs and culture?"

The same student two days later: "The [particular] culture is absolutely fascinating. From the first day in [host country] when we went to the museum and saw the kind of intricate artwork and the figurines, I was captured by culture. That has led me to focus my paper on the culture instead of the government like I originally planned."

On International Issues of Development and Economics

"After dinner our group began throwing ideas around for a management plan for [local people]. Since tourism and herding seem to be in constant flux, I suggested weaning herding slowly out of the area. Since tourism is the only industry that will become developed and bring profits to the area, I felt we should have a plan biased towards it. Of course, that reaction is one of omnipotence, standing on a pedestal from the Western world telling others what is right or wrong. For the [local people], herding is their culture. Taking that away would be cultural suicide to them. That was the reaction of my group members and we were left debating the rest of the night."

"The theme for this family farm is similar to the farms in NZ – they don't grow for themselves they grow for the world. This is such a new concept for me, global economics. So many times I think we are stuck in our own 'little worlds,' ignorant of what is happening around us."

Transcriptions of Focus Group Comments

On Personal Development and Tolerance

"I was so nervous about everything, about going in with a host family, speaking the language . . . I wasn't sure that all those years of Spanish classes would really actually put me where I needed to be, with every day communication, with people. But when I came back I realized I could do it. I realized that I'm a lot more independent than I thought I was. I left to study abroad like at a really funny time in my life where there were a lot of changes going on and I wasn't sure if I should do it or like even just getting on the airport like getting on that plane I'm just crying right oh what am I doing, I [sic] so stupid. But, I mean getting off the plane was a totally different experience. I thought like, you know, independent woman, I can do this and I mean it just changed my outlook on things."

"It [study abroad] has made me, I don't know, made me patient with foreigners that visit this country . . . I've seen people in restaurants . . . just totally irate at a foreigner who doesn't speak English very well and you know, being over there I didn't speak [the foreign language] very well, even towards the end. You know, just to have your waitress slow down her speech and point at the menu to help you out is so much more helpful than, you know, having somebody just get away from me, you don't speak [the language]. . . . And my roommate is [a foreign student] right now and she doesn't speak English very well. And I've been very patient with her and things like that. You know, once you are in the other, in their shoes you see it from both sides."

On Drinking Abroad
As are many schools, MSU is concerned about the way in which its students deal with alcohol while studying abroad. The following is an extended excerpt from a focus group conversation:

"I got drunk for the first time in Europe, you know, I had never done that before.

"Yeah. You have to do that while you are over there, but I just meant that in my relationship with her, I don't like what she is doing. I don't like that she is drunk every weekend. And stuff like that. And I don't know if I'm noticing it more now because, because I've grown up maybe."

Another student: "I party a lot. I don't consider myself that grown up. I just, I think I don't necessarily think my experiences [in study abroad] make me, they may make me more [inaudible] but I'm still just as much of a kid as in high school."

Student: "All I did on study abroad was drink, drink, drink."

Different student: "It's part of the culture, you've got to get to know the people, the people drink, you've got to drink with them."

Student: "Oh, that's part of my personal culture, so . . ."

Different student: "That's part of your persona."

Student: "I didn't really want to switch out just because I crossed the ocean."

Another student: "Americans tend to be very extroverted typically. They go out to play, they are just like whoa just have a good time. . . . Whereas the middle Europeans, especially the Germans are used to drinking so we'd go out and we'd party. And there, they are socializers, I mean they have a beer, what they are doing

[is] let's have ourselves a big old conversation, you know. They just love talk. And you know, I saw parties in Europe, I watched Americans come in. What, you talking? Turn the music up. It's like, let's go.

"If I could just leave it, I think it is just a party culture at Michigan State and just party culture in general in colleges. Um, you just go out and you just go. It was just a much more free and open, I don't know if it is open-minded, but just more open [over seas]."

On Language Study
Oddly enough, it seems as if the traditional function of study abroad – to increase one's facility at a second language – is not nearly so important as it once was for many students. However, for those who have an interest in improving their language skills, it still can be dramatically successful. Here is a slight twist on the usual testimonial:

"We had the Spanish class at the regular university, which was nice. [Another student in the class was] a girl from Korea, who was living in [the host country] with her husband. That was interesting, because she didn't know English. So we really, to communicate with her, had to communicate in Spanish. So that was really good."

And a Bit of Criticism
"Well, I'm much more critical ah, about the educational system over here, especially the language departments. I have to say . . . I did not feel prepared going over, I really didn't. Um, it is because the language departments are catering to a student population that does not really want them. . . . If we make the language courses too hard and too strenuous, then students will just . . . do something else, because this is not a big deal, you know. . . . The language classes over there are extremely rigorous because you can't really say oh, and go to something else, because you have to have these languages to get around to talk to people. . . . And over here it is not such a big deal. It is kind of like a game, that's what I really felt it was."

New Perspectives on the World
"I had a totally different outlook on the globe when I came back. Probably the most interesting place I've ever gone to because these people lived under Communism for so long . . . it was really neat to talk to them because they had totally different experiences, totally different ideas about how things should go, totally different everything than anybody I'd ever met . . . I really value their ideas because they are coming from a totally different world than I came from. And it really just kind of helped me get a perspective and say look, when I go here, this is what I've got, this is what I've had growing up, and this guy from over here didn't have that. Or he

come up with something totally different and just really helps you put everything into perspective."

On the Effects of Study Abroad on Search for Employment
"I did a couple of interviews just from the Career Fair . . . And before I didn't have it [study abroad program] bulleted on my resume, but then I bulleted it and it is just like, I don't know, people's eyes went to it. So, and it [the study abroad program] gives you a story, it makes them understand that you can communicate with different types of people, you know, and you can understand different types of people and I think in advertising that's a big bang, you know, just being able to look at all kinds of aspects of it. So I think it has really helped me. It just gives you something more to talk about than the average."

On the Effect of Study Abroad on the Way Students View their Careers
"It's [study abroad has] made me look at my priorities a little differently, of what I want to do. It's even made me kind of look at my career options. Do I want to do this? You know. Do I want to live abroad? Do I want to stay here? What do I want to do? I'm not quite sure. I have a good idea . . . I've just always seen myself growing up in Michigan, staying in Michigan teaching, but, and I'm pretty sure that's what I'll end up doing, but I'm always thinking, well, I could get a job in London or France or something. Even working with the military and traveling around as a teacher, but I don't know if that's how I'd want to raise a family, traveling a few months here, and a few months there. So it's made me think about that, and I never thought about that until I got back this year, and looked at, you know, what do I want to do with my life? Do I want to be here, or do I want to be there? It's, it's made me have some choices to make."

"When you go to look at companies that you want to work [for] . . . one of my first questions is: Do you have abroad opportunities?"

"I just feel like I can make myself at home anywhere in the world and that's pretty important to me. 'Cause you know, I'm going to do business with all types of people, not just Americans."

NEXT STEPS

The committee feels that in addition to the areas it has begun to study there are many other important questions and issues that unlimited time and money would allow it to pursue.

First, there is the matter of assessing what students learn while studying abroad and how much value is added to their education as a result of studying abroad, a difficult but important task.

Then there are the major areas of impact not directly related to students:

- faculty
- MSU as a whole
- the host institutions and their countries
- national security
- business climate of the State of Michigan and the country

Finally, there remain many interesting areas of student-related matters that need to be explored more deeply. A few of these are:

- "Times outside the country" prior to study abroad. Since only 16% of students in study abroad programs are going abroad for the first time and a third have been four or more times, is the pool of potential study abroad students being defined by those who have already had the opportunity to travel abroad? What is the "times outside the country" rate for the MSU student population at large? What factors play a role in students' opportunities for travel abroad – financial, family history?
- Knowledge of international issues and affairs. Could study abroad students and students who did not participate in study abroad be compared through an achievement test designed by a faculty member?
- Male students. Why are the percentages of men participating in study abroad lower than those of women? Would encouraging male students to help in identifying study abroad areas that fit their academic and career interests increase enrollment?
- Socialization and drinking. More assessment is needed. On the basis of the data available now, students could experience difficulties while abroad. Could OSA increase alert to availability of alcohol in certain countries and offer tips in ways to reduce potential problems? For example, telling students about Shandy's and the social acceptability of drinking half rather than full pints.

CONCLUSION

This project being about a year old, it is apparent to this observer that Michigan State University is well on its way to making assessment of the impact of study abroad a regular part of its study abroad operation. It is equally apparent that the process of usefully interpreting the information gathered has only just begun and that it may take some time before we will reach confident and revealing conclusions. However, much of the early evidence suggests that the folklore in the field about the benefits of, as well as the difficulties posed by studying abroad is accurate. As this project continues through the years, it will be of compelling interest to see with increasing clarity just what are the aspects of the impact of study abroad, which of them remain stable, and which change.

NOTES

1. During the first six months of this project, it became increasingly clear that this project was not yet ready to tackle the full range of its charge and so it has focused on assessing the impact of study abroad on the student participants, leaving the impact on faculty and the institution for later.

2. Whenever appropriate, authorization to proceed was obtained from the University Committee on Research Involving Human Subjects.

3. The "participation rate" numbers game is a quicksand of shifting definitions and "apples and oranges" comparisons. The IIE *Open Doors* definition (which is the basis for nationwide comparisons) essentially takes the number of students who study abroad at any institution in a given year and divides that number by the number of graduates of that institution in the same year. While this definition has its advantages, it suffers from the numerator coming from a radically different group than the denominator. Another (perhaps more naïve) definition is to take the number of graduates of an institution in a given year and divide it into the number of *those* graduates who studied abroad. This has the advantage of accurately reflecting progress towards institutional goals that are stated in terms of a certain percentage of graduating students having studied abroad. A third approach is to calculate the participation rate as was done in this case (11.9%) by taking an entering class and looking at it over the long run of six years and finding out the percentage of those students who studied abroad at some time during those six years. We are not prepared to advocate one over the other of these definitions but we do caution the reader when discussing participation rates to be clear as to what definition is being used.

4. To no one's surprise, our study of the 1994 cohort shows that only 23% of the students who studied abroad did so for the first time during their first two years after matriculation.

ACKNOWLEDGMENTS

This paper is based on the progress report of the Study Abroad Impact Assessment Committee at Michigan State University submitted in late May 2001 by the project director, Professor Emeritus Joy Curtis. She deserves unlimited praise for leaving the freedom of retirement for a six-month return to schedules and deadlines in order to ably oversee getting this project on its feet. I'd like to acknowledge as well her assistant, Debra Peterson, for her indispensable contribution. Finally, Bill Sperber of MSU's Office of Planning and Budgets made an especially valuable contribution through his study of the 1994 cohort.

APPENDIX A

"Post-Only" Questionnaire Analysis

"POST-ONLY" SURVEY 1999–2000 STUDENTS

STATEMENTS

ASSESSMENT OF THE IMPACT OF STUDY ABROAD ON STUDENTS

Post Study Abroad Survey: Sent spring 2001 to 1475 undergraduates who participated in study abroad during the 1999–2000 academic year. 437 surveys returned and analyzed.

Asked to indicate agreement: 1 – Not at all; 2 – Very little; 3 – Some; 4 – Quite a bit; 5 – Very much

	Mean	STD
1. Academic Progress/Intellectual Development:		
A5. My study abroad experience has led to an improvement of my academic performance	3.09	1.17
Questions asked negatively about academic progress:		
A23. Considering all the effort I put into participating in study abroad, I gained very little	1.19	0.56
A7. Studying abroad has delayed my graduation	1.4	0.87
A18. I could have accomplished a lot more academically if I had stayed on campus rather than studying abroad	1.42	0.9
2. Attitudes:		
A13. Study abroad has increased my appreciation of human difference	4.17	0.89
A20. Study abroad has enhanced my self-reliance	4.17	0.89
A27. Study abroad has enhanced my independence	4.11	0.97
A26. As a result of my study abroad experience, I have become more open-minded	4.01	0.9
Attitudes about study abroad and MSU:		
A30. I will recommend (have recommended) study abroad to my friends	4.68	0.69

A19. I think that every college student should have at least one study abroad experience   4.66   0.74

A15. MSU is an institution that I will recommend (have recommended) to others   4.28   0.93

A24. I think that MSU is an institution with a strong international emphasis   4.14   0.9

Questions asked negatively about study abroad:

A12. Studying abroad was a waste of time for me   1.08   0.45

A34. I wish I had used the money I spent on study abroad on something more beneficial   1.18   0.55

3. Skills:

A32. Studying abroad has increased my ability to cope with unfamiliar situations   4.19   0.84

A6. Study abroad has increased my feeling of personal effectiveness   3.9   0.92

A17. My study abroad experience has increased my level of comfort with people different from myself   3.84   0.94

A29. My study abroad experience has increased my ability to interact effectively with people from different backgrounds   3.82   0.88

A31. Studying abroad has helped me develop leadership skills   3.59   1

A10. Studying abroad has enhanced my critical thinking skills   3.47   1.01

A22. My study abroad experience had improved my problem-solving skills   3.37   1.03

Language skills:

A36. Studying abroad has contributed to my desire to begin learning a foreign language   3.14   1.44

A35. As a result of my study abroad experience my ability to speak a foreign language has improved   2.46   1.52

4. Appreciation/Understanding of the World and One's Place in it: 4.5   0.67
A4. Studying abroad has contributed to my understanding of my host country

A14. My study abroad experience has increased my curiosity about other cultures   4.45   0.73

A21. Study abroad has contributed to my understanding of other cultures	4.34	0.74
A8. My study abroad experience has enhanced my understanding of international issues	4.14	0.85
A11. My study abroad experience has increased my understanding of my own culture	3.89	0.94
A9. Study abroad has encouraged me to seek out a more diverse group of friends	3.35	1.08
Questions asked negatively about Appreciation/Understanding of the World, etc. A28. I have no desire to travel/work/study abroad again in the future	1.19	0.72

5. Effect on One's Place in Society:

A33. My study abroad experience has favorably impressed potential employers	3.66	1.07
A25. Studying abroad has helped me find professional direction	2.91	1.09
A16. Studying abroad has made me reconsider my career plans	2.84	1.29

APPENDIX B

"Pre-post" Questionnaires

Study Abroad
Post-Program Survey (Pre-Post Sequence)

P0. From which Study Abroad Program have you most recently returned?

P0.a. Program Name: _____

P0.b. Location: _____

P0.c. In which academic term did you study? (please check)
    [   ] Winter Break [   ] Fall Semester [   ] Spring Semester [   ] Summer
    [   ] Academic Year

Prior Experiences Abroad

P1. In what kind of study abroad program(s) have you participated in the past and earned academic credits (if none before this program, skip to Question 2)

P1.a. The FIRST time I studied abroad, it was: (check both: type of program and length)

[   ] an MSU program with courses taught by MSU instructors
[   ] an MSU program at an institution abroad with courses taught by host country
       instructors
[   ] a Non-MSU program offered by another institution (including high school
       abroad)

P1.b. It was: [   ] 1–3 weeks; [   ] 4–6 weeks; [   ] 7–9 weeks; [   ] 10–18 weeks;
               [   ] 5 months +

P1.c. The SECOND time I studied abroad, it was: (check both type of program and length)

[   ] an MSU program with courses taught by MSU instructors
[   ] an MSU program at an institution abroad with courses taught by host country
       instructors
[   ] a Non-MSU program offered by another institution (including high school
       abroad)

P1.d. It was: [   ] 1–3 weeks; [   ] 4–6 weeks; [   ] 7–9 weeks;
               [   ] 10–18 weeks; [   ] 5 months +

P2. About how many times have you been outside the United States for any reason (not counting trips to Canada)?

[   ] Never [   ] Once [   ] Twice [   ] Three times [   ] Four times or more

P3. Not counting study abroad for college credit, what other kinds of international experiences have you had? (check all that apply)

a. _____ Served in a professional assignment overseas (e.g. worked abroad or in
           the military)

b. _____ Lived overseas for other than professional reasons
c. _____ Participated in an international internship program abroad
d. _____ Participated in a high school exchange abroad
e. _____ Regularly interacted with foreign students, acquaintances, friends here in the USA
f. _____ Hosted international visitors/students in my home
g. _____ Other (please describe)_____

Now that you have returned from your study abroad program, we are interested in how you believe your time in the host country has affected you. There are no right or wrong answers. Please indicate on a scale from 1 (not at all) to 5 (very much) the degree to which you believe each statement reflects your experience.

1 – Not at all 2 – Very little 3 – Some 4 – Quite a bit 5 – Very much

P4. _____ Study abroad has contributed to my understanding of the host country.
P5. _____ As a result of study abroad, I expect to improve my academic performance.
P6. _____ Study abroad has increased my feelings of personal effectiveness.
P7. _____ Study abroad has enhanced my understanding of international issues.
P8. _____ As a result of the study abroad experience my critical thinking skills will improve.
P9. _____ As a result of study abroad, my understanding of my own culture will increase.
P10. _____ Study abroad has increased my desire to travel/work/study abroad in the future.
P11. _____ Study abroad has increased my curiosity about other cultures.
P12. _____ I expect my comfort level around people different from me to increase as a result of study abroad.
P13. _____ Study abroad has enhanced my self-reliance.
P14. _____ Study abroad has contributed to my understanding of other cultures.
P15. _____ As a result of study abroad, I expect my problem solving skills to improve.
P16. _____ I expect that the study abroad experience will help me find professional direction.
P17. _____ My study abroad experience will lead to an increase in my open-mindedness.
P18. _____ I have become more independent as a result of study abroad.

P19. _____ As a result of study abroad I will be able to interact more effectively with people from different backgrounds.

P20. _____ I expect that having had the study abroad experience will help me develop leadership skills.

P21. _____ As a result of study abroad, I will be better able to cope with unfamiliar situations.

P22. _____ I expect my study abroad experience to favorably impress potential employers.

P23. _____ Study abroad has improved my ability to speak a foreign language.

P24. _____ Study abroad has contributed to my desire to begin learning a foreign language.

Now we would like to ask you a few questions about your perceptions of your host country. Using the key below, indicate the degree to which you agree with each statement.

1 – Strongly agree; 2 – Agree; 3 – Neither agree nor disagree; 4 – Disagree; 5 – Strongly disagree

P25. _____ I found locals to be very friendly toward me.

P26. _____ Locals do not like the way the United States uses its world power and influence.

P27. _____ The average local person knows less about world issues than the average American.

P28. _____ The host country's standard of living is much lower than the American standard of living.

P29. _____ The locals are more informed about current issues in their own country than is the average American about current issues in the U.S.

P30. _____ The overall quality of life in the host country is not as good as in the United States.

P31. _____ I found the host country to be a place where I would want to live for a year or longer.

P32. _____ Americans do not have much to learn from the locals.

P33. _____ Local people generally don't like Americans.

P34. _____ I found locals to be very different than Americans.

Please respond to the following questions about your expectations regarding your study abroad experience

P35. What were the TWO THINGS that happened during your study abroad program that were the MOST EXCITING for you?

P36. What TWO THINGS happened during your program that caused you the MOST CONCERN?

P37. What are the THREE BIGGEST DIFFERENCES YOU FOUND between the host country and the USA?

APPENDIX C

Graduation Percentage as of 4th, 5th, and 6th Year

FALL 1994 COHORT: GPA Control Group

GRADUATION PERCENTAGES AFTER 4, 5, AND 6 YEARS

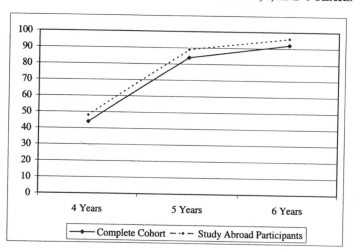

The Complete Cohort comprises those 4,426 students from the Fall 1994 cohort who attended MSU Fall Semester 1997 with a GPA of 2.0 or higher. Of these, 650 studied abroad and comprise the Study Abroad Participants.

THE CASE FOR ASSESSING EDUCATIONAL OUTCOMES IN STUDY ABROAD

Michael Vande Berg

Over the past fifteen years, U.S. study abroad enrollments have increased by 160%, with nearly 130,000 students earning credit abroad during the 1998–1999 academic year. The growth has been especially striking during the past five reporting years, as the number of participants has swelled by an astonishing 70% (Davis, 2000, p. 16). During the past fifteen years or so, our discussions about study abroad have come more and more to be dominated by this sort of self-congratulatory number-crunching: we've come to regard each successive annual increase in participation as a worthy achievement in itself, and much of what we do, and much about what we report to each other, focuses on our challenges and successes in pursuing this goal at our individual institutions, and on the national level. Thus, we identify the obstacles that stand in the way of greater student participation; we report about our institutional successes in administratively overcoming those obstacles; we commit ourselves to increasing the participation of African-American, Hispanic, disabled, natural science, business, math, engineering, and other "non-traditional" students; and we relish the gains we make in encouraging more of our students to study in "non-traditional" destinations in Africa, Asia, Latin America and elsewhere.

This is not to say that there's anything inherently unhealthy about wanting more of our students, of whatever background, to study abroad, whether in traditional or non-traditional locales. Students are often transformed in very positive ways through their experiences abroad, and I've had the good fortune to work, throughout

Study Abroad: Perspectives and Experiences from Business Schools
Advances in International Marketing, Volume 13, 23–36.
ISSN: 1474-7979/PII: S1474797902130031

my career, at institutions which have vigorously promoted international programs and have been especially successful in increasing the numbers of students going abroad. I am, however, concerned that in our zeal to increase access to study abroad, we've lost our focus as educators, and have become all too willing to measure success through the very crudest of metrics: the number of students enrolling in programs abroad. It's time for us to move away from this over-preoccupation with the numbers, and to shift our primary focus from the on-campus marketing, promotion and recruitment of students to the design, delivery and evaluation of quality educational experiences abroad. When we describe our future successes, we'll take more pride in having provided our students with opportunities abroad that allow them to acquire the knowledge, skills and awareness that benefit them after their return to campuses than we will by having increased our institutional participation rates. And we'll take an important first step, as international educators focused on providing quality experiences, by committing ourselves to identifying and documenting the educational outcomes of our students while they are abroad.

Advocating that we shift our focus from increasing the quantity of participants to designing and delivering quality programs abroad of course begs the question: what do we mean by quality? The rapid and continuing increases in enrollments these past fifteen years have accompanied, both driven and been driven by, the evolution of a great variety of study abroad program models and types. We now offer students a broad assortment of different types of long- and short-term experiences. We provide them with courses taught in English as well as in the language of the host country; we enroll them in courses at host universities and in courses we specifically organize for them; we arrange for them to be taught by faculty from host universities or from our own home campuses; we allow them to earn credit through traditional classroom methods and through experiential activities. In short, we offer our students a veritable cornucopia of options, all under the increasingly strained and probably insufficient rubric of "study abroad."

Twenty and more years ago, when fewer than a third as many students were annually participating, "study abroad" still called up the relatively unified images and objectives of the Junior Year paradigm. Back then, students majoring, for the most part, in the Social Sciences and in the Arts and Humanities typically prepared themselves for sojourns by studying foreign languages prior to departure; once abroad, they often enrolled in courses for at least a semester, if not a year. Framed against the educational values and ideological pre-occupations of the Cold War, studying abroad provided students with learning opportunities that would allow them to develop the skills and attitudes which they – and presumably the United States – would need in order to be successful players on the world stage. Those who went abroad, whether directly enrolling in a host university or studying within an academic island designed for U.S. students, aimed to fulfill two goals, acquire two useful skills: to become proficient in a foreign language and to learn about and adapt to another culture.

We can appreciate the extent to which the goals of an American sojourn abroad were, in the post-War period, defined very specifically in linguistic and intercultural terms through turning to the opening pages of *When Americans Live Abroad*, a booklet produced by the U.S. State Department in 1956, at the height of the Cold War. The publication served to prepare Americans prior to their departure for a foreign assignment:

> ... the person living abroad has a much more profound problem before him than the delights of new foods and charming folkways, proper though an active interest in these may be. His effectiveness depends on an ability to make a clear and accurate interpretation of the behavior of the people that make up a 'foreign' society, whether to conduct official business or to adjust to the physical and social conditions of life around him. He also needs an insight into what happens when human interaction is complicated by cultural differences. Among the thousands of Americans working abroad, many have developed this very specialized skill through long experience and successful mastery of foreign languages. There are also Americans who have not been able to understand the reasons for the differences they find and have tried to continue working with the same assumptions and approaches they would use in the United States, often decreasing their achievement and their personal satisfaction with their assignment (Fisher, 1956, pp. 1–2).

A simple and reasonably unified consensus governed the expectations of the American going abroad, whether diplomat or student: success meant acquiring "abilities," "insights" and "specialized skills" – specifically, mastering a foreign language, and through the exercise of this foundational skill, learning to interpret and to adapt to the cultural differences that he or she would inevitably encounter. It was also understood that this linguistic and intercultural skill-building would emerge through an experience abroad that would last for more than a few weeks – a semester, if not a year, where study abroad participants were concerned.

The consensus that found one of its strongest expressions in the Junior Year paradigm has of course broken down where current study abroad programming is concerned – even if the language we typically use to describe our programs, including our use of that over-stretched rubric "study abroad," does at times create the impression that we're still embracing some vague unity of purpose in sending our students overseas. Much of the growth in study abroad participation these past fifteen years has been driven by our interest in developing programs for students in business, the physical and life sciences, math and other under-represented majors, and of our consequent development of numerous programs of short duration. Fifteen years ago, only 28% of students went abroad for eight weeks or less; in 1998–1999, nearly half of all students participated in such short-term programs (Davis, 2000, p. 19). We unfortunately have no data that will allow us to trace precisely, during this same period, the accompanying decrease in the percentage of programs requiring students to demonstrate a reasonable degree of foreign language proficiency prior to departure – but decrease there has been, and it's been significant. Against the continuing erosion of foreign language requirements at our colleges and universities; the conviction of faculty in many academic disciplines that foreign language instruction cannot reasonably be incorporated within already tight curricula; and the increasing use abroad of English in commerce, industry, government and in educational institutions, well over half of all our students now participate in programs that require no development of foreign language proficiency at all.

Nor do we any longer share a belief that our students will, or should expect to, adapt interculturally while abroad – even if many of our promotional program brochures continue to assure students they'll be learning about the "host culture" with which they'll come into contact. It is ironic that the period that has witnessed the coming of age of intercultural communication as an academic discipline, and a corresponding strengthening of our knowledge about intercultural adaptation and learning, should be the same period during which we've developed study abroad programs that often show so little interest in applying these insights to the benefit of our students' learning. The growing perception that English is fast becoming a truly universal language has certainly contributed to the weakening of the traditional views that language and culture are inextricably linked. The perception that "everybody over there speaks English," or in its more ethnocentric form, that "everybody over there *ought* to speak English," has undermined the traditional assumption that the foreigner who wants to understand and to function well in a new culture can accomplish those goals only by acquiring a reasonable degree of proficiency in the local language – an acquisition that, two decades and more ago, was associated with spending a significant amount of time living, working or studying abroad.

As John and Lili Engle have pointed out, the on-going, world-wide homogenization of consumer culture – the ubiquitousness of McDonald's, U.S. popular music, television and films, along with the blue-jeaning of fashion and the multinationalizing of product brands at every turn – is doing its part to convince our students, and some of our faculty as well that learning about another culture isn't necessary or at least isn't particularly challenging, when so much of the world seems bent on adopting the trappings – and apparently the underlying values – of U.S. culture (Engles, 2001). The steady decline of reporting about international events in the U.S. media is clearly implicated as well in the increasing ethnocentrism of our students. The number of international stories U.S. television networks reported on declined more than 50% between 1989 and 1995; a single issue of *Time* magazine in 1968 carried as many internationally focused articles as a month's worth of the magazine's issues in 1998 (Baughman, 1998, p. 125).

In calling attention to the problems that have emerged as the old study abroad consensus has weakened, I'm not bewailing the emergence of new study abroad program *models* per se. I have nothing against short-term, faculty-led study abroad, and I have during my career participated in the development and operation of numerous programs, and particularly short-term programs, that require no foreign language proficiency of participants, and that do not focus on culture learning in any sort of profound or focused way. It's obvious to all of us who send students abroad that a number of those students, whether for financial, academic, or personal reasons, will not be able to, or simply won't, participate if we don't provide creative alternatives to the traditional semester and year-long models that promoted only foreign language study and cultural integration.

It's also obvious, however, that in developing new programs for under-represented student populations, we've left behind the educational objectives of the older paradigm without giving sufficient thought to what the new objectives ought to be. The weakening of the assumptions underlying the older models has unfortunately confronted us with what amounts to an educational void – with students in too many cases filling that void by valuing study abroad more for its entertainment than for its educational possibilities. It's not that students haven't always wanted to go abroad to experience the new, the different, the exotic, and to have the proverbial good time; it's that we used to expect them do this *and* to acquire a language and learn about and adapt to another culture.

Our institutions – which is to say, the faculty, academic advisers, and international administrators who collaborate in designing and delivering programs – are unfortunately too often responding to the erosion of traditional linguistic and intercultural values by simply replacing these with the narrower academic values that prevail on our home campuses. That is, we're now too often framing study abroad for our students as primarily an *academic* activity, simply an extension of on-campus course work that will allow them to earn credits they can use to fill major and university graduation requirements, rather than as a broader *educational* opportunity that will allow them to develop skills that will prove useful to them after they graduate. The conversations that we have with students in meeting with them to plan their experiences abroad, and the professional activities we pursue on our campuses do at least suggest that we've come to value our study abroad programs principally for the academic course work that our students will complete while abroad. We do of course need to work with students to make sure that the management or engineering or international relations courses they will take while abroad will fulfill their graduation requirements, as we need to devote ourselves to working on campus to develop processes that limit the pain involved in providing course equivalencies or transfers for the formal academic work the students complete. However, in focusing more and more on the purely academic side of overseas study, we are doing little or nothing to identify broader and equally important educational objectives for the programs, objectives which clarify the personal, intellectual, professional and intercultural gains we expect our students to make abroad.

Identifying these broader educational objectives requires that we first recognize that different sorts of programs allow for different sorts of learning to take place. This is not a criticism of any sort of program model, simply the recognition that students learn differently when placed in different sorts of learning environments. A student can complete formal academic work in a classroom, whether enrolled in a faculty-led, four-week Political Science program in London or in a year-long, direct enrollment program at a host university in Quito. We would not, however, expect that a student would learn either the same sorts of things, or in the same way, during the four weeks in London as he or she would during the nine months in Quito. The challenge here is to come up with a classification of study abroad program types, one that might eventually be adopted as a national and even an international standard, that will enable us to identify the learning outcomes appropriate to each of the various types. Establishing a standardized classification system will allow us to advise students about what they can realistically expect to get out of a program. They *will* likely increase their foreign language and intercultural proficiency when they enroll in courses taught by host-institution faculty, complete their course work in the local language and live with a host family; they *won't* likely accomplish either when they take courses taught in English by an accompanying home-institution faculty member and live in apartments with other U.S. students. Having that classification system will also allow us to refine the question I posed earlier, replacing "What do we mean by quality in study abroad?" with, "What do we want and expect our students to get out of this particular *type* of study abroad program?"

The first step, the elaboration of a classification system, has already in fact been undertaken: John and Lilli Engle have proposed a five-level classification, with programs being designated, at level one, as "Study Tours or Visits," at level two as "Short Term Study," at level three as "Semester, Academic Year Immersion Programs," and so on (Engles, 1998). In this system, individual programs fall into one or another category according to their design characteristics across seven key elements, or variables: first, the length of the sojourn; second, the relative foreign language proficiency of the students prior to departure; third, the language used in course work abroad; fourth, the context of the course work abroad (that is, whether U.S. or host-country faculty do the teaching, whether students directly enroll or take courses specially arranged for them, and so on); fifth, the type of housing provided; sixth, whether active, guided culture learning is required on site; and seventh, what sort of pre-departure and on-site orientation is provided. As the Engles point out, the way that we manipulate these variables in designing programs provides the parameters within which our students learn. The decisions we make about something as seemingly inconsequential as the type of housing we make available to our students doesn't turn out to be so innocuous after all: whether our students live with a host family, in a dormitory with host-country roommates or in an apartment with other U.S. students determines in important ways what, and how, they learn while they are abroad – and, arguably, even after they return to the U.S.

The Engles' creation of this system is important not only because it articulates the felt need to distinguish between various sorts of study abroad experiences, but because it specifically identifies combinations of key variables that affect student learning for each type of program and thereby points up several specific questions we need to research in order to better understand educational outcomes abroad. Future research may reveal that there are still other variables than those the Engles have identified that significantly affect student learning abroad, or that some of the variables they have identified do not play as salient a role in student learning as the Engles suggest that they do. Nonetheless, their classification system provides an important first step toward gaining a better and more persuasive understanding of what "study abroad performance" means. It points up a way for us to begin to gather information about what works and what doesn't work, from an educational perspective, in study abroad programming – to identify and measure what it is that study abroad is doing for our students.

The Engles' identification of key variables affecting student learning resonates profoundly among those of us who send students abroad. We carry with us a set of beliefs, a loose consensus arrived at through long experience working with students prior to their departure, during their sojourns, and after their return to campus, about how the presence or absence of most, perhaps even all, of the variables identified by the Engles does in fact lead to strikingly different student learning outcomes. However, our knowledge about these outcomes is at this point intuitive, based on personal experience and student and faculty anecdote. Our shared beliefs about the nature of these likely outcomes, which amount to largely untested hypotheses about study abroad performance, can and need to be stated as testable questions that will form the basis of future research. These include:

- Do students participating in direct enrollment programs at host universities abroad indeed become more interculturally proficient than those enrolling in academic travel or in U.S. "island" or "enclave" programs?
- Are students who become interculturally proficient while abroad more likely to perform well in the traditional disciplinary courses – history, biology, marketing,

mathematics – they enroll in, both during their programs and after their return to campus?

- How much does acquiring a reasonable degree of foreign language proficiency, prior to, or during sojourns, academically benefit our students, and especially those studying business, engineering, and other technical and professional subjects that are increasingly taught in English abroad?
- Does the duration of the sojourn in fact play a significant role in student gains in disciplinary knowledge as well as intercultural competence?
- Do students indeed learn foreign languages most effectively and efficiently while enrolled in study abroad, rather than in language classes back on the home campus?
- What role does the presence or absence of a trained on-site program coordinator or resident director play in increasing the intercultural and disciplinary learning of students?
- How does the type of housing a student opts for abroad affect his or her learning?

In evaluating programs, we have in the past all too often designed instruments that, in measuring student satisfaction instead of student learning, have failed to address these and other questions related to learning outcomes. A recent survey of leading U.S. study abroad institutions found that 96% of the questionnaires students are asked to complete after returning from a program abroad are measuring student satisfaction. Less than a third of the responding institutions indicated that the questionnaires they use assess gains in academic achievement, only 13% that they assess intercultural competence, and less than 10% that they measure "career-related outcomes" (Davis, 2001, p. 1). There's no question that understanding how students consciously respond, emotionally and intellectually, to the various elements of a study abroad experience, from selection and admission through pre-departure and on-site orientation, to coursework, independent projects and right on through to re-entry de-briefing, is important. However, measuring degrees of student satisfaction alone won't tell us what students are learning abroad or how they're learning it. Nor will they provide us with the sort of data we need to be able to convince skeptical colleagues at our institutions about the values of studying abroad, or to be able to make adjustments in the design of the programs we organize for our students abroad.

A number of institutions and individuals have, however, recently begun developing research projects and applying instruments which shed light on these and other questions related to learning outcomes. The University System of Georgia is in the early stages of a comprehensive study which aims to identify several factors involved in providing for quality study abroad: the potential cognitive, affective and behavioral outcomes for students enrolling in both short- and long-term programs; the specific program characteristics that maximize the benefits of different types of programs; the characteristics of successful study abroad participants; and more (Rubin & Sutton, 2001). The Institute for the International Education of Students (IES), in its "Model Assessment Project for Study Abroad," or MAP, provides a valuable framework for planning and evaluating academic quality in study abroad programs. The MAP focuses, among other things, on student learning and the development of intercultural competence, identifying educational outcomes in five discrete areas: intellectual development, development of language and communication skills, cognitive growth, interpersonal growth, and intrapersonal growth (IES, pp. 9, 21–22).

The School for International Training (SIT) is focusing on the development of intercultural competence during study abroad as well, completing the first phase of a pilot program to assess gains in this area. SIT is relying on two instruments designed to measure increases in student ability to interact with those of other cultures, the Intercultural Development Inventory (IDI), developed by Milton Bennett and Mitch Hammer (discussed in Hammer, 1999), and the Cross-Cultural Adaptability Inventory (CCAI), developed by Colleen Kelley and Judith Meyers. The IDI is based on Milton Bennett's "Developmental Model of Intercultural Sensitivity," a well-known and frequently cited linear model that identifies six progressive stages that individuals apparently pass through in adapting interculturally (Bennett, 1986); the results of the IDI place an individual at one point or another along this six-stage developmental continuum. The CCAI provides measures of four dimensions – emotional resilience, flexibility/openness, perceptual acuity, and personal autonomy – which are held to be predictive about the extent to which an individual can work with people in a culture different than his or her own (Kelley & Meyers, 1992). Extensive field testing and analysis of both instruments have shown that they are valid and reliable; this testing supports their use in measuring student gains in intercultural competence during study abroad. Both instruments have been administered, on a pre-and post-test basis, to students enrolling in a number of SIT programs.

A pilot study administered by the Institute of International Education (IIE) promises significantly to broaden the scope of research on the intercultural impact of studying abroad. Students whose participation in programs abroad has been supported through National Security Education Program (NSEP) funding are now completing an instrument designed to measure their relative capacity to integrate interculturally. The study, which grows out of work in student development theory, has important implications for future research on the relationship between study abroad and intercultural proficiency (Davis, 2001, pers. com.). If it can be shown that some individuals have a stronger capacity, innate or learned, than do others for learning interculturally while enrolled in study abroad, this variable will need to be taken into account in designing future studies. Students who, whether innately or through previous experience, are "gifted" intercultural learners, presumably make intercultural progress even in those learning environments abroad whose characteristics – in terms of program duration, amount of prior language training, type of housing – would limit the learning of less interculturally inclined students.

A number of studies are also attempting to measure and document the impact of study abroad on foreign language acquisition. The National Foreign Language Center at the University of Maryland, in partnership with the National Security Education Program, has since 1996 been using the Oral Proficiency Interview (OPI), a measure of spoken language proficiency developed in the early 1980s by the American Council on the Teaching of Foreign Languages (ACTFL), to document foreign language gains of undergraduates who have studied abroad after receiving NSEP scholarships. While the study is still on-going, the preliminary data indicate that "study in country is in fact the key to the attainment of functional proficiency," and that "any program that has true functional ability in a foreign language as its goal must include a study abroad component" (National Foreign Language Center, 2000, pp. 28–29). The School for International Training has been relying on the OPI as well in a pilot program designed to measure and document gains in foreign language proficiency of students enrolling in SIT programs. Comparisons of participant results in the National Foreign Language Center and SIT studies with the results from control groups of students who have remained in the U.S. and studied the same foreign languages on their home campuses will provide much-needed data about the relative effectiveness of studying languages abroad. The American University Center of Provence (AUCP) has begun to use another instrument, the *Test d'Evaluation de Français*, developed by the *Chambre de Commerce et d'Industrie de Paris*, to measure language proficiency gains of U.S. students enrolling in the AUCP study abroad program in Aix-en-Provence (L. Engle, 2001, pers. conv.).

These studies and efforts, sponsored for the most part by individual institutions and organizations, point up several future research needs. First, it is clear that we need broader inter-institutional efforts to identify educational outcomes appropriate to different types of study abroad programs. The recruitment of students is becoming ever more competitive, with individual institutions and third-party providers maintaining that their particular approach to organizing and running study abroad programs is superior to all others. We hear claims that students learn best when they enroll in island programs designed specifically for U.S. students, when they are enrolled directly in host universities abroad, when they are enrolled in programs featuring extensive fieldwork or other experiential activities, and so on. The results of studies designed by single institutions or organizations, in focusing only on students enrolled in their own particular "brand" of programs, will at the very least inevitably risk being perceived as self-serving. The results of inter-institutional research, designed collaboratively by colleagues from more than one institution – particularly institutions whose student profiles and philosophies about study abroad are to some degree different – will prove more reliable and convincing than will the results of efforts focusing on students sent abroad by a single institution.

Second, faculty, advisers and study abroad administrators from two or more institutions, committed to working collaboratively, will need to begin their research efforts by identifying a study abroad classification system that provides a common way of thinking about and describing their students' experiences abroad, one that will clearly identify the variables whose impact on learning they want to measure. The Engles' system will serve as a useful point of departure in this regard, proceeding as it does by identifying those very program variables – foreign language preparation, delivery of courses in the target language, type of housing provided, and so on – which many, probably most, international educators intuitively believe are significantly implicated in student learning abroad. As institutions work with this classification system, the results of their research may produce refinements in it over time; at this point, it's the best classification that's been proposed and will prove very helpful in framing research questions.

Third, faculty representing specific disciplinary areas at each of the institutions involved will need to participate actively in the design of these inter-institutional studies. While study abroad administrators from each of the institutions involved will of course participate as well, they need to partner with faculty and academic advisers who will be able to identify study abroad learning outcomes appropriate to the needs of students in their respective disciplines. Faculty members in Business will, in the long run, be supportive of study abroad programs whose design characteristics permit students to learn the knowledge and acquire the skills and awareness that will both allow them to do well in their Business courses after their return to campus and, more broadly, prepare them for careers after graduation. The knowledge and skills needed by Business students will, of course, differ in significant ways from the needs of Chemistry, Engineering or International Relations students. The faculty in each disciplinary area will be interested in research that focuses on program design characteristics that will presumably most directly benefit their students. Business faculty, for example, need data that shed light on a series of questions being asked in Business colleges and schools across the U.S.: what type of study abroad experiences provide optimal opportunities to acquire the interpersonal, intercultural, leadership, team-building and other skills that lead to success in an increasingly global economy? How important is it for Business students to become proficient in a foreign language? What type of language-learning program abroad provides the best language-learning results? What role does program duration play in the acquisition of interpersonal, intercultural and foreign language skills? How does the type of housing provided abroad impact the learning of knowledge and the acquisition of important skills? (Keillor, 2001, pers. comm.)

Fourth, any research design needs to include one or more instruments capable of measuring the intercultural learning of our students. All of my experience as an international educator tells me that the constellation of knowledge, skills and awareness which are brought together through the terms "intercultural competence" or "intercultural proficiency" is profoundly implicated in all aspects of effective student learning abroad. This conviction, which I share with many other international educators, is as I've noted before, intuitive and based, like most of our current knowledge about learning abroad, on our own observations and experience. The *sine qua non* of *any* study abroad experience is that it occurs abroad, in a different country and culture. It follows that if we are to understand what our students are learning in this new and different culture, and how they are learning it, we must necessarily begin by focusing our research efforts on the *intercultural* character of the learning that is taking place. Our conviction about the inevitable intercultural nature of learning abroad can, as we have seen, be stated as a series of fundamental propositions, or hypotheses, that can and need to be tested, whatever the disciplinary background of the students: that students who study abroad become more interculturally competent than those who stay on the home campus; that students who become meaningfully proficient in a foreign language, before or during their sojourns abroad, are more likely to become interculturally competent than those who speak only English; that students who become interculturally competent will academically outperform those who do not, both in their courses abroad and in those they take back on the home campus after their return; that interculturally competent students will be more successful in their careers after graduation.

Fifth, institutions collaborating in the design of studies need to make an early decision about whether to develop their own instrument to measure and document intercultural learning, or to rely on one or more which have already been developed. Anyone interested in implementing a study in the short run will be well advised to rely on already existing instruments: the field testing and analysis that will be required to confirm a newly developed instrument's reliability and validity will require expertise in intercultural communication and in assessment, significant financial resources and considerable time. The two instruments I discussed earlier, the Intercultural Development Inventory (IDI) and the Cross-Cultural Assessment Inventory (CCAI), have been shown to be valid and reliable measures of intercultural learning; faculty and administrators designing studies should study both and decide whether one or both will be able to serve the needs of their particular study.

Finally, long-range study abroad impact studies, of the type that the University System of Georgia (Rubin & Sutton, 2000) and Michigan State University have launched (Ingraham, 2000, pers. conv.), need to be designed inter-institutionally as well. Such studies will provide other useful forms of data by measuring such things as the overall and major GPAs of students who have participated in study abroad, the amount of time it takes them to graduate, their career choices and income levels after graduation, and so on. Impact studies allow us to begin to answer those questions that can't be easily or thoroughly be tested through pre- and post-testing of students: the extent to which the development of foreign language proficiency is important to Business students can, for example, be examined by compiling long-range data about the career paths of students after graduation. Like reluctant faculty members, administrators on home campuses who are focused on the very apparent costs of study abroad – lowered enrollments in majors courses on campus, reduction in enrollment-based college or departmental allocations, loss of institutional revenue to foreign institutions, empty dormitory rooms on campus – will need these sorts of impact data, in addition to evidence that students are becoming interculturally proficient, or that their foreign language skills are significantly increasing, if they are to become meaningfully supportive of study abroad programs when these require increases in institutional resources over time.

There are structural challenges ahead, as many of our institutions face the task of re-aligning offices and operations so that study abroad can better be designed and promoted for its educational value to students. For many institutions, shifting the primary focus from recruiting students to developing, delivering and evaluating programs abroad will prove difficult, given the reality that sufficient budgetary support for study abroad activities is often tied to expectations of annual increases in overseas enrollments. Those study abroad offices which are administratively organized under an institution's student affairs wing, rather than under academic affairs, may also find it challenging to convince those faculty colleagues who regard "the academics" of study abroad as their exclusive domain that it is necessary to identify and focus on educational outcomes – on the development of those specific skills, attitudes and knowledge that will benefit students in particular disciplines after graduation. Our success in meeting these and other challenges will depend on our ability to articulate to colleagues across our institutions a vision of what quality study abroad can mean for participating students, and to provide research data that clearly document the range of potential learning outcomes that occur across different types of programs.

REFERENCES

Baughman, J. (1998). The return of isolationism: The decline of global reporting in the American news media. *Communiqué, 8*(2), 1–4.

Bennett, M. J. (1986). Toward ethnorelativism: A developmental model of intercultural sensitivity. In: R. M. Paige (Ed.). *Cross-cultural Orientation: New Conceptualizations and Applications* (pp. 27–70). New York: University Press of America.

Davis, T. M. (2001a). Personal conversation, June 1.

Davis, T. M. (2001b). SECUSSA/IIE electronic sampling of "Outcomes assessment and study abroad programs." Retrieved April 22, 2001 from the World Wide Web: http://www. opendoorsweb.org/Lead%20Stories/Assessment.html, 1–6.

Davis, T. M. (2000). *Open Doors 2000*. New York: Institute of International Education.

Engle, J., & Engle, L. (1998). Study abroad levels: Notes toward a classification of study abroad program types. Published NAFSA Conference Paper. Presented June 2, 1998 by John and Lilli Engle at the 1998 NAFSA: Association of International Educators Conference in Washington, D.C.

Engle, J., & Engle, L. (2001). Globalization, the hermetic American self, and 'authentic' study abroad. Presented by Lilli Engle May 30, 1991 at the 2001 NAFSA: Association of International Educators Conference in Philadelphia, PA.

Engle, L. (2001). Personal conversation, June 12.

Fisher, G. H. (1956). *When Americans Live Abroad*. Washington, D.C.: U.S. Government Printing Office.

Hammer, M. R. (1999). A measure of intercultural sensitivity: The Intercultural Development Inventory. In: S. M. Fowler & M. G. Mumford (Eds), *The Intercultural Sourcebook:* (Vol. 2, pp. 61–72). Yarmouth, ME: Intercultural Press.

Ingraham, E. (2001). Personal conversation, June 1.

Institute for the International Education of Students (IES) (2000). "The IES MAP for study abroad." IES informational brochure, 1–28.

Keillor, B. (2001). Personal communication received August 9.

Kelley, C., & Meyers, J. (1992). *The cross-cultural adaptability inventory manual*. Minneapolis, MN: National Computer Systems.

The National Foreign Language Center (2000). Impact of in-country study on language ability: National Security Education Program undergraduate scholarship and graduate fellowship recipients: draft report vol. 1.5, pp. 1–33.

Rubin, D., & Sutton, R. (2001). Study abroad learning outcomes assessment. Presented at the American Association for Higher Education Assessment Forum Conference in Denver, Colorado, June 25, 2001.

SUCCESSFUL RECRUITMENT OF BUSINESS STUDENTS FOR STUDY ABROAD THROUGH PROGRAM DEVELOPMENT, CURRICULAR INTEGRATION AND MARKETING

Kathleen Sideli, Marc Dollinger and Sharon Doyle

One of the major growth aspects of my international experiences was that it gave me a different view of people and the world. I realized there are many different types of people and perceptions. We have views and stereotypes of them and they have views and stereotypes of us. But the key is overcoming those stereotypes and making a working relationship and friendship with others quite unlike you. There is no space for xenophobia in the new world order. If I started an international company today, now I realize I would hire more non-Americans than Americans because that is what is more representative of the world. It is a competitive advantage to have a work force that can tailor itself to the local customs and social aspects (Jack Ross, 1998).

This comment was made by an Indiana University (IU) Kelley School of Business (KSB) Computer Information Systems major who studied on a summer program in Cambridge in 1997, followed by a semester-long internship in Information Technology, which took him to offices in Belgium, Denmark, England, Finland, The Netherlands and Spain. He made this statement to a packed group of students who came out one evening in the spring of 1998 to attend a recruitment meeting about international opportunities. Jack is hardly unique at the KSB at IU. Over a quarter of all IU students who study abroad today are business majors, yet in 1981,

Study Abroad: Perspectives and Experiences from Business Schools
Advances in International Marketing, Volume 13, 37–57.
Copyright © 2003 by Elsevier Science Ltd.
All rights of reproduction in any form reserved
ISSN: 1474-7979/PII: S1474797902130043

IU had only one business program abroad that attracted just 20 students. How did this remarkable change in recruiting so many business students to study abroad take place in the past two decades?

RECRUITMENT FOR STUDY ABROAD THROUGH PROGRAM DEVELOPMENT

Throughout the early 1980s, schools of business struggled with ways to internationalize their faculty, students and curriculum. In the face of an increasingly global economy, it was necessary for schools to meet this challenge. Various strategies were employed: infusion of global topics into the classes, creation of International Business departments, the implementation of the CIBER program (Center for International Business Education and Research) and faculty exchanges. Although the Kelley School of Business tried all of these, our most successful efforts to internationalize students has been by facilitating overseas experiences through organized study abroad programs.

Although the Office of Overseas Study, which centralized study abroad programs in 1970, offered a number of academic year options and a few semester and summer programs, business students rarely participated in them. This was not surprising since most of the programs required a background in a foreign language. Therefore, KSB early on decided to develop its own programs. Beginning with a semester-long program at Tilburg University, The Netherlands, in 1981, we began to focus on how to give our students the greatest opportunity to experience global business trends. We created these opportunities in order to ensure that our students would be better prepared for careers which are increasingly international, experience the type of personal growth and maturation which are key to higher-level managerial success, become more sensitive to issues of cultural diversity, speak – or at least appreciate – other languages and develop special skills for life-long learning. In short, our goal has been to ensure that the Kelley graduate would be, as much as possible, a citizen of the world. To that end we developed a close partnership with the Office of Overseas Study on our campus so that jointly we could offer students a wide range of interesting possibilities overseas.

When looking at the progression of the development of the various program models we now have, it appears that there may have been an organized plan for their development. Although there was never a long-range formalized plan, the pioneers who developed study abroad programs in the Kelley School of Business ultimately envisioned programs which would one day entail advanced language ability and even involve direct enrollment with host country students. However, those same faculty members intuited that they needed to start more modestly, so they began with programs of special courses taught in English. Only when students were successful with this early model did the faculty venture to create more complex models. They then looked to direct enrollment, first in countries where English was the native or second language, and then eventually to programs requiring an advanced level in a foreign language. Along the way they tackled the creation of business internships for credit in challenging environments and ultimately created a dual degree program involving not only direct enrollment in a foreign language but also the ability for KSB students to earn a degree abroad simultaneous with their IU degree.

The opportunity for the first program model came from entrepreneurial Dutch colleagues who agreed to create a range of special courses in English for our students. These focused on business from an international perspective, emphasizing the evolution of the European Union and the role of The Netherlands, which historically needed a conciliatory perspective to do business with its neighbors. Although the Office of Overseas Study had a series of year-long programs in Europe at that time, this one was the first which would be a semester in length, offer courses in English, and would offer credits that could be used towards a business degree. This special profile became the standard design of KSB programs for quite some time. Additionally, the program model incorporated an IU business professor who functioned both as an on-site director and a faculty member since all students were required to take his or her course. This rotation of KSB professors provided faculty development at the same time that it built support for the programs. That is, the faculty took advantage of the intellectual opportunities available to them abroad and upon their return promoted the experience to their future students.

The semester program soon relocated from Tilburg to the University of Maastricht. With the advent of ERASMUS (European Regional Action Scheme for the Mobility of University Students) a decade later, U.S. students benefited by having English-speaking European students alongside them in special courses and also gained access to regularly offered courses, taught in English, with their Dutch counterparts. Due to the growing popularity of the Maastricht program, KSB decided to create a summer program at the same location to accommodate the growing numbers of interested students. Creating the summer program model also recognized the reality that certain students would only venture abroad for a shorter period of time outside the months of the regular academic school year. A second summer program – three courses taken during 9 weeks abroad – was later initiated in Mikkeli, Finland, again to give students the opportunity to view business from the perspective of northern Europe. Although the location has never attracted as many applicants as Maastricht, Mikkeli has proven to be a serious and successful program.

The model for direct enrollment began with a semester program in Singapore in order to give students the advantage of viewing business and economics within the Pacific Rim. Due to the fact that English was the language used at the National University of Singapore, IU students at first were easily recruited for this program that, for a number of years, was led by an IU faculty director who also taught a course for the IU students and their Singaporean peers. Unfortunately, due to many academic and cultural differences between the two systems, we were increasingly unable to recruit enough students to make this program viable. We eventually replaced that program with a small exchange at the City University of Hong Kong so students can continue to learn about business from an Asian perspective.

A decade after our initial foray into creating special programs in English for business majors, KSB also began to realize that an increasing number of our students had sufficient language background to warrant the creation of programs requiring language ability. The first of these, a direct enrollment exchange program in Santiago, Chile, suffered from low enrollment in the years before Santiago became a popular site abroad for American undergraduates. The Santiago program was replaced by a more successful semester program, also requiring Spanish language, launched at ITESM (Instituto Tecnológico de Estudios Superiores de Monterrey). Similarly, IU students with a significant background in French enroll at the École Supérieure de Commerce in Rouen, France where they take business as well as culture courses, both in French and English, with students from all over the world.

The most innovative and challenging KSB venture that combines foreign language and business is the dual degree program at the Fachhochschule Reutlingen which gives program participants (from both institutions) a B.S. degree from KSB and a Diplom-Betriebswirt (FH) degree from Reutlingen after spending a full year at the foreign institution and a semester doing an internship. An earlier semester program in Ljubljana, Slovenia could not be sustained because of its proximity to the various political upheavals in that part of Central Europe. However, the contacts there have led to a successful summer internship program in the same location. Equally successful summer internships operate in Erlangen-Nurnberg and Pforzheim, Germany which require a significant background in German language.

KSB's most recent additions include a direct enrollment semester at the University of Manchester in Great Britain and a summer or semester option at Denmark's International Study Program at the University of Copenhagen. The long-standing relationship with the University of Maastricht has also resulted in an extended degree program where students from IU can graduate in five years with a B.S. from IU and a special MBA from the University of Maastricht.

Although the progression of program models has moved towards more challenging learning environments – beginning with programs of special courses in

English and ending with full immersion experiences in a foreign language – KSB currently maintains programs involving the entire range of models since they are appropriate for different kinds of students.

Despite having this broad range of program models available to KSB students, our students need an even wider range of options, including non-business focused programs. Therefore, the active partnership on campus between KSB and the Office of Overseas Study has resulted in our students having access not only to our business programs but also those available to the entire Indiana University student body. The Chair of the Undergraduate Program in KSB, who is responsible for the undergraduate business programs abroad, sits on the university-wide Overseas Study Advisory Council which reviews and approves all proposals for study abroad programs that take place under the auspices of Indiana University. A close working relationship has evolved between KSB and the Office of Overseas Study as they share managerial functions for all aspects of the business programs. This collegiality and cooperation fosters trust in both directions, and allows both units to share their expertise across all areas, from recruiting, screening, advising and orienting the students to visiting, reviewing, and collaborating with the programs overseas. While KSB staff and faculty recruit, select and advise students for its own programs, Overseas Study reviews, confirms and processes the dossiers, which includes having student disciplinary records screened by the Dean of Students. The two units collaborate to create the written promotional and orientation materials, which are distributed by Overseas Study, and plan the recruitment and orientation programs, which are led by KSB. The Director of Overseas Study and the Chair of the Undergraduate Business Programs in KSB together plan program site visits and reviews, within the context of the Overseas Study Advisory Council that monitors all visits and reviews. Meanwhile, the manager/advisor of international programs in KSB works closely with the study abroad advisors at Overseas Study. This dynamic relationship between KSB and Overseas Study benefits the students on all levels.

RECRUITMENT FOR STUDY ABROAD THROUGH CURRICULAR INTEGRATION

The Value Proposition for Undergraduate Business Majors

If a value proposition is the motivating factor that compels a customer to a product, in this case, the customer is the undergraduate business student and the product is study abroad. As we have reviewed, KSB has developed an interesting portfolio of diverse study abroad programs specifically designed for students of business.

But what has really motivated the Kelley undergraduate to participate in study abroad?

The availability of a wide range of program options of varying lengths and models abroad did not by itself result in the successful recruitment of business students for study abroad programs. Our commitment to internationalization also led us to a number of curricular innovations that, in turn, have led to increased numbers of students seeking study abroad programs. Students began to clamor for study abroad opportunities once they viewed them as being related to their overall degree requirements.

(1) International Dimension Requirement

The creation of the International Dimension Requirement (IDR) grew out of our inability to thoroughly internationalize the curriculum without a specific requirement. Like many business schools, we went through a period of study where we looked at ways to internationalize our courses. We examined and adopted a number of different models, such as specialized international functional area classes. Thus we created classes like *International Management, International Business*, and *Global Financial Strategies*. We also were determined to infuse global business topics in every class where it was appropriate. So marketing classes frequently talk about how marketing issues differ from country to country and entrepreneurship classes provide examples of non-American entrepreneurs.

While the infusion strategy and the adoption of specialized courses were considered progress towards the goal of internationalizing our students, most of our students still had little exposure to global topics, and issues, and many missed classes with international content by majoring in Accounting, Operations and Production, Computer Information Science and the like. Consequently, the next step was to make some form of international exposure and global study a requirement.

Consequently, we created the *International Dimension Requirement* (IDR) in 1988 for all students in KSB. The Chair of the Undergraduate Program proposed this requirement to the Undergraduate Program Committee of KSB. It then needed the approval of the Academic Council before the proposal was put to a vote by the entire faculty of KSB. It had wide support from the start and received unanimous approval because of the importance given to globalization. Students also reacted favorably to the requirement since it could be fulfilled by one of four interesting options:

(a) two years of language study;
(b) six hours of international business and economics courses;
(c) a set of area studies courses or;
(d) a study abroad program with at least six credit hours of course work.

Of the four options, all involving six credit hours, our experience has been that many students find the study abroad option very compelling.

Option 1: Language Students need 6 credit hours of a language at the 200-level or above. Since many students come to us with some competency in a foreign language, they are required to do further study, pass a confirmation test, or start a new language in order to meet our requirement for second-year proficiency. Almost 30% of KSB graduates have two years of a language by the time they graduate and most of them use this language proficiency to satisfy the IDR. There was a movement in the early 1980s, by our internationally minded faculty who developed KSB's programs abroad, to have a foreign language requirement for all business students but this initiative failed. Nevertheless, language is highlighted and promoted throughout the various internationalization efforts evidenced here.

Option 2: International business and economics Six hours of international courses are usually fulfilled by a sequence of International Business and Economics courses. These are frequently taught in large lecture sections and, although the level of instruction is excellent, these courses resemble most of the other courses students will take at the Kelley School of Business. This is the option which students choose the most often to satisfy the IDR.

Option 3: Area studies Six hours of area studies courses can be selected from seven different divisions: African, Central Eurasian, East Asia, Latin America and the Caribbean, Near Eastern, Russian and East European, and Western European Studies. This option is the one least selected by students.

Option 4: Overseas programs As long as the credits from a program abroad articulate back to IU as 6 hours or more, a student can fulfill the requirement for the IDR by going abroad. In addition to the rich array of KSB's study abroad programs administered within the School, students can choose from dozens of excellent study abroad programs that are administered or co-sponsored by Indiana University's Office of Overseas Study. Finally, those students who cannot find the exact geographical location desired in IU's vast selection choose to go abroad through a program offered by another university or a program provider. Approximately 15% of graduating seniors use a study abroad program to satisfy the IDR. From its inception, the IDR has resulted in an increase in business students going abroad.

(2) International Field Specialization
In 1996, two other important curricular options were introduced to further allow students an opportunity to emphasize international issues in their degree program:

an *International Field Specialization*, which is part of the general education curriculum, and an *International Studies Concentration*, which can be added to another major. Once the *International Dimension Requirement* served as the catalyst that demonstrated our commitment to giving our students a global perspective on business, it became easier to introduce other international curricular elements to our degree programs.

All KSB students must complete 27 credits in general education requirements to complement their business requirements. They can satisfy this requirement in two ways:

Option 1: Nonspecialization general education option Many students choose to complete their 27 credits in a non-specialized way, that is, selecting courses from a wide range of courses under the categories of arts and humanities, social and historical studies and natural and mathematical sciences, choosing a concentration of 15 credits (6 at an advanced level) in one of these three broad areas, with 6 credits in each of the others.

Option 2: Field specialization option The field specialization option is a second, more focused way to satisfy this general education requirement. Instead of splitting their credits among the three areas described above, students select a combination of 27 credits taken in one of five areas (Communication, Environmental, International, Arts and Social Service or Science and Technology). Students increasingly see the benefits of selecting the *International Field Specialization* since it allows them to focus on one or more international topics (e.g. African Studies, Jewish Studies, Spanish, French, Germanic Studies, etc.). They all soon discover how well it works out to combine the *International Field Specialization* with a program overseas since they can easily pick up the necessary area studies programs for their field, by selecting the appropriate program. (Note: During the academic year 2001–2002, this field specialization will be renamed '*Global Studies and Languages*' rather than '*International*' to more accurately describe its composition.)

(3) International Studies Concentration

The third international option, the *International Studies Concentration*, is a concentration that can be added to any major but cannot be a stand-alone major. It comprises 15 credits. Students fulfill this concentration by completing the *International Dimension Requirement* and then 9 credit hours of further course work from one of the four areas not used to satisfy the IDR. Students with a strong language background (two years), typically use their language work to satisfy the IDR and then use a study abroad program to complete the *International Studies Concentration*.

How well have these three curricular initiatives worked in internationalizing our students? By the time they graduate, approximately 30% of the graduates of the Kelley School of Business have completed an overseas study program of 6, 15 or 30 credit hours and about 10% of the students complete the International Studies concentration, and many others complete the International Field Specialization as a means of fulfilling their general education requirements. The students clearly recognize the value of internationalizing their worldview.

If we believe that study abroad is the optimum way to internationalize KSB students of the world, then these curricular initiatives have gone far in helping us achieve that goal since these academic incentives have led more and more business students to study abroad.

Yet there certainly has to be more to the value proposition than just meeting requirements for graduation. Below are some of the other arguments and benefits for study abroad that we put forth in advising sessions, information sessions and in our recruiting literature.

RECRUITMENT FOR STUDY ABROAD THROUGH MARKETING

In addition to embedding study abroad into the curriculum, KSB articulates a variety of convincing benefits and values to compel students to consider going overseas as part of their undergraduate studies.

Careers Are Becoming More International

We are, after all, a professional school and students come to us for professional and career training with the expressed intention of graduating from IU and beginning a good job. We have long recognized the fact that the world of business demands professionals who can work and succeed in an international environment. Now many students are being similarly persuaded. The undergraduate business student is a pragmatic thinker who will pursue the means to the ends, that is, the better job.

Although few students, other than our foreign born nationals, move directly into international assignments, many of our fast track undergraduates anticipate and welcome an overseas transfer early in their careers. Employers understand that students who have successfully navigated the international waters in study abroad are usually well prepared to accept an overseas assignment and thrive in it. These students have already experienced the problems of culture conflict, language difficulty and problem solving under difficult circumstances. While study abroad is not a perfect indicator of professional success, the student has demonstrated a tolerance for ambiguity, a willingness to take personal risk and an ability to survive in an uncertain environment. These are the keys to higher-level managerial success.

Personal Growth and Development (Maturation)

Another of the value propositions for study abroad is that the student will return to IU more mature, more seasoned and with a better sense of self. We see students returning from a study abroad experience better able to handle the vicissitudes of campus life. They have developed a feeling that sometimes patience is required, that things do not work out as intended and that personal flexibility can be a positive characteristic. The intense nature of the cultural shock of study abroad brings students face to face with their limitations. By confronting them, they seek to overcome them.

We have been, unfortunately, negligent in documenting the degree of personal growth achieved by these programs. There are two reasons for this. First, personal growth is difficult to measure. Second, the resources do not exist for this type of follow-up. But our observations and anecdotal evidence tell us that this is one of the benefits of overseas study and we communicate this to the students in orientation sessions.

Sensitivity to Diversity Issues

Most of the students at KSB are majority male students. Therefore, our students abroad finally begin to feel what it is like to belong to an ethnic or cultural minority. Their behavior, their skin color, their accents, or their t-shirts call attention to them. Although there are many resources on campus which are dedicated to providing the training needed to sensitize these students to the special problems and issues of being a minority, there is nothing like walking in another's shoes to empathize with the experience. No matter where our students study their attention is drawn to the cultural diversity prevalent in other societies around the world. And minority students themselves can gain new perspectives on diversity. Damian Peoples, who studied for a year at the University of Madrid in 1997–1998, was hired upon graduation as a finance associate by Baxter International, Inc. to work first in Maurepas, France and then in Brussels, Belgium. In his own words, "My year abroad was an eye-opening experience that prepared me for a future role as an international businessman. Never have I learned more about people, culture and language. Never have I learned more about myself and my own abilities. Studying abroad made me appreciate diversity, think independently and relate with others. These are probably the three skills I have found most valuable in my business career."

Additional Values Promoted By Study Abroad

There are a number of other benefits of study abroad and arguments in its favor that we make with students or that students recognize without our counsel.

- Study abroad promotes life-long learning since it demonstrates that learning is not limited to Indiana University, the United States, or a college campus. Living in another culture makes many people curious about the language, society, folkways, and ethics that they encounter. Curious people continue to learn and also learn how to teach themselves. They develop strategies to gather information and rules to process this information that develops complexity in their thinking. The overseas study experience is a strong stimulus.
- Study abroad promotes strong friendships with the people who are sharing the experience with you. This is particularly true of our large program in Maastricht. People who share difficulties, fun and exploration, learning and problem-solving over a long period of time with each other will become friends. These relationships may last long periods of time because the bonds of these activities are so meaningful to the participants.
- Study abroad gives students access to other academic contexts where they learn a variety of different perspectives regarding the various subjects and disciplines they choose to study while abroad. This is particularly critical in the area of business that is often approached differently in other cultures.
- Students are exposed to all-important cultural cues and different attitudes, manners, etc. that are of critical importance and cannot be thoroughly learned any other way.
- Study abroad provides students with opportunities to network while they are abroad since they are in classes with students from business backgrounds from other countries. Some of these networking experiences result in future employment opportunities.
- Study abroad can connect students with international IU alumni. We always take the opportunity to bring the students together with alumni living in foreign countries. This often gives the students a model for a career overseas or just shows them that Indiana University Kelley School of Business has a worldwide reach. Alumni also appreciate being brought into these activities. It bonds them with the school and enables them to pay back with kindness and commitment the debt they incurred when they were the guests in our country.

OTHER RECRUITMENT STRATEGIES

KSB uses numerous recruitment strategies, besides the programmatic and curricular elements outlined above, to reach students with the message that they should consider studying overseas. While these are not necessarily innovative, the combination of all these methods, in combination with the curriculum requirements, results in an increasing number of business students going abroad.

Returnees

The best marketing tools are the students who have participated in the programs. Word of mouth, that is, student satisfaction, is by far the most widely-used means of spreading information about study abroad in the KSB. Students love to talk about their experiences. Special presentations that advertise the programs incorporate returnees but it seems that student-to-student discussions are, by far, the most effective means of recruitment.

Meetings

Informational meetings are held to promote the programs for which selection is being made that semester. Former participants are invited and encouraged to bring their photo albums and videos to these meetings. The discussions that emerge from the students in attendance often center on "what's in it for me." They invariably want to know what they can do while on the study abroad program in addition to attending classes. While they are interested in knowing what courses they will be taking and how those will fulfill degree requirements, they also want to know the other benefits of study abroad. In this case, the former participants are the best source of information available regarding extracurricular activities, travel, networking, etc.

Displays

The Kelley School of Business has displays on all of its business programs abroad throughout the building – in key areas such as the advising offices and the commons areas. The Office of Overseas Study also promotes university-wide programs to the business students in these areas.

Web Presence

The Office of Overseas Study and the Kelley School of Business Web sites give copious information on the programs offered and the Kelley web site links to the Office of Overseas Study site to avoid repetitive information. http://www. indiana.edu/~overseas/http://pacioli.bus.indiana.edu/ugrad/overseas.html: There is a special informational flyer available in the Overseas Study Information Center and it is also posted on the Web (http://www.indiana.edu/~overseas/han_bus.html) to inform students how to combine their interest in study abroad with an interest in business. This handout also suggests ways to combine a B.A. degree with a business curriculum or a business degree with a humanities curriculum since it can be quite complex to combine majors/minors or double degrees in these areas.

Students can also easily contact returnees who have agreed to serve in this capacity through the Overseas Study Web site.

Advising

The business advisors are actively involved in recruitment for programs during the normal advising process. For example, when they discuss the International Dimension requirement, the topic of study abroad naturally comes up. When they talk with students with a foreign language background they immediately mention the venues abroad where they can further their language study and how those can also satisfy the International Field Specialization in addition to the International Studies Concentration. Interested students are then guided to the Manager of Undergraduate International Programs to learn more about the options available through Indiana University and, in particular, about the programs sponsored by the Kelley School of Business to see how beneficial the individual programs will be for their own academic needs. Students are also informed about going abroad through external programs, that is, programs offered by other institutions. These discussions also include information sharing about various scholarships and other financial aid opportunities for students going abroad.

Overseas Study Information Center

The Office of Overseas Study, in the administrative services building across campus from KSB, has a large Information Center with flyers, videos, handbooks, extensive notebooks with photos, course equivalency lists and student evaluations, which describe programs offered by Indiana University. It also has a wide selection of promotional brochures and reference books describing programs offered by other institutions. The Center maintains a list of courses from external programs for which students have received credit and student evaluations to assist future students select the most appropriate program for their needs.

Students can talk to former participants who work in the Office of Overseas Study as peer counselors who assist them in understanding the array of programs or in answering many of their basic questions. One of the peer counselors is always a business student. The peer counselors go through rigorous training with the staff of Overseas Study so they understand what information they can give and when they should guide the student to make an appointment with the advisors in the Office of Overseas Study. If the students decide on programs sponsored by other institutions or organizations, the advisor and/or peer counselors make available to them a special packet of forms to ensure the transfer of credit and financial aid, where appropriate, and to explain registration and other university-related activities associated with being off campus.

Ensuring Progress Towards Degree

While all advisors in the Kelley School of Business can assist students in their initial planning to go abroad, once the students have narrowed down their choices, the Manager of Undergraduate International Programs in KSB does most of the detailed advising for participants in the business programs. The basic premise underlying all advising for study abroad at IU is that students who go abroad will make normal progress towards their degree programs. It is the task of the advisor to organize the student's schedule in such a way that the student will be satisfying requirements while abroad so that he or she will be on track for graduation.

IU Business Programs
Most of the approved KSB study abroad programs have a limited group of courses from which the student makes selections. The Manager of Undergraduate International Programs determines, in conjunction with faculty, the appropriateness of a student's course selection for a certain program and determines how best to incorporate those courses into the degree requirements of his or her program of study at IU. Students on the business programs usually satisfy a few courses in their major(s) in addition to general education requirements. The articulation is facilitated by the fact that, for all IU overseas programs, the credits are considered direct credit and actual course numbers from the regular curriculum can be applied to the courses from abroad. The grades also count in their overall GPA which we find is an incentive for students to apply themselves more diligently to

their courses while abroad. An ongoing analysis shows that the average GPAs of the groups accepted to the programs are very similar to the average GPAs of the groups' performances on the programs.

IU Non-Business Programs
Students accepted on the wide array of non-business programs offered by Indiana University meet with an advisor at the Office of Overseas Study after acceptance to determine how the general education courses from those programs will count towards their degree requirements. The Manager of Undergraduate International Programs in KSB reviews the course selections on the advising sheet prepared by Overseas Study to corroborate the applicability of those courses towards the students' minors, general education requirements and/or second-degree requirements. The students also earn 'direct' credit for such courses, although occasionally exceptions need to be made by KSB to allow undistributed general education courses to count towards degree requirements. Students participating in non-business programs are typically taking courses to fulfill their general education requirements, either the non-specialized option or the Field Specialization. Since many of these non-business programs involve foreign languages, business students are also often completing minors in those languages and/or completing the International Studies concentration. A number of them will select a year-long program which concentrates on language and area-studies courses taught in the language and, although the year will put them behind for a 4-year degree in business, many of them will earn a 2nd degree, usually a B.A. in a language area. Students believe that a dual degree (B.S. in Business and a B.A. in a language) will make them more marketable.

Non-IU Program
Students going on external programs meet with both the advisors in Overseas Study and in KSB since exceptions allowing their transfer credits from abroad are made on an individual basis. The Office of Admissions transfers courses from external programs by designating the specific departments of the courses taken abroad but does not make distinctions that would categorize the courses under the various rubrics established for general education requirements (e.g. Arts and Humanities, Social and Behavioral Sciences, etc.). Therefore, the Undergraduate Program Director in the Kelley School has given permission to the business advisors to make these exceptions and substitutions regarding general education requirements rather than trying to get these approved by various department advisors in the College of Arts and Sciences. Petitions to earn credit in their majors for business courses need to be evaluated directly by the faculty responsible for similar courses on campus. Without this type of accommodation there would be fewer business students studying abroad.

It is common for students choosing external programs to focus on their general education requirements while abroad, selecting the non-specialized option. Nevertheless, they put together an interesting assortment of humanities and social sciences courses that often focus on the politics, arts, literature and culture of the country where they will be studying. So, even the non-specialized general education option ends up giving the business students who go abroad a very coherent, focused area studies approach to their intellectual formation. In that sense, they have a stronger background in general education than their counterparts in KSB who do not study abroad.

Recruitment Strategies Summary

It is our belief that KSB students are very aware of the wide range of supports in place to enable them to study abroad. The combination of curriculum requirements, marketing materials, information meetings and advising sessions to ensure progress towards their degrees convey to students the seriousness with which we hold our internationalization efforts. Likewise, they also feel informed enough to select a program abroad, with the confidence that investing academically and financially in the experience will have a positive long-term impact on their lives and their careers.

ORIENTATION AND REENTRY

Our strong support for study abroad, coupled with our belief that students need to have as much information as possible to help them profit on both academic and personal levels while abroad and when they return, have resulted in our providing detailed orientation materials and sessions and a reentry program.

All program participants receive a comprehensive packet of materials including a set of forms (e.g. release from liability, health, scholarship, course selection, etc.) and a program handbook. Orientation meetings for each individual program are held for program participants. These meetings are intended to prepare them as thoroughly as possible for their experience abroad. At such meetings the conveners include the following:

(1) Get acquainted activities for the group.
(2) Overview of forms that need to be filled out and forwarded to the program site.
(3) Review of the program handbook prepared by the Office of Overseas Study.

(4) Discussion of what to expect when they arrive.
(5) Speaker from an appropriate department to give an overview of the country.
(6) Discussion of program policies, including healthy, safety and responsibility issues, (i.e. behavior expected, drug and alcohol usage abroad, ramifications of various risky behaviors, etc.).
(7) Discussion of the academic program: pedagogical methods abroad, what faculty expect from students, how exams are administered etc.
(8) Resident Director introduction (where applicable) and expectations for the group.
(9) Discussion of travel, packing, finances, housing, etc.
(10) Panel of returnees to assist with questions and answers.

While Abroad

Overseas Study continues its orientation efforts by sending a monthly e-mail newsletter to all program participants, keeping them informed about campus activities and posing a set of questions and concepts for them to consider during various times of the year. Again, this is done to urge students to seriously reflect on the experiences they are having while they are having them. Early on in the year, the newsletter reminds them about the various stages of culture shock and how they can cope with them. We also remind them about registration matters, both abroad and for the semester of their return, so that they can take appropriate steps to register in the appropriate classes. We later prepare the groundwork for re-entry adjustments, reminding them how they can best prepare themselves for reverse culture shock, particularly since their families and friends will be encountering a more experienced, well-traveled, hopefully more broad-minded and matured son, daughter, or friend.

Re-entry

In our ongoing attempt to have students reflect on their experiences so that they maximize the impact of study abroad on their lives, the Office of Overseas Study holds a welcome back reentry session, providing detailed information about how to build on a study abroad experience and how to seek out an international career. Unfortunately, business students have rarely taken advantage of these re-entry opportunities. The KSB has also tried a variety of activities, including a welcome back session with a guest speaker to discuss how to incorporate study abroad into the job search. At these sessions there are refreshments, a photo contest, and a list of activities of what students can do on campus to keep active in the area of international interests. However, it has been increasingly difficult to get returnees interested in re-entry activities. They immediately get involved in classroom activities, clubs and interviews for jobs, thus putting re-entry at the bottom of their list of priorities. Some of the students volunteer to assist at information and orientation meetings. Nevertheless, many returnees from study abroad programs promote the programs on an individual basis. Overseas Study has just begun to communicate regularly with returning students via e-mail newsletters, circulating information to help them reflect on reintegrating into their personal and academic lives as they begin to make post graduation plans.

Some returnees work as peer counselors or outreach coordinators in the Office of Overseas Study. With training by Overseas Study, they are able to use their expertise from abroad to assist prospective students. The outreach coordinators give presentations on campus, staff tables in various classroom buildings, and post information on bulletin boards or elsewhere. The peer counselors work in the Information Center where they assist students at the inquiry stage or those who have selected a program. They frequently serve on panels at information and orientation meetings.

IMPACT ON ENROLLMENT TRENDS

Over the past 15 years, KSB students represent an increasingly larger proportion of the undergraduates at IU who study abroad. From representing only 13% of all IU undergraduates abroad in 1986 (the first year Overseas Study computerized its records), in 1998–1999 business majors accounted for 27% and then 23% in 1990–2000. These statistics surpass the national trend that shows that in 1986, 11% of U.S. students abroad had business majors while in 1998–1999 the percentage had only increased to 17.7%.

The increase in participation rates among IU business students has been fairly steady throughout the 1990s as the KSB implemented each of its curricular innovations. As Fig. 1 shows, the increased participation has occurred not only in programs administered or co-sponsored by Indiana University but also in programs offered by other institutions or providers. This shows that IU business students are convinced that the international experience itself, not just the programs designed by KSB, have intrinsic value for their degrees. KSB and IU have been generous in accepting course work from a wide range of programs, allowing students to make progress in their degrees which is the greatest factor motivating their selection of programs.

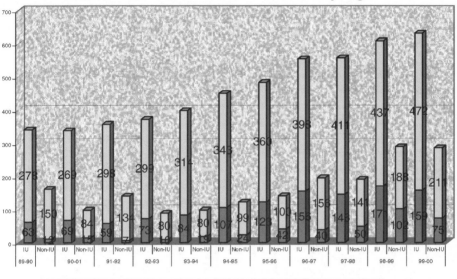

Fig. 1.

Figure 2 shows the types of programs that the business majors have selected in the past eleven years. While they rarely go abroad for an academic year, either through IU or external options, the program duration most popular among business students at IU is the semester. This is impressive since, according to the national statistics published in the Institute for International Education's *Open Doors* survey, 50% of U.S. undergraduates today participate in short-term study abroad programs, that is, those whose duration is *less* than a semester (i.e. summer, quarter, January term, etc.). Sixty percent of the IU business students who studied abroad in 1999–2000 chose programs which were a semester or longer.

They are also diversifying their choices more than before. In 1989–1990 the vast majority of business majors who studied abroad (71%) chose to go abroad with KSB programs. However, as the curriculum innovations evolved over the decade, students began to see that they could satisfy a wide array of related academic requirements on non-business programs (i.e. International Dimension Requirement, the International Field Specialization and the International Studies Concentration). They began to choose from among IU's other administered and co-sponsored programs and from choices outside Indiana University. In fact, in 1998–1999 more

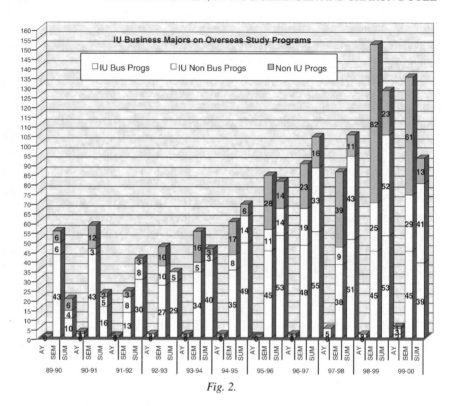

Fig. 2.

than half the business students (54%) who went abroad for the semester chose an option offered by an institution or a provider other than IU. And in that same year 65% of the entire group of business majors abroad chose a program outside KSB programs. Aside from the fact that many KSB business programs have reached capacity, we also know that the students select other programs because they have the confidence that their international experience will be incorporated by IU into their degree program.

CONCLUSION

As is evidenced here, students in Indiana University's Kelley School of Business find an atmosphere that strongly supports study abroad. Prior to the development of the various curricular innovations that now embed internationalism into the degree requirements, business students at IU were wary about going abroad, fearing that such an activity would be considered extraneous to their degree program. Often they felt that their desire to study abroad was frivolous or, worse, a waste of time. However, since the KSB introduced the International Dimension requirement, the International Field Specialization and the International Studies Concentration, students flock to the Office of Overseas Study in search of programs that will help them satisfy these various requirements. Their parents support their choices because they are an integral part of their degrees, and their advisors encourage their participation as well since they will not be delaying their graduation by going overseas. In fact, students often believe now that if they do not study abroad, they will be missing out on a critical life-changing event while also jeopardizing career opportunities in the future. Despite this strong track record of having over 250 business students a year engaged in study abroad, IU needs to further study the demonstrated outcomes. Although a number of us have wonderful anecdotal stories from our students, a more systematic study could prove the impact that study abroad has had on our students.

A favorite example we use to show students how influential study abroad can be on one's life is that of David Hodge, an IU School of Business graduate from 1989. He studied for a semester in KSB's program in Tilburg, The Netherlands, a semester in Seville, Spain and a year in Lima, Peru. He graduated from IU with a B.S. in Business and a B.A. in Spanish and went on to complete a Master's Degree at Georgetown University's School of Foreign Service. In the past decade he has been stationed in Rio de Janeiro, Lisbon, Brasilia, and Buenos Aires, where he is currently the U.S. Consul General. Although David did not pursue a conventional career in business, his training in business coupled with his training in liberal arts and his three stints overseas have given him the broad and balanced perspective that a successful U.S. diplomat needs. When asked recently about what he remembers most about his three study abroad experiences, David said, "There's no doubt in my mind that one cannot be as effective as a foreign affairs practitioner (in business, government, or whatever field) without foreign language skills. ... All three programs were instrumental in my intellectual development by forcing me to look at international issues from a foreign perspective which was great for critical thinking and analysis." Although few IU graduates will have the opportunity to experience three different programs in three countries, students in the Kelley School of Business will know from the moment they start their studies at IU that study abroad is considered an integral part of their degree programs, because they need to train themselves on various levels – academic, professional and personal – to become part of the globalized citizenry who will shape the world of tomorrow.

PARTICIPATION OF MINORITY AND LOW INCOME STUDENTS IN STUDY ABROAD: THE ILLINOIS-NSEP INITIATIVE

Joan D. Solaun

INTRODUCTION

Why is there a need for initiatives such as the one which will be described in the following pages, designed to increase the participation of minority and low income students in study abroad?

Study abroad plays a major role in undergraduate education today. The patent advantages that exposure to new cultures, on-site practice of a foreign language, travel to new places – all of which are mind-expanding and involve some degree of risk-taking have been seen to ultimately promote greater achievement in returning students (Solaun & Goldstein, 1986). The interest at the federal and state level in promoting a greater awareness of our place as citizens of the world has led to new scholarship opportunities and ventures (the National Security Education Program, the Gilman, a grant from the Illinois Board of Higher Education for example, for internationalizing at the K-12 level). The current numbers of U.S. students abroad have increased dramatically. Between 1993–1994 and 1999–2000 we have seen an increase of 58%. The words "globalization" and "internationalization" are current buzzwords at all levels of education. For most U.S. post-secondary educational institutions it has become a necessary tool for educating their students and even for recruiting incoming freshmen to their campuses.

Study Abroad: Perspectives and Experiences from Business Schools
Advances in International Marketing, Volume 13, 59–69.
© 2003 Published by Elsevier Science Ltd.
ISSN: 1474-7979/PII: S1474797902130055

The student population that chooses to study abroad has been relatively stable over the years in terms of ethnic and gender breakdown, however: 85% of participants are white, 65% are female. Although the general impression is that most students tend to be middle class, I do not have actual data to this effect. There is a perceived need to increase the participation of targeted minority groups. According to the statistics provided for 1998–1999 by the Institute of International Education in their publication *Open Doors,* which compiles data from U.S. universities and colleges on international education, minority student participation represents a total of 14% of all students studying abroad for that year. No one questions the need to provide targeted minority students equal opportunity to participate in the "American dream," which now includes a college education. The need to bring minority students into the mainstream, to enable them to become meaningful leaders in their communities, employment and academic fields, now also means that opportunities for them to have an overseas experience must be part of their undergraduate academic training.

Barriers to Minority Participation

The percentage of students at the University of Illinois who studied abroad in the past year who chose to report membership in one of the minority categories listed on our materials is 18%, slightly higher than the national average. In fact, the percentages since 1993–1994 have varied between 15% and 18%, despite the fact that overall numbers have increased on our campus by 58% between 1993–1994 and 1999–2000. (This figure is not reliable in that there were many students who did not report their ethnic status. If, in fact, we take the percentage who do report and base the minority reporting on that figure, the number can be considered considerably higher – 22%). The minority categories are defined as the following: American Indian/Alaskan native; Asian/Pacific Islander; Black (non-Hispanic) and Hispanic (regardless of race). At a large state university such as the University of Illinois, where study abroad numbers this past year were over 1,400, this is indeed a concern. Pondering the factors that we at the University of Illinois considered to be barriers to increased participation by students in these categories, based on advising sessions with students in these categories over the past years, our Office of International Programs targeted the following factors as being the greatest impediments: perceived or real prohibitive cost; lack of knowledge on the part of students and their families about these opportunities; perceived cultural barriers, including fear of the unknown, of encountering prejudice; and concerns over separation from the familiar, including family and friendship ties; linguistic challenges and in many cases, administrative barriers which can be considered as a lack of encouragement by institutions such as ours. Not only recruitment of students, but devising strategies to increase retention was also an important conclusion.

THE FIRST PHASE OF THE ILLINOIS-NSEP PROGRAM ("PHASE ONE")

To address this, in 1995 the University of Illinois developed an initiative which ultimately became a grant proposal to the National Educational Security Program. This I will call "Phase One," as the proposal was successfully submitted a second time with some significant modifications ("Phase Two"). The proposal was designed to enable a large group of minority and low income students to study abroad. It is important to note here that we did not have total flexibility in the design and implementation of this proposal, as we needed to follow NSEP guidelines. These steered us toward both program development and consortium building – in other words, to cast a wide net among a group of institutions in the State of Illinois to enable the funds allocated to have a greater impact.

The program design targeted:

- Minority and low income students (as defined by our admissions and financial aid criteria).
- Underrepresented academic fields in study abroad at the time (international business and education).
- Foreign language and culture (Spanish and Japanese).
- A consortium of 4-year public institutions in Illinois, some of which had little familiarity with study abroad.

The result was an 18-month long program in which a group of students was to prepare for and successfully complete a study abroad experience of an entire semester in Mexico and Japan. A total of 55 minority and low-income students began and completed participation in Phase One, of this first initiative.

It is important to point out that the overall purpose of this program was not to produce totally bilingual individuals or area specialists, although this might be the end result for some students. Instead the program was designed in the hope that the acquired international skills and knowledge would enable the participants to become "global citizens" in the sense that they will be better able to function in the global marketplace, and be better equipped to participate in the political process and the important international issues which face the United States now and in the future.

Furthermore, the program design was developed along lines which we felt would minimize the impact of the barriers to participation by students in our target categories, as follows:

- The program design structures did not require any previous foreign language proficiency. Classes overseas were taught in English, with an intensive required course in the language of the country (Spanish and Japanese) both in the pre-departure orientations and during the programs.
- A set of special classes were designed in each site, related to the area, and to the participants' majors in business and education.
- Housing was pre-arranged with local families and/or residence halls.
- Costs were minimal – students were required to cover only some personal expenses.
- Extensive pre-departure preparation. This included two, two-week orientation programs on the University of Illinois campus, which led to group bonding, less attrition, and increased confidence among participants and their families.
- A total program length of 18 months, from beginning to end. The purpose of this time frame was to familiarize students with what to expect abroad, to increase the self-confidence of the participants and permit the group to "feel like a group" for retention purposes in the intervening year back at their home institutions, and to enable their institutions to feel pressured to support this initiative by providing the necessary foreign language classes and the administrative support.

Thus this first NSEP grant, or Phase One (1995–1996)), not only intended to facilitate an international experience among an underrepresented group of students in study abroad in two underrepresented fields at the time of education and international business, but to involve public educational institutions that lacked experience in the field. The grant was awarded to Illinois as the lead institution in the ICIE (Illinois Consortium for International Education) which consists of the twelve 4-year public institutions in the State. The program was attractive to this organization because the Consortium had been seeking sources of funds for study abroad programming. The grant provided funds for two to four students from each institution to participate. It was expected that each institution would contribute additional scholarships from their institutional funds to enable a greater number of students from their institution to join the program.

By awarding the funds to the Consortium there was another purpose, however. The grant was intended to develop, test and evaluate models for strengthening these institutions in international learning experiences. Each institution was expected to develop an administrative structure to deal with study abroad issues, such as transfer of credit and financial aid. Some of the institutions were further ahead in this regard than others. An important aspect of the institutionalization of the international component was the requirement of each institution that it provide continued instruction in Spanish and Japanese (depending on which language or languages their students had begun in the initial, two-week orientation) for the intervening year between the two summer institutes. This resulted in arrangements having to be made at some institutions to teach Japanese, and in one case, Spanish.

In sum, the program length of 18 months was considered important to familiarize participants with the concept of becoming internationalized, to build group cohesion, to prepare students in intensive language and culture of the overseas sites, and to thus build confidence and a "can do" feeling among the group, their families and their teachers through the increased visibility this federally funded grant afforded.

The program design included two, two-week early summer orientations or workshops at Champaign-Urbana with an academic year in between. The second orientation was followed at the end of the second summer by a semester abroad. In other words, the lengthy pre-departure elements were considered essential not only in the usual sense of study abroad pre-departure nuts and bolts and cross-cultural exercises; they were geared toward building self-confidence and prevent selected students from dropping out. It was made clear to participants that this was an "all or nothing" proposition: students could not join the program once it had begun. Use of technology – a chat room and a web page – in the intervening year was an additional factor in promoting retention among students in the lengthy pre-departure period.

The Summer Orientations

These are worthy of special attention as they proved to be enormously successful for this target group of students for a variety of reasons. Intensive foreign language classes were held in the mornings, and taught by teaching assistants already employed by their respective departments at the University of Illinois. Afternoons were packed tightly with lectures on topics related to the host countries. There were social activities, movies, tai chi and program dinners. Visitors from the host universities overseas visited the groups as well, which was a big help in making the final destination seem more real. Many students found it a good opportunity to allay concerns held by their parents as well as themselves, particularly those related to safety and security. A larger panel discussion with students of color who had studied in the host countries and overseas in general gave students a chance to address specific concerns related to race both in the U.S. and abroad. (During the summer orientation of the first NSEP grant, two women from Spelman College visited Urbana to specifically talk to the groups about their experiences in Mexico and Japan). The first institute provided a sort of "shake down cruise" for the program. It became clearer where and with whom the problems lay, and friendship patterns became established. During the intervening year, some students communicated among themselves via the webpage, and program-related assignments were also put on the web. It opened the program to family members and served as a form of communication with our office.

Selection Criteria
The first group of NSEP scholars, for that was how they became known, were selected by their institutions. As mentioned elsewhere, the cost of their program was almost fully, though not totally, covered by the NSEP grant, while matching institutional funds enabled a greater number to participate. There were originally 69 students who arrived in Champaign-Urbana for the first orientation in 1995. Had the overseas portion of the project taken place immediately after this orientation, possibly we would have lost fewer students; as it was in the intervening year that 12 of the 69 students dropped from the program. Most cited academic concerns – tight curricula that made a semester abroad risky in terms of time lost toward graduation; others withdrew for personal and health reasons.

The Host Institutions Overseas
Of the two institutions overseas which hosted the initial program, one was a program in Japan already up and running, administered by Southern Illinois University as part of their campus in Japan. Most of this campus' students were Japanese, planning to transfer to the United States. This made it relatively easy to manage, from the perspective of everyone but those in charge of the program in Carbondale and Japan! The study abroad advisor at SIU commented that the onslaught of 20 new American students in what was a relatively small program until that point was like a boa constrictor swallowing a pig!

But the program had advantages, such as the fact that our minority low-income students shared dormitory rooms with Japanese students. Fortunately, there were course descriptions and all kinds of pre-departure information already available – a large plus for the institutions in the ICIE struggling with what many saw as the ambiguities of this new concept and new programs.

The other host institution – the Universidad Panamericana – was a private university in Mexico City, with a branch campus in Guadalajara. The cost to the lead institution – the University of Illinois – was high in the sense that we based cost of this portion of the program on an exchange agreement, which provided tuition waivers to incoming students from the Panamericana to our College of Business and Engineering. The Mexican host institution worked hard to deliver the program as outlined, but it was difficult. The instruction was not on a par with expectations; students were not motivated to attend classes. As with study abroad students elsewhere, there were students whose enjoyment of newfound freedom, in at least one case from her husband and children, were at odds with the traditional family values of their hosts. Here we also found that we had not prepared this group of students well enough in terms of host standards of behavior – there were many cases of rudeness and lack of acceptance of food prepared for them by their families. In retrospect in the excitement of this special program we felt that there had been too much of a tendency to "coddle" them and not lay down some tough ground rules.

An important note to mention is that while the program structure in Japan followed a more familiar pattern, with staff from Carbondale in Japan to oversee the operations of the program and serve as "resident directors," in Mexico this task was delegated entirely to the host institution. The decision not to fund a "resident director" for this portion of the program was considered to be viable, given the close relationship between the designers of the program and personnel at the Mexican institution, and it enabled more funds to be used for scholarships.

"PHASE TWO"

The second NSEP grant (1998–1999) was an expansion of the first. Although the basic structure of the two summers followed by a semester abroad was kept, based upon experiences learned in the administration of the first grant, the goal in Phase One related to the development of administrative structures was eliminated. This had proved to be immensely challenging: frustration and even acrimony developed among the administrations at Illinois and some of the ICIE consortial partners!

Another item eliminated from the first grant was the requirement that students be majors in specific fields of study: students could be majors in any field. This became a necessity especially because of the difficulties encountered in the transfer of credit in the field of education. Some students received very little credit for their semester abroad, and unfortunately, it was assumed that upon return "everything would work out." Schools of Education around the state were not as compliant with the greater goals of the project as we had originally hoped. One reason that this was particularly frustrating was the difficulty in obtaining adequate, or in some cases, any course descriptions, not to mention syllabi from the host institutions overseas in advance. This time, at the request of NSEP, the grant was expanded to a national pool, with all of the administration centralized at the University of Illinois. Ten of the original ICIE institutions provided matching funds for additional scholars from their institutions for the second NSEP grant. The ICIE institutions which chose not to participate cited the inability to provide the needed language instruction as the main reason for doing so (Spanish or Chinese).

An additional change in the second phase was the substitution of China for Japan, because of the lower cost advantage. The new institution was Tsinghua University in Beijing. The second group of NSEP scholars came from institutions as far away as the University of California and the University of Pennsylvania. Promotion and final selection was handled by the Study Abroad Office at the University of Illinois. In the short time between notification of receipt of the grant and the deadline established to enable students to participate in the first summer institute, 115 applications were received. Had we had an earlier start, there would have been more applicants.

For these students an application form, transcript, two letters of recommendation, a statement of goals addressing their interest in this program and other personal and academic information was used. Eligibility for the program was based upon the same minority categories and on financial need ("low income" defined here as a student who relied on financial assistance, including monies to fund more than 75% of his or her education); U.S. citizenship; freshman, sophomore or junior standing; strong statement of goals; recommendations and a strong grade point average (3.0/4.0 or higher preferred). Thirty-three schools were represented in the final selection; 61 students were chosen in April 1998 and eight alternates, as from experience we knew that it could be expected that some students would not complete the entire program. Participants in the second grant, were able to be fully funded for everything but personal expenses. The University of Illinois again contributed "exchange" spaces for program students, this time at both host institutions abroad, whereby tuition was waived in toto or partially to lower the overall program cost. Illinois was thus contributing tuition wavers for incoming students from these Mexican and Chinese institutions on a set ratio based on the costs and numbers of students these institutions had been asked to receive.

The Overseas Experiences in "Phase Two"

As we, in study abroad administration know, whether there are complaints or not, it is rare that a student tell us that they would not do it again! The experiences varied greatly in some respects. At Tsinghua University the 27 students lived together in a residence hall. In Mexico, where the same institution – the Panamericana – agreed to take on the program for a second time, they were apportioned out to individual families carefully selected by the International Programs unit at that university. Each setting had its own individual problems and benefits. As with "Phase One" the University of Illinois chose to use all of the funds possible for scholarships to cover both domestic and overseas costs, including travel, thus requiring the host institutions to assign an individual or individuals as "resident directors" to take charge of the students. This is not to be recommended for future programs of this sort. There were issues requiring expertise in conflict resolution because of living in such close quarters in China; there continued to be needs in Mexico. U.S. students need a buffer and an advocate. Our model resulted in local institutional employees having to deal with uncomfortable pressures. Furthermore, both in China and Mexico, the students did not feel that there was someone of trust to whom they could turn.

A semester is a long time. Many of the difficulties were academic in nature because of the requirement that all courses, except intensive language, be taught in English. Except for a handful of students in Mexico with a higher level of Spanish, who enrolled in some regular courses at the Panamericana, most students merely skirted along on the surface of the culture they were visiting.

EVALUATION AND SUMMARY

The Negatives

We found that in addition to dissatisfaction with the academics in the host institutions abroad, caused in great part by difficulties in finding faculty able to teach the curricula effectively in English, the length of the program also presented challenges (as well as advantages). While the 18-month long program (from start to finish) made it a problem to recruit students, it did help those who participated, develop the necessary confidence and skills to venture abroad, and resulted in an 81% retention rate of accepted students, which can be considered excellent in study abroad programs in general. The design of the program enabled us to send 11%. more African Americans; 5% more Hispanics and 10% more Native Americans than national averages in study abroad.

The Positives

We found, however, that because of the length of time spent together both physically and electronically, the groups bonded together to the point that once overseas, participants found it difficult to go their separate ways. Lack of foreign language proficiency also contributed to this. However, there was a most unexpected benefit to this close interaction among participants: the multicultural makeup of the group provided an amazing opportunity for them to learn to know and appreciate each others' cultural differences.

Participants expressed over and over how much it meant to have made these friendships between Americans with different racial and ethnic backgrounds. The second grant enabled us to expand the applicant pool to the national, as opposed to just the state level. This was a definite plus for the student mix, as participants were able to learn about different regional cultures within the United States, as well as the different cultural groups that the minority participants represented. The mix of public and private institutional participants provided additional insights for this group.

ALTERNATIVE MODELS AND THE FUTURE

The fact is that this project was relatively unique. Its impact has been tremendous. We continually receive phone calls from institutions around the country asking about it. For this large number of underrepresented students, it was a life-changing opportunity. The University of Illinois is committed to continuing the concept that the NSEP grant enabled us to begin. With an important grant from the Office of the Provost at the University of Illinois, we are looking at the exciting opportunities ahead of us. A campus committee will assist us in determining which options we finally select.

We are contemplating programs which would enable us to modify various aspects of the existing model, such as program length, amount of pre-departure preparation, involvement of our own faculty in program leadership, and programs in locations which do not require a foreign language. One which we are already exploring in an English-language environment is a group program in South Africa. Here we would remove the foreign language barrier, which did prove to be a stumbling block to greater academic and cultural integration, while at the same time provide a very different set of challenges.

But an important question for our field is: why should we continue to develop "special" programs for target groups such as the ones described above as opposed to simply providing more open scholarships for students to enable them to study on the program, and in the country of their individual choice? It depends, in my opinion, upon what students are being targeted. This brings us back to the idea of creating international opportunities as part of our educational mission for students in minority categories. It can be argued that just as we had special "bridge" programs for minority applicants to our universities in the past, given the low percentage of minority students and the importance of these students to the future of the nation, we should duplicate this concept initially in study abroad. There is no doubt that for students who would otherwise not have considered study abroad, such as most of the students we targeted, the safety in numbers, the security for students who have in other settings complained to me "mine is the only black face here" is extremely important. The impact of a multiracial group gives credence to the idea that "If they can do this, I can do this!" The fact that these programs were almost fully funded enabled us to attract students for whom the opportunity to study abroad was indeed a totally new concept.

On the other hand, the success of this program is yet to be properly evaluated in terms of where the participants are now, and how has this experience affected their lives. We are in the process of collecting data from the participants themselves, but this could benefit from a longitudinal study. Such a study would also benefit from a comparison with some of the other minority scholarship groups, such as the Council on International Educational Exchange's Bailey Scholarship program.

While the benefits to the participants overall are reportedly great, the implementation of such special group programs are not easy. The need to determine appropriate sites and determine the focus of the program requires a good deal of thought. Levels of immersion (and thus language levels) and an interest in appealing to "heritage learners" comes into play as well. Then there are the logistics of finding accommodations in certain parts of the world for students, which requires a special effort and commitment on the part of a host institution; identifying that institution in the first place and expecting that it can or is already teaching a special curriculum is also asking a great deal. Cultural barriers also include the tendency to please in this regard. In this case, do we sacrifice academic quality to the overall benefits of the experience of being abroad for the participants?

These are some of the concerns of which we must be aware based upon our experience. Linking a special opportunity program such as this to a more integrated academic experience, such as a new study abroad course that Latino/Latina Studies at the University of Illinois is looking to develop for its majors, could well provide a solution to the concern for academic quality as well as the opportunity to study abroad for minority students with a specific academic focus.

THINKING OUTSIDE THE BOX: STUDY ABROAD IN THE TARGET LANGUAGE AT BUSINESS SCHOOLS OVERSEAS

Steven J. Loughrin-Sacco and David P. Earwicker

If an unfriendly foreign power had attempted to impose on America the mediocre educational performance that exists today, we might well have viewed it as an act of war. . . . We have, in effect, been committing an act of unthinking, unilateral educational disarmament (*A Nation at Risk*, The National Commission on Excellence in Education, 1983).

INTRODUCTION

The U.S. faces unprecedented challenges to its economic, political, and military pre-eminence as it proceeds into the initial years of the 21st century. During the Cold War era, the superpowers viewed countries as either enemies or friends. The era of globalization, however, has transformed friends and enemies alike into competitors (Friedman, 2000). The U.S., the chess master of the Cold War era, has encountered great difficulty in adapting to the new geo-political and socio-economic realities brought about by the era of globalization. As this new era celebrated its coming out party in 1989 with the fall of the Berlin Wall, the U.S. has witnessed its own economic decline. In 1945, the U.S. accounted for over 70% of the World's GDP. Today, that figure has shrunk to 19% (cited in Kedia, 2001).

For many years in the second half of the 20th century, the U.S. had a monopoly on its own domestic market. In the post-World War II era, our relative wealth and

Study Abroad: Perspectives and Experiences from Business Schools
Advances in International Marketing, Volume 13, 71–84.
© 2003 Published by Elsevier Science Ltd.
ISSN: 1474-7979/PII: S1474797902130067

economic power allowed the United States to avoid having to focus much attention on the two-way nature of international trade. In 1958, when Congress passed the National Defense Education Act, it was the first overt indication by the federal government toward a new level of awareness of foreign cultures, languages and environments. The first chords of globalization were beginning to echo, and the first round of government intervention into enhancing the foreign language and area studies abilities of universities had begun.

Today, over 75% of U.S. firms face import competition but only 10% of U.S. firms export. United States exports remain sluggish and each month economists report record trade deficits. As a result of this decline, World Bank economists predict that China will surpass the U.S. as the world's largest economy before 2020 (World Bank, 1992).

Recently it was noted that only nine states require foreign language classes as a high school graduation requirement. More disturbingly, the report also noted 53% of U.S. ninth-grade boys who say we should stop "outsiders" from influencing American traditions and cultures (Harper's Magazine, Fall 2001).

The Association to Advance Collegiate Schools of Business (AACSB-International) has identified cultural and linguistic illiteracy as a major cause of the U.S.' sluggish exporting performance. Despite the ascension of global inter-dependence during the last quarter century, U.S. companies have reacted slowly to the reality that the knowledge of other languages and cultures is a prerequisite for conducting business in other countries. Pallemans (2001), for example, reports that 80% of U.S. international business practitioners admitted that their foreign language skills were inadequate. It is ironic that the U.S., which has historically led the world in business education, has been among the slowest to revise business curricula to reflect the growing need for international expertise. According to Douglas D. Danforth, former CEO of Westinghouse, "the failure to recognize that we're in a global economy is the biggest failure of American chief executives today" (cited in Branan & Hergert, 1992). In recognition of the problem, the AACSB-International has strengthened its call for internationalizing the business curriculum: "The business leaders of tomorrow should be able to operate effectively and comfortably in an increasingly complex multicultural, multilingual, global environment" (cited in Branan & Hergert, 1992). Unfortunately, many U.S. business schools have not yet heeded the AACSB's call. Not surprisingly, Webb et al. (1999) reported that only 29% of global managers surveyed agreed that U.S. business schools graduate an adequate supply of qualified entry-level international business personnel.

Recent studies, most notably Webb et al. (1999), have identified the curricular components that multinational companies are seeking in U.S. business students. Global managers were asked: "How important are these features in producing employable international business graduates?" The top-rated features were:

(1) language training;
(2) student internships with firms abroad; and
(3) student foreign exchange program.

Since World War II, the nature and structure of work in the world has undergone an enormous transformation, matched only by the rapidity of recent work context changes brought about by globalization and technology in the last decade. We know that knowledge is the key factor in value production, that technology has the capacity to amplify the abilities of the intellect, and that creative, problem-solving and strategic-brokering skills must be utilized in globalized business practices. We also know that the organizational form of the corporation is evolving rapidly, and that network, horizontal, boundary-less or virtual corporations, however you call them, will increasingly form the basis for global business.

Being able to access the decision-making level of other firms is critical, and for this language and cultural knowledge is absolutely critical. Immersion and experience in the language and culture of competitors and partners will illuminate the role of perception, the nature of decision-making and the attention to detail of the environment, all factors utilized to form contextual knowledge and clear risk assessment. From these factors flow the competitive edge necessary for understanding the integrated mechanisms of globalization, and the most effective means of preparation is still immersion via study abroad in the target language in a business classroom.

We must train our students not for today but for tomorrow, for a world in which it is brutally apparent that the competition brought by globalization exacts a necessity of discipline, clarity and thought that cannot be acquired through traditional methods, and without which the firm cannot and will not survive.

The American Council on Education (ACE) reports that university students and the general public concur with global managers on the importance of student foreign exchange ("Student Poll," 2001). In the ACE study, 75% of the general public favored a study abroad requirement and 65% of students stated that they would study abroad if it were required. Forty-eight percent of students polled stated that they planned to study abroad. Despite their recognition of the importance of study abroad, only 3% of currently enrolled students actually participate in some form of study abroad during their college education.

The enthusiasm for studying abroad clearly wanes because of the realities of college life. Work obligations, the lack of financial aid, and prohibitive program costs eliminate a large percentage of students from studying abroad. Inflexibly packed curricula in business and engineering schools transform study abroad into an extracurricular activity forcing participating students to extend their four-year college education to $4\frac{1}{2}$ or 5 years. San Diego State University's International Business program has overcome these obstacles by making study abroad a required and integral component of its undergraduate international business curriculum. The goal of this paper is to describe this cutting-edge program and to assist colleges and universities to "think outside the box" when it comes to study abroad.

THE SDSU MODEL: STUDY ABROAD IN THE TARGET LANGUAGE AT BUSINESS SCHOOLS OVERSEAS

Overview of SDSU's International Business Program

The SDSU International Business (IB) Program enrolls over 725 students making it the largest undergraduate program of its type in the nation. Recently, *U.S. News and World Report* (September 10, 2002) ranked the program 12th in the nation. The IB curriculum melds business, foreign language, and regional studies into a 128 semester-hour program. The IB degree (128 semester units total) includes 51 semester hours of business and international business courses, 40 hours of foreign language study, and 19 hours of regional studies. Innovative features include a working proficiency in at least one of nine foreign languages, a semester-long internship in a global firm, and, most importantly, a minimum semester-long study abroad component. San Diego's strategic location at the edge of the Pacific Rim and as a gateway to Latin America makes it imperative that SDSU graduates be capable of conducting business in a global context. In our view, study abroad is the most important ingredient in preparing future business practitioners for the global marketplace.

Study Abroad for International Business Majors

Study abroad models abound in U.S. colleges and universities, but SDSU has carefully crafted a model that ensures foreign language fluency, international business acumen, and work experience. SDSU places its students at business schools where coursework is taught in the host country's native language. These languages include Spanish, French, German, Italian, and Portuguese. (IB majors specializing in Chinese, Japanese, and Russian enroll in intensive language courses in their respective countries.) They cannot satisfy their study abroad requirement at an English-speaking university. SDSU IB majors enroll full-time in business and regional studies courses as their native counterparts do and SDSU IB majors are graded on the same criteria and scale as the host country's students.

All IB program study abroad takes place through exchange agreements, which enable SDSU students to pay their annual tuition and fees of $1,854. SDSU IB students are generally housed with families or in dormitories/apartments with non-U.S. roommates. In all, SDSU IB sponsors study abroad in 50 institutions, in 15 countries, on four continents. SDSU's partners include the *Instituto Tecnológico de Estudios Superiores de Monterrey* (ITESM), the *Fachhochschule Reutlingen*, the *Ecole Supérieure des Practiciens en Commerce International* (EPSCI), the *Université du Québec à Chicoutimi*, the *Scuola Europea di Economia* (Italy), the *Pontificía Universidade Católica do Rio de Janeiro* (PUC-Rio), and the *Universidad de la Habana* (Cuba) among many others. Around 150 SDSU IB majors will study abroad this year, the most of any international business program or business school in the U.S.

Transnational Degree Programs

SDSU IB majors also have the opportunity to participate in transnational degree programs where students complete coursework and an internship abroad for much longer periods. In a transnational degree program, IB students complete coursework and an internship in a business school abroad with a time frame ranging from 15 months to two years. At graduation (after four years of coursework), program participants receive degrees from the host and the home institutions. SDSU offers, or will soon offer transnational programs (dual and triple degrees) in six countries: Brazil, Canada (Quebec), Chile, France, Italy, and Mexico.

SDSU's most famous transnational degree program, MEXUS, was established in 1993 and has graduated over 120 students. In the MEXUS dual-degree program, SDSU students complete general education and business coursework at SDSU their freshman and senior years and at one of several Mexican universities during their sophomore and junior years. Participants graduate receiving both the Bachelor of Arts in International Business from SDSU and the *Licenciatura en Negocios Internacionales* from the Mexican university and they are equally prepared to conduct business in Mexico and the U.S.

Luis Hernandez (1996), one of the program's first graduates, offers the typical profile of the MEXUS student. Shelley Herron relates Hernandez's experience in the Spring 2001 issue of *Business: the SDSU College of Business Alumni Magazine*:

After graduation, with two internships under his belt, he landed a job as a trade representative for the U.S.-Mexico Chamber of Commerce in Washington, D.C. The Orange County native enjoyed a view of Pennsylvania Avenue from his office window when he wasn't traveling to Mexico to set up internships as part of his job. He also worked with the textile industry and translated environmental laws. The language skills he developed are especially useful in his new position as export coordinator for the Costco Wholesale, Mexico Division in San Diego (p. 8).

Hernandez reminisces on his MEXUS experience:

MEXUS magnified my realm of learning in many, many ways. I not only learned a different view of international business, but I also sharpened my language skills, made contacts I maintain to this day, and gained a unique background that gave me a competitive edge with my current and previous employers... What I liked most about the program was the experience of complete immersion into a new culture and environment. This allowed me to learn much more than just what was being taught in the classroom. I lived in Tijuana for two years and was active at the university by playing soccer and participating in school events... Although my educational experience was by far most important, my cultural experience has proven to be a key factor as well, as I found out through my employers. The whole experience made me more well-rounded and prepared for the tasks and challenges I confront in the professional arena (p. 8).

SDSU has recently developed the nation's first transnational triple-degree program in international business or any other undergraduate discipline. Project CaMexUS, short for Canada, Mexico, U.S., is designed to prepare future business managers to conduct business effectively in all three NAFTA countries. In Project CaMexUS, SDSU will place its undergraduate international business students for one academic year each in two North American institutions outside of the U.S. Specifically, CaMexUS students enroll in 10 business courses (taught in Spanish) at the *Universidad Autónoma de Baja California* (UABC) and 10 business courses (taught in French) at the *Université du Quebec à Chicoutimi* (UQAC). CaMexUS students also complete an internship in all three countries. Upon graduation (after four years of coursework), CaMexUS students receive three bachelor's degrees awarded by the three NAFTA countries and they will be prepared to work effectively anywhere in North America as a result of their language skills and intercultural expertise. Project CaMexUS is an extension of the FIPSE-funded MEXUS Program that former presidents Clinton and Zedillo cited in 1999 as a model for transnational cooperation in higher education.

Project CaMexUS, recently funded by a U.S. Department of Education FIPSE Comprehensive Program grant for $210,000, will become the North American version of the highly successful ERASMUS and CEMS programs developed in the European Union. The European Union created dual- and triple-degree programs because it realized that economic interdependence also implied social, political, and educational interdependence. ERASMUS and CEMS require students to study and intern at one or more foreign universities as part of their degree programs. The objective has been to create a distinctively "European" manager. Project CaMexUS, which involves 24 months of study and internship in two foreign North American countries, in addition to home university requirements, is designed to create a distinctively "North American" manager.

The "Deliverables" of the SDSU Model

SDSU's IB study abroad programs equip participating students with a globalization skill set that other types of study abroad programs cannot provide. Some programs, known in some quarters as "island" programs, transport U.S. students to the host country where coursework is taught by the home campus' faculty in English. These programs unwittingly or in some cases purposely segregate U.S. students from the local population and its culture by encouraging fraternization with other Americans and limiting American students' contact with native speakers. An SDSU MBA alumnus, who did not participate in an SDSU IB study abroad exchange, expressed his displeasure with the "island" program he attended:

> In my opinion, this program was little more than a prolonged vacation because students were accommodated in ways that created a comfortable bubble for them to live in. Without involving oneself in the language, culture and people the experience is very limited in its advantages (Jack Tyndall, SDSU MBA class of 2001).

The RAND Corporation Report *Global Preparedness and Human Resources: College and Corporate Perspectives* (1994) also critiqued "island" programs. United States corporate executives canvassed in the RAND Report remarked "those who go abroad should not confine their association to other expatriate Americans" (p. xv). "Island" programs often provide an excellent cultural enhancement to their education but they do not adequately prepare students to compete successfully in global business. Other programs offer coursework at English-speaking business schools which can be very enriching. However, these programs limit business majors to perspectives from the English-speaking world and only prepare students to conduct business in countries such as Great Britain, Ireland, Canada, and Australia. SDSU's IB Program provides an expansive globalization skill set that includes the following:

(1) Academic training in the finance, management, and marketing practices of the target country;
(2) Fluent foreign-language skills beyond the level of proficiency attainable at the home campus;

(3) Knowledge of, and sensitization to, the target country's cultural values, norms, and taboos as well as its political, linguistic, historical, and economic heritage;
(4) Experience working in a multinational firm while in the target country;
(5) Experience working effectively in multicultural teams through group class assignments with the host university's business students and;
(6) Experience dealing effectively with ambiguity and resolving intercultural problems through everyday life encounters abroad.

One of the key "deliverables" (number 4) of the SDSU IB study abroad model is the work experience that many students gain through internships. The internship, which is rapidly becoming a prerequisite to employment in global business, enables students to apply the knowledge they have acquired in the U.S. and foreign classroom. Furthermore, the internship enables them to study business culture up close through the completion of tasks and interaction with company employees.

"Deliverable" number 6 "dealing with ambiguity" is a particularly interesting skill SDSU students gain through study abroad. International business practitioners must cope with vagaries pertaining to time, negotiations, government regulations, and the like. However, how does one prepare future international business practitioners to acquire this skill on the home campus? Business professors, for example, cannot teach tolerance of ambiguity in their classes through unclear syllabi, grading criteria, and assignments because students will exact their revenge in their course evaluations. However, through study abroad at business schools, ambiguity is a natural part of the education process; SDSU students must cope with each country's educational philosophy, which naturally trains them for dealing with ambiguity in the global marketplace. For example, at EPSCI outside of Paris, Jaymi Koch (2001) relates what it was like to deal with an ambiguous educational situation:

> They weren't kidding when they said there'd be no quizzes and only one exam at the end of the semester. I had to figure out right from the beginning how to get a good grade in each of my four classes. There were no midterms to let you know where you stood grade-wise. There wasn't any attendance policy and you didn't even have to go to class if you didn't want to. There were minimal course materials like textbooks, which I counted on back home.
>
> In the final analysis, I got good grades but I had to figure out what study groups to be in, what library resources to read, when I needed to attend class, and most importantly, how to answer essay questions on my final exams the way French students do. All of which had to be done in French. It was frustrating and challenging but I'm glad I went through the experience. Dealing successfully with the French education system was a cultural experience as rich as studying French business practices and consumer behavior.

A secondary benefit of the SDSU model is the contribution of international business faculty of partner universities to the development of SDSU IB majors.

Not only do the faculty of partner universities provide multiple perspectives of global business practices, they in essence serve as at-large faculty attached to the SDSU College of Business Administration at no cost to SDSU. The converse holds true for the partner institutions when SDSU faculty teach their students.

FIPSE'S FOCUS ON SUBJECT MATTER-ORIENTED STUDY ABROAD IN THE TARGET LANGUAGE

The U.S. Department of Education's Fund for the Improvement of Post-Secondary Education (FIPSE) concurs with SDSU's philosophy of study abroad and has initiated three special grant initiatives to promote subject matter-oriented study abroad in the target language. These include the North American Mobility in Higher Education Program, the European Union/United States Joint Consortia Program, and the U.S.-Brazil Higher Education Consortia Program. All three of these programs share common goals and strategies. All are run cooperatively between the U.S. government and the Canadian, Mexican, Brazilian, and European Union governments. All three programs have 4-year funding cycles and support student-centered curricular development. To receive funding, colleges and universities must "improve the quality of students in undergraduate and graduate education in both countries (or groups of countries) and to explore ways to prepare students for work through:

(1) the mutual recognition and portability of academic credits;
(2) the developed of shared, common, or core curricula;
(3) the acquisition of the languages and exposure to the cultures (of the countries in question);
(4) the development of student apprenticeships or other work related experiences;
(5) an increased cooperation and exchange among academic personnel; and
(6) the development of joint research projects aiming at the improvement of graduate training and formation of personnel at higher academic levels" (pp. 5–6).

SUGGESTIONS ON ESTABLISHING STUDY ABROAD IN THE TARGET LANGUAGE AT BUSINESS SCHOOLS

Over the last dozen years, SDSU's IB Program has negotiated study abroad agreements with 50 business schools worldwide. All U.S. business schools engage study abroad exchanges around the world as well, but establishing agreements like SDSU's add several new wrinkles to negotiating and managing agreements. These wrinkles include determining course equivalencies, fees, student support, foreign language preparation, student financial aid, and internships. Additionally, few successful agreements seldom take place without adequate staffing either centrally within a college or university or within a business school.

Course Equivalencies

If a business school seeks to fully integrate study abroad into its curriculum, it is imperative that all coursework completed abroad count for credit back on the home campus. The process of determining course equivalencies begins with each business school (the U.S. business school and its counterpart abroad) examining the other business school's curriculum and then selecting a group of courses it would like to propose for the study abroad curriculum. Sometimes the courses at both schools have the same title and course content (e.g. International Marketing), while other times the courses are only slightly different (e.g. SDSU's International Business Finance versus EPSCI's International Investments). Still others have no equivalencies in which case each business school must decide what courses can serve as substitute course. For example, EPSCI's ECON 400 European Economics can be substituted for any one of several SDSU courses categorized as regional studies.

Student Support and Services

SDSU sponsors well-established study abroad and student service offices that facilitate study abroad annually for hundreds of incoming and outgoing students. To help students navigate the variety of study abroad programs, SDSU provides numerous services for all incoming and outgoing students. For outgoing students, SDSU's International Business Exchange and Dual-Degree Programs Office advises students on course selection, assists students in securing visas and health insurance, distributes special pre-departure materials, and conducts a pre-departure orientation and a student debriefing and reorientation upon return to the home campus. Pre-departure materials at SDSU comprise a thorough orientation of issues that includes immunizations and medical precautions, exchange rates, culture shock, emergency contacts, consulate information, baggage tips, code of conduct, living with a family or other students, communication home, etc. For incoming students from partner institutions, SDSU provides them with academic support, arrival assistance, counseling, tutoring, housing referral, information on establishing a bank account, honor societies for international scholars, and relevant student organizations.

Foreign Language Preparation

Study abroad at a business school in which coursework is taught in a foreign language requires extensive foreign language preparation as well as a commitment from the business school. Students need at least $3\frac{1}{2}$ years of college-level language study to succeed in a foreign business school. The IB Program requires three advanced-level foreign language courses (conversation and composition, business language, culture and civilization) before they can apply to study abroad. Before leaving the home campus, all students must pass a language interview demonstrating advanced-level listening skills and intermediate-high speaking skills according to the American Council on the Teaching Foreign Languages (ACTFL) proficiency guidelines (Higgs, 1985).

Some students bypass traditional foreign language coursework and condense their language study by attending summer intensive foreign language instruction abroad. Intensive language courses normally run six hours per day, five days a week coupled with a homestay residency. A five-week intensive French course at the *Université du Quebec à Chicoutimi* is the equivalent of one year of classroom instruction at SDSU. A full summer in Chicoutimi is worth two full years of home campus language instruction. SDSU Spanish-speaking students wanting to study in Brazil have access to a six-week Portuguese language course designed for them. After six weeks of accelerated Portuguese, SDSU students enroll in business courses taught in Portuguese at the *Pontificia Universidade Católica* in Rio de Janeiro. Summer intensive courses are available at most of SDSU partner institutions and some institutions such as the *Fachhochschule* in Reutlingen, Germany require students to complete a two-week intensive orientation in which language and business skills are strengthened.

SDSU's foreign language policy has worked well in most cases. Reading course materials and listening to course lectures have seldom caused a problem for SDSU students. Developing adequate speaking and writing skills, necessary to make PowerPoint presentations, to participate in class discussions, to interact successfully with native classmates, and to pass examinations, has been the most challenging problem. SDSU recently added a third advanced-level course, which some of SDSU's partner schools strongly recommended. Students not passing the oral exam or demonstrating inadequate writing skills at SDSU have the option of enrolling in an intensive language course prior to commencing business coursework at the host institution.

Student Financial Aid

A critical part of integrating study abroad fully into the business curriculum is to make study abroad affordable to all business majors. For many U.S. colleges and universities, foreign exchange programs provide the least inexpensive option for business majors. Additionally, if a U.S. business school requires study abroad, like SDSU's IB program, it might feel obligated to provide financial aid through university-wide financial aid and scholarships. Even though SDSU's IB majors pay their home annual tuition and fees of $1,854 regardless of where they study abroad, they still face the cost of generating funding for tuition and fees as well as roundtrip airfare. SDSU provides financial aid to its students studying abroad. Additionally, study abroad scholarships, generated through private fundraising, exist for approximately 10 of the 180 IB majors studying or interning abroad. Federal grants, emanating from the U.S. Department of Education, and foundation grants from the Coca-Cola Foundation, have provided students with much-needed funding during the duration of the grant. SDSU has recently embarked on a scholarship campaign to assist study abroad for a much larger body of participants.

Internships

Gaining work experience with internationally oriented firms is a critical part of an international business student's education. In the past, quality internships were difficult to obtain but SDSU has found that partner business schools abroad will locate and place its students if their study abroad experience lasts more than one semester. The *Pontificía Universidade Católica* in Rio de Janeiro, for example, will place U.S. business students in Brazilian firms where they intern six hours every day from noon to 6:00pm. Afterwards, they attend night classes at PUC-Rio. In a 16-week semester, business students compile 480 hours of invaluable work experience. In SDSU's transnational dual degree program, IB majors garner 1,460 hours of work experience in addition to completing 10 business courses. Not every partner business school provides such a unique coursework-internship combination but other creative internship opportunities exist. The *Université du Québec à Chicoutimi*, for example, will soon place students at ALCAN, the Canadian aluminum manufacturer. ALCAN is especially interested in placing SDSU Hispanic-Americans to assist them in expanding sales in Mexico. SDSU interns will work with *maquiladores* and other potential purchasers in Mexico. The internship dimension of the exchange agreement will work best if the U.S. business school supplies internships for its partner business school's students.

CONCLUSION

Albert Einstein once said: "The world that we have made, as a result of the thinking we have done thus far, creates problems that we cannot solve at the same level as the level we created them at." In this era of globalization, we must exhort our students to "think outside the box" through study abroad, the single most significant global experience that they can have. Business students cannot learn to solve global problems if they do not step outside their sphere of comfort and understanding and experience, truly experience, the world as others see it and live it. Our institutions are the "box" and if we do not expose our students to multiple global voices and perspectives beyond the box, then we are selling them short. This is why study abroad can be the single most transformational experience that we can incorporate into a business student's program. Every year, SDSU IB alumni trumpet the benefits of having studied abroad and describe its benefits to their current jobs. Study abroad in any form will enhance an international business student. However, we sincerely believe that SDSU's model of study abroad will best prepare students to become the next generation's global managers.

The authors understand that each college and university approaches the issue of study abroad and program options using a calculus that incorporates history, resources, faculty relationships, geographic considerations, campus politics, and student demographics. No two institutions can approach the issue in a like manner, however lessons can be drawn from the experiences of others and melded to fit different environments.

On October 12th the House Committee on Labor, HHS and Education Appropriations released a report that noted, in part, *"The Committee believes that foreign language skills and international expertise are essential factors in national security readiness. Ensuring U.S. security, foreign policy leadership, economic competitiveness, and our ability to solve global problems that affect the nation's well being depend on Americans who have an understanding of and ability to function effectively in other cultural, business and value systems, as well as foreign language proficiency."*

REFERENCES

Bikson, T. K., & Law, S. A. (1994). *Global Preparedness and Human Resources: College and Corporate Perspectives*. Santa Monica, CA: Rand.

Branan, A., & Hergert, M. (1992). Project MEXUS: Preparing for business without borders. Funded by the U.S. Department of Education's Fund for the Improvement of Postsecondary Education.

Friedman, T. (2000). *The Lexus and the Olive Tree*. New York, NY: Anchor Books.

Global Economic Prospects (1992). Washington, D.C.: The World Bank.

Harper's Magazine (Fall 2001), p. 13.

Herron, S. (Spring, 2001). *Business*: SDSU College of Business Alumni Magazine. *Internationalization of U.S. Higher Education: Preliminary Status Report 2000* (2000). Washington D.C.: ACE.

Higgs, T. V. (Ed.) (1985). *Teaching for Proficiency, the Organizing Principle*. Lincolnwood, IL: NTC.

Kedia, B. (February 15, 2001). International business and developing a global mindset. Keynote Address. *The University of Memphis International Business and Foreign Language: A Workshop for Foreign Language Educators.*

Pallemans, G. (April 19, 2001). Foreign Language Trends in the U.S. and the Economic Growth of the Pacific Rim: Possible Initiatives for Foreign Language Departments. Kentucky Foreign Language Conference.

"Student Poll" American Council on Education (ACE) (2001). Vol. 4, number 3.

U.S.-Brazil Higher Education Consortia Program (2001). Information and Application Materials.

Webb, M., et al. (1999). Internationalization of American business education. *Management International Review: Journal of International Business*, *39*(4), 379–397.

THE ROLE OF FOREIGN LANGUAGE INSTRUCTION AND PROFICIENCY AS RELATED TO STUDY ABROAD PROGRAMS IN BUSINESS

Orlando R. Kelm

INTRODUCTION

The object of this brief paper is to discuss the balance between business content and language proficiency in study abroad programs related to business. When blending these three activities, the challenge is to balance each appropriately. If the study abroad experience contains little or no business content, students lose out on the opportunity to learn elements of international business. If the study abroad experience contains little or no language content, students miss out on the cultural integration that is essential for international interactions. And if "study abroad" becomes too loose (i.e. party on the beach) or too rigid (i.e. no different than taking classes back home), students miss the essence of studying in a foreign location. Of course, there are excellent business study abroad programs that are conducted in English (e.g. see Keillor & Emore for the roundtable discussion regarding English language programs). The focus of this paper is the role of foreign language instruction and student proficiency in foreign language, as it relates to business study abroad programs.

The good news is that undergraduate business students are participating in study abroad programs at significantly higher numbers. For example, at the University of Texas at Austin where I am employed, of the nearly 1,500 undergraduate students

Study Abroad: Perspectives and Experiences from Business Schools
Advances in International Marketing, Volume 13, 85–97.
© 2003 Published by Elsevier Science Ltd.
ISSN: 1474-7979/PII: S1474797902130079

who studied abroad last year, over 20% were business majors. This is second only to liberal arts majors, who represent 34% of all of the students who studied abroad. The increase among business students has steadily risen every year over the past 10 years. If we believe that experiential learning is a vital part of education, then the internationalization of our students, by definition, requires international experience. Study abroad is one of the most effective ways for students to gain this international experience. Especially for undergraduate students, study abroad is often a life-changing event. Similarly, for graduate and MBA students, study abroad can be a career-shaping event.

When we talk about study abroad programs, there is a wide spectrum of options. For some students, study abroad may be a brief study tour to specific sites over a period of a few short weeks. For others, a summer intensive program may be the easiest way to fit study abroad into a specific curriculum. Semester- and year-long programs provide opportunities for greater interaction and integration, but for many students this may not be feasible given academic and financial limitations. Besides the duration of programs, study abroad programs differ in focus and purpose, for example, geographic location, foreign language, and business content.

To help introduce these topics, what follows is a brief description of short-term programs with and without foreign language components and then semester- or year-long programs with foreign language.

SHORT-TERM PROGRAMS WITHOUT FOREIGN LANGUAGE

Simultaneously with the general increase in the number of students who are studying abroad, the number of short study abroad programs has also increased. Summer programs that run 4–6 weeks are very popular, as are brief study tours. As the duration of these programs decreases, the issue of foreign language proficiency becomes more difficult to delineate. When a student spends a year, or a semester in Chile, for example, there is little doubt that this student will need to have a level of proficiency in Spanish that correlates to the courses offered at the foreign university. However, when a student spends only 5 weeks in a foreign country to take a summer course, parameters change. What we observe is that the short business content courses that are taught abroad are frequently taught in English, something that would be difficult for students who enroll in regular semester-long courses at non-English speaking universities. If we want to teach a short summer course in a foreign language, we need to suppose that the potential audience of interested students already possesses sufficient proficiency in the local language. The truth is that such a pool of foreign-language speaking students is limited, especially beyond those programs that could be offered in Spanish, French, and German. As such, the alternate route is to teach these courses in English, while taking advantage of local contacts, guest speakers, regional assignments, and cultural observations.

At the University of Texas at Austin, for example, we experienced a scenario a few years ago related to this issue, which I repeat here for illustrative purposes. We had hoped to offer two summer courses (one in marketing and another in finance) that were to be taught in "friendly Spanish" to undergraduate business students. This course was to be taught in Barcelona with our partner school ESADE using a mix of faculty from both institutions. The idea behind friendly Spanish was to teach the course in Spanish, but have faculty be aware that the students were still in the development phases of language proficiency. Immediately we came across the problem of defining what we meant by "friendly Spanish" and what level of Spanish we required. In the end it was a moot point because only a few students signed up for the course. In order to attract more students we then lowered the language requirement and the number still remained low. We then changed strategy and decided to offer the courses in English. Within a few weeks the courses were filled to capacity. We recently completed our third year of teaching the marketing and finance courses and it has been extremely successful, providing students with a unique view of marketing and finance from a mixed American/Spanish perspective.

What did we learn from this experience? First of all, the pool of undergraduate business students who wanted to take the content courses in marketing and finance, and who also had sufficient proficiency in the Spanish language, and who wanted to study abroad, was limited. These courses were designed for juniors and seniors who had already completed other prerequisite core classes. There simply were not enough interested juniors and seniors who had fulfilled the prerequisite. Second, if the material of a "content" course is perceived to be vital to the student's academic preparation, students are reluctant to put themselves in a situation where they will misunderstand or not learn the content. In other words, students make comments like, "I would love to take this class in Spain, but I think it's more important for me to make sure that I understand marketing and finance really well. I don't want to take the chance of not understanding the concepts." Given a higher proficiency in the foreign language, this would not be an issue, but in the absence of proficiency, students are not willing to take the risk. Third, we learned that students are apprehensive about endangering their home institution's GPA. We frequently see requests to take a course on a pass/non-pass basis. Although there is nothing wrong with taking a course on a pass/non-pass basis, in some instances the lure to travel, to see sites, and to be a tourist, take their toll on academics. Quite honestly, performance suffers when the student's objective is to merely pass a course. Fourth, and on a more positive note, we have seen that the content of the marketing and finance courses is strengthened by team teaching these courses with faculty from the host institution, ESADE, in Barcelona. Students are exposed to a new perspective, receive insights into European thought, make visits to local companies, receive guest lectures from Spanish professionals, take tours of the Barcelona stock market, etc. In other words, their educational experience is enhanced with activities that would be impossible to duplicate at home.

So where does foreign language fit in? The students who have participated in the program themselves have provided several insights. Given the positive cultural and academic experience, they perceive that something is missing. We hear comments such as, "I really need to come back here to study Spanish." or "It's weird that they all have to speak English to us, and we're here in their country." As a result of the summer course, we have seen students who come back home and enroll in additional Spanish language courses. Other students have signed up for semester-long study abroad programs, seeing the need to return and increase language proficiency. This is precisely the catalyst that one would hope to see in the students. Short programs serve as a foundation for future international experiences.

Summary observation no. 1: Short-term business programs abroad that are taught in English have the potential of providing students with an international context for a unique academic and cultural experience. These programs also serve to help students see the need for increased proficiency in foreign language.

SHORT-TERM PROGRAMS WITH FOREIGN LANGUAGE

Student comments such as those cited in the paragraphs above help strengthen the need for study abroad experiences where students receive instruction in the host country's language, even for short-term programs. As such, continuing with the example of our summer program in Barcelona, we still sensed a need for courses that are taught in Spanish. Rather than design another purely business content course, we followed up with a proposal for two new courses: One to develop advanced-level business language skills (business vocabulary, oral ability to discuss business content), and a second course on specific cultural aspects of doing business in Spain. This proposal responds to the lessons learned from the marketing and finance courses. First, we changed the content from core business to language and culture. Students are willing to focus on finance and marketing or focus on language and culture, but for short-term programs they are not in a position to focus on both. Second we increased the pool of potential students. Instead of offering an upper-division course for business majors who are also advanced speakers of Spanish, the language and culture program is designed for intermediate-level speakers who want to become advanced. Students are required to have the equivalent of two years of university-level Spanish. Now we draw from all students, Business majors, Spanish majors, and double-majors, anyone who has completed the basic core language courses. In many ways, this summer course provides the students with the necessary tools to enroll in future semester-long programs. That is to say that it helps them obtain the necessary vocabulary and proficiency to be able to take business content courses abroad.

A third lesson learned relates to how much we observed that the students in the English language finance and marketing program valued the cultural perspectives gained from the experience. This is equally true for the Spanish-language students. The language and culture courses are taught in Barcelona during the same dates as the finance and marketing courses, and again with a mix of faculty from ESADE and the University of Texas. Students participate in many of the same types of local tours, receive visits from local business professionals, and gain a European perspective on all of the cultural issues. And the result, unlike our initial attempt to offer business content courses in Spanish, enrollment in the business language courses filled up right away.

One caution, there is a limitation related to progress in foreign language proficiency and short-term summer courses: progress in foreign language proficiency takes time. National guidelines and standards from the Foreign Service Institute advise that learners of category II languages (e.g. Spanish, French, etc.) need about 240 hours of instruction to go beyond a beginning survival-level to exceed intermediate levels of proficiency. Students need an additional 240 hours to get to beyond superior levels of proficiency. (Feel lucky, category III languages (e.g. Japanese, Chinese, etc.) are estimated at 2700 hours to get to superior levels of proficiency.) To put this in perspective, most university-level programs that require students to study a foreign language only provide students with 240 contact hours after four semesters. Of course, students study more than just contact hours, but the example illustrates the high level of commitment that is required to progress. True beginning-level students, those who begin at zero, still need to go through the beginning levels of language acquisition. Verb conjugations, grammar, pronunciation, comprehension, fluency, all of the initial stages require focused memorization and hard work. These initial stages may be enhanced by a foreign experience, but many of the advantages of studying a foreign language abroad are seen only after the initial foundation has been established. In other words, beware of false expectations.

Beginning-level students who study a foreign language abroad will still only be intermediate-level speakers when they return from short intensive programs. As intermediate-level students, they still do not possess the proficiency necessary to perform the linguistic tasks required to study or conduct business in a foreign language. No doubt, true beginners will make progress, but they will not become advanced speakers simply because their study was conducted in another country. The best advice is that short-term intensive language programs are better suited for intermediate-level and advanced-level students who already have a foundation. Let them use the time abroad to build on their linguistic foundation, not to construct it from scratch.

Summary observation no. 2: Short-term business programs abroad that are taught in the host foreign language are more successful when focused on language and cultural topics, and when they are geared for students at intermediate and advanced levels of proficiency. These programs also serve to help students prepare for long-term study abroad experiences, including business content courses.

Summary observation no. 3: Students need to have realistic expectations on the speed and depth of language acquisition. Short-term intensive language programs abroad are best suited for intermediate- or advanced-level students and not for true beginners.

SEMESTER- AND YEAR-LONG STUDY ABROAD PROGRAMS AND FOREIGN LANGUAGE

Language instructors are frequently asked to fill out language evaluation forms for students who are applying for study abroad programs. One of the questions is generally summarized as follows: Does this student possess the foreign language proficiency necessary to perform the required project, research, or course work? This question is vital because it helps establish the role of foreign language within the objective of study abroad, namely, a tool to help fulfill a specific task. (Granted, for some students, the task may be limited to increased proficiency in a foreign language; but this is seldom the true nature of semester- and year-long programs, even when increased foreign language proficiency is a welcome by-product of the study abroad experience.) Students participate in long-term study abroad programs to increase international competence, to gain insight into cultural realities, and to develop an ability to analyze social, economic, and political issues from an international perspective. As such, foreign language proficiency is simply a tool, albeit a very important one, to assist in helping a student to accomplish a specific objective.

To illustrate how the tasks and objectives of business study abroad programs may differ, forgive another example from our programs at the University of Texas. We offer a number of undergraduate and MBA Spanish-language programs with our partner schools in Latin America. One of our strongest partnerships is with ITESM in Monterrey, Mexico. Given the proximity to Texas, the technical expertise of its faculty, and the prestige of its program, many students are attracted to it. A large number of faculty members at ITESM were trained and educated in the United States. As such, they understand American-style education and American students. A large percentage of the advanced textbooks and reading materials that are used in their curriculum are written in English. Even the Mexican students have to read a lot of the materials in English. As a result, American students who attend classes at ITESM have access to English language materials and to professors who speak English (and who sometimes allow students to turn in written materials in English). Consequently, one of the major linguistic tasks for these students at ITESM is to be able to understand course lectures. Reading, writing, and speaking Spanish are not as essential at ITESM as they might be at some of our other partner schools. Of course we are talking about a matter of degree and not the complete absence of reading, writing, and speaking, but if there is a student in business who is apprehensive about his or her language ability, ITESM may actually be the best possible option. On the other hand, there are other students who want to minimize exposure to English and to be as far away as possible from Texas. For these students, a study abroad program in South America may be more to their liking. The point is that an understanding of the tasks involved help establish the appropriate levels of foreign language proficiency that are required to be successful.

In addition to participating in class lectures, writing papers, and doing research at foreign institutions, study abroad students also participate in field projects and internships. In these instances it is also important to focus on the object of the project in terms on what needs to be done. Sometimes I see students who only think in terms of language ability, "How much Spanish will I learn at this internship?" It is as if they are using the internship as an excuse to get better at Spanish. Again, this is a great by-product of the experience, but it should not be the main focus.

Summary observation no. 4: In order to determine the role that foreign language proficiency will play in a business study abroad program, focus on the tasks and objectives that the student will perform.

COLLABORATION BETWEEN LANGUAGE AND BUSINESS EDUCATORS

Truth told, sometimes there is a misunderstanding between business and language educators as related to the role of foreign language proficiency in business-related study abroad programs. From a language educator's perspective, without understanding the business objectives, there is a tendency to focus exclusively on the linguistic and literary elements of language development. It is easy to lose sight of the true business objectives that students have in studying abroad. For better or for worse, we live in a society of narrow specializations. If an educator in accounting is unaware of many details related to finance, imagine how much more difficult it is for the language educator. This is what Steven Loughrin-Sacco (2000, pp. 107–119) has identified as "building a bridge to Liberal Arts." He encourages business educators to assist by locating interested language faculty, discovering common professional interests, building working relationships, seeking approval from superiors, and developing successful projects. Study abroad is an ideal example of an area where business educators can contribute to building that bridge. Language educators have experience in proficiency-based language instruction and they also have expertise in literature and civilization, which brings a foundation for understanding the cultural aspects that affect business. Coupled with information about business objectives, they are in a position to contribute their areas of expertise as they guide students to appropriate study abroad experiences.

From the other end, there is also a need for language educators to build a bridge to Business. There are potential misunderstandings from the business educator's vantage point too. For example, sometimes business educators follow a thought process as follows: If there is a need to get a general foundation in accounting, take a semester of accounting; if there is a need to get a general foundation in economics, take a semester of economics; if there is a need to get a foundation in German, take a semester of German. The problem is, of course, that one semester of a foreign language instruction will not result in enough proficiency to be of practical use in professional settings. Consequently, a business educator is apt to conclude that it is either not worth the time and effort to have students become proficient in another language or it is not "cost effective" to put that much energy into foreign language because everyone speaks English anyway. Given the context, there may even be some truth to this conclusion. However, clearly there are limits placed on a monolingual professional who is unaware of the cultural aspects of international business. It is easy to underestimate the value of language and cultural proficiency.

Summary observation no. 5: Business educators can take an active role in assisting language educators in understanding the foreign language needs of students enrolled in business study abroad programs by helping to identify the business tasks and objectives.

Summary observation no. 6: Language educators should build a bridge to business to help establish realistic expectations, both in time and quality, regarding language and cultural proficiency.

ESTABLISHING FOREIGN LANGUAGE PROFICIENCY AS A PREREQUISITE IN BUSINESS STUDY ABROAD PROGRAMS

In all study abroad programs, setting the criteria for how proficient a student must be in a foreign language is actually a fairly difficult assignment. As seen in the previous sections of this paper, the single greatest factor in assessing appropriate levels is to know about the tasks and activities that the students will actually be involved in. Additionally, it is difficult to get this information out to all who need to know it. For example, I have seen instances where the program coordinators and instructors know what the courses entail, but the academic advisors and language assessors do not. A second difficulty is to know the format of the student's courses. That is to say, will the student be taking regular courses at a foreign university, special courses for foreign students in the host language, or special courses for foreign students in English? There is also a tendency for students to mix and match these three possibilities, taking both regular courses and also courses for foreign students.

After we understand the student's activities abroad, we have two major options in determining their foreign language proficiency. The first is to set a formal study prerequisite. That is to say, if students have successfully completed a specific course with a specific grade, it is assumed that the student will be able to handle the study abroad course.

Sample wording: Prerequisite: Students must have an overall GPA of 2.75 and be in good academic standing. Students must have successfully completed Spanish 300, or its equivalent, with a grade of B (or have permission of the program coordinator).

Formal study prerequisites are structurally and organizationally straight forward, but there will always be exceptions and there will be students who did not take the prerequisite course for one reason or another. Because of this, the other way to determine proficiency is by interview or by some sort of language evaluation. Once again, however, the interviews are only possible when the language evaluator has an idea of what the students will be actually doing abroad. What follows are some rules of thumb for these interviews. In simplified terms, the ACTFL guidelines categorize language proficiency in all areas (speaking, listening, reading, and writing), into four general levels (novice, intermediate, advanced, and superior). (Note: Readers unfamiliar with the oral proficiency interview and ACTFL guidelines are encouraged to visit their site for more information at <actfl.com>.) The characteristics of the proficiency levels coincide nicely with the language tasks in which students studying abroad are involved. That is to say, the novice-level speaker is limited to small memorized chunks of language, and their study abroad tasks would also be limited to basic needs and social niceties that are memorized. The intermediate-level speaker is limited to sentence level-tasks and their study abroad tasks would also be limited to general descriptions that do not include well developed paragraphs. The advanced-level speaker expands language use to paragraph-level tasks and similarly the study abroad student who needs to tackle paragraph-level tasks needs to be at an advanced level. Finally, the superior-level speaker expands the paragraph-level tasks to include specialized, hypothetical, and manipulative tasks. Students who need to use specialized vocabulary or conduct abstract analyses need to be superior-level speakers. These characteristics are summarized in the following table.

ACTFL Level	Language Ability	Study Abroad Task
Novice	Limited to memorized chunks	Student's use of language is limited to basic needs and social niceties.
Intermediate	Limited to sentence level tasks	Student's use of language is centered on general descriptions and daily tasks.
Advanced	Expanded to paragraph level tasks	Student's use of language includes speaking, reading, writing at paragraph level and with larger chunks.
Superior	Expanded to specialized, hypothetical, and manipulative tasks	Student's use of language includes specialized vocabulary and language manipulation, analysis, etc.

ASSESSMENT OF STUDY ABROAD PROGRAMS

As we have observed in this paper, the type of assessment of business study abroad programs will depend on the presence or absence of a foreign language component. If the program focuses on language acquisition, our assessment will be more related to the quality and level of the language instruction. If the program focuses on the business content, our language assessment will focus more on making sure that students have the appropriate language proficiency to participate fully in the program.

Among the different ways to assess a study abroad program, I have been impressed with the guidelines within a pamphlet produced by the Institute for International Education of Students (IES, formerly called the Institute of European Studies). IES has developed a very complete set of guidelines to assess the quality of their study abroad programs. IES has grown to the point where they enroll over 2,000 students annually from over 125 affiliate and associate institutions. The guidelines are excellent and serve as a model for all study abroad programs. Interested readers may obtain a copy of the complete guidelines in a document entitled, "The IES MAP (Model Assessment Practice) for Study Abroad: Charting A Course for Quality." (See their Internet site at <www.IESabroad.org> for details.) The MAP is actually divided into four major sections: the student learning environment; student learning and the development of intercultural competence; resources for academic and student support; and program administration and development. I will limit my observations to those related to language instruction, but the MAP also provides related suggestions regarding non-academic issues such as housing, travel, food, social activities, etc.

The student learning environment section of the MAP contains the following guidelines as related to language instruction:

(1) Language instruction, when appropriate, is integrated into all courses and IES activities.
(2) In language development courses, students gain a perspective of the host country's values, history, culture, and current status.
(3) Students are provided with out-of-classroom opportunities to develop oral, listening, and writing skills in the language of the host country.
(4) The center environment strongly encourages use of host country language through a student pledge.
(5) Tutoring and/or other forms of academic assistance are available.

The student learning and development of intercultural competence section of the MAP contains additional guidelines as related to language instruction:

(6) Students systematically report on how, and what, they have learned about the host country's language.
(7) Students engage in periodic self-evaluation of their communication skills in the language of the host culture during their course of study.
(8) IES sponsors periodic oral proficiency interviews to measure oral skills according to the American Council of Teachers of Foreign Languages or similar guidelines.

(9) IES language faculty prepare students at highest language levels for appropriate in-country exams that demonstrate mastery.

Finally the Resources for Academic and Student Support also contains an item related to foreign language:

(10) Students have access to collections of videos, slides, music, and language tapes or CDs.

Given these ten items listed in the MAP, we have concrete and consistent suggestions for assessing the foreign language components of existing study abroad programs. We also have a checklist of sorts, for those who are designing new programs or exploring new projects with international partners.

For the business content programs that assume initial language proficiency, the MAP also provides additional items for assessment. Dr. Jon F. Wergin, in his introductory comments about study abroad within the mapping pamphlet describes the objectives of study abroad in terms of three challenges, "First, the program's mission and goals need to reflect cross-cultural learning experiences, such as access to educational, cultural, and political institutions. Second, the evaluation's scope should include such non-academic elements as interactions between U.S. students and people in the host country. And third, the evaluation must respect differences in academic cultures, including pedagogical practice and student assessment and grading." Once again, the MAP is extensive and I recommend it for all interested readers.

CONCLUSION

Those of us who deal with business language education are forced to confront the issue of how much learning one foreign language will be of benefit to a person who then has to work professionally in a country of a different foreign language. In other words, will the student who becomes proficient in French for example, have any advantage when asked to conduct business in Japan? The challenge, of course, is that so many people speak English and it is so difficult to learn another language, that there is a question about whether or not it is worth it. I believe that the answer is yes. The student who learns French and who is aware of the cultural factors that affect people will take that experience of learning French to Japan. This individual will be more aware of the linguistic and cultural issues at hand. This person will be more sensitive to misunderstandings and to the limitations of interpreters. This learner will have experienced the need to speak slowly and will know how to avoid idiomatic expressions and false cognates. There will be a host of techniques that assist in being sympathetic to language communication. This person will know what types of questions to ask and the easiest and most direct way to ask them. A person who has learned one foreign language will have experience in circumlocution. It sounds easy, but being able to communicate the same idea by using various different words is actually a developed skill. Furthermore, the Japanese counterpart will also recognize that this individual has gone through the process of learning another language, similar to the way that he or she had to learn English. If it does become the case that the learner needs to learn Japanese too, he or she will have experience from learning French that will help in taking on a new language. It is definitely true that it is not as difficult to learn a third language as it is to learn a second.

There are also the cultural advantages and insights that come into the study of a foreign language that can be transferred to another culture and language. So, even if the learner ends up needing other languages, the French speaker in this example will still have an advantage over the monolingual professional who never has experienced the process. In many ways we are talking about an issue of competitive advantages. A bilingual or multilingual professional will have an advantage over the monolingual speaker.

There is no question that students can build a foundation in finance and marketing within an academic setting by studying at a university, but it must be followed up with practical, real-world experience to obtain mastery. Similarly, international cultural competence and foreign language proficiency can only developed via international experience. Study abroad offers the conduit for this equally important mastery.

REFERENCES

Loughrin-Sacco, S. J. (2000). Building a bridge to liberal arts. In: R. F. Scherer, S. T. Beaton, M. F. Ainina & J. F. Meyer (Eds), *A Field Guide to Internationalizing Business Education* (pp. 105–119). Austin, Texas: Center for International Business Education and Research.

The IES MAP (Model Assessment Practice) for Study Abroad: Charting A Course for Quality (2000). Chicago, Illinois: Institute for the International Education of Students.

THE IMPORTANT ROLE OF FACULTY INVOLVEMENT IN STUDY ABROAD

Annagene Yucas

INTRODUCTION

From a traditional institutional perspective, the ultimate customer of the university is the student and perhaps his/her parents. From the perspective of a business school, however, the ultimate customer is the employer. Thus, a school's goal, in particular a CIBER school, should be to develop and provide international programs that deliver expertise and experience to meet the needs of firms, not students. The students are the products, and the study abroad program is the means by which this product is developed and improved. Faculty are key players in the development and quality control of the student product.

THE IMPORTANT ROLE OF FACULTY

In order to prepare business majors for the highly competitive job market, the acquisition of international expertise must be an essential component of their undergraduate years. Speakers on career panels at any American campus undoubtedly stress the need for language and culture learning, as well as work abroad experience. To further convince undergraduates of this need, faculty must play an active role. While most business schools or programs implicitly support the need for international competence, it is much more effective to have in place an explicit promotion plan and to offer students a range of relevant options. Better yet, the

Study Abroad: Perspectives and Experiences from Business Schools
Advances in International Marketing, Volume 13, 99–113.
© 2003 Published by Elsevier Science Ltd.
ISSN: 1474-7979/PII: S1474797902130080

integration of study abroad into the business curriculum is the most effective assurance of student participation in overseas experience.

The importance of faculty involvement in study abroad cannot be over stressed. Various student surveys have cited the significant impact of faculty on a student's decision to study abroad. Even with on-campus resources such as a study abroad office or international resource area where encouragement to study abroad is readily available, the suggestion, if not outright encouragement, from faculty can be even more influential, particularly with goal-oriented, success-driven undergraduate business majors.

THE VARIOUS ROLES PLAYED BY FACULTY

Institutional efforts to "internationalize" can move in a number of different directions and can identify a variety of priorities. Faculty should be engaged in all activities supportive of the institution's mission and goals for internationalization. *NAFSA's Guide to Education Abroad for Advisers and Administrators* provides a fairly thorough list of important roles for faculty:

- Members of international education policy, advisory and overseas scholarship committees.
- General advocates of education abroad and promoters of campus-sponsored, affiliated, and other overseas programs.
- Advisers and pre-approval and transfer academic credit evaluators in conjunction with the study abroad office and/or registrar.
- Resources in program development and administration, including cost analysis and budget preparation.
- Area studies resources in pre-departure orientation and post-return reentry programming.
- International consultants to other campus committees.
- Campus-based or overseas program directors.
- Overseas teachers in institutional study abroad programs and exchanges.

It is worth noting that most of these roles are related to study abroad.

ADVOCACY

General advocacy on campus for study abroad is a role that can be played very effectively by faculty. It is also an excellent starting-off point for an interested faculty who wants to become involved. Without strong advocacy efforts on a campus, the internationalization process can lag, and progress can be slow and halting. An informed and committed faculty member can serve as an international "spokesperson" in a variety of contexts. Participation on an international education committee or study abroad advisory committee is the appropriate venue for supporting study abroad. Any ad hoc committee or task force to assess international activities is best served by supportive, internationalized faculty.

Faculty also play essential roles in the review of course content for new and existing courses. They can advocate for the inclusion of more comparative, regional and global content. In academic advising, faculty can encourage students to take courses with international foci and to augment their coursework with study abroad and/or internships abroad. Finally, by seizing any opportunity to speak formally or informally with students, faculty can provide affirmative views of the worth of study abroad.

THE "BEST FACULTY"

The "best faculty" should have international research interests and a passion for study abroad. Not all faculty are well suited for participation in study abroad programs. However, as just noted, there is a range of involvement, and faculty do not necessarily have to participate in every possible role, although that would be optimal. Without a doubt, staunch supporters of international expertise and experience can be very effective spokespersons on international education policy and advisory committees. They can guide institutional discussions and direct change in favor of internationalization. These same faculty, or others, can lobby for scholarship support for study abroad from internal sources, i.e. departments, colleges, deans' offices, provost's office, even the president's office, as well as minority affairs, disabled student services, etc. External sources of scholarship support can also be approached with the assistance of faculty advocates. Furthermore, faculty can identify appropriate internship placements abroad as well as stateside.

The "best faculty" to work in program development and administration and then to continue on as overseas program directors are those who are considered the most "student friendly". These are the faculty who receive consistently strong student evaluations and who are the recipients of teaching awards. They are the dedicated teachers who place the greatest importance on this aspect of their academic careers. Above all, these are the faculty who genuinely like students, enjoy their company, and want to impact their learning process, thereby developing a marketable product – the student. They are the true student advocates.

Faculty who can relate to the student experience abroad are best able to develop relevant, appealing curriculum and also address the practical needs of the students.

They understand the kinds of courses that work best on the host site and they effectively link them to the host culture. They recognize that on a study abroad program a portion of the learning experience takes place in the classroom; the field component provides an equally, if not more, important learning venue. They delight in the creative challenge of developing exciting, stimulating courses that take full advantage of the overseas site, integrating students, to the greatest extent possible, into the host culture.

The academic experience is only part of a study abroad program, however. Faculty need to have an understanding of student life issues and a willingness to assume the responsibility of crisis management on site. Identifying and securing safe, clean housing, determining how meals will be provided, and committing to a group flight are among the easier tasks. Typically, most faculty are removed from student life outside of the classroom on the home campus and can be quite taken aback at the amount of sexual activity, alcohol and drug use, and the variety of oftentimes distressing complications that ensue from them.

In addition to a range of potential accidents and illnesses, it is not uncommon to be faced with sexual assaults, drug arrests, and alcohol-related traffic accidents. A willing, empathetic faculty member may find him/herself at a hospital bedside or in a police station with a very distraught student. Such situations can be time-intensive and emotionally draining. They also make it difficult to maintain other teaching and/or administrative responsibilities. Yet when the faculty can remain the calm, competent "adult-in-charge" and provide support to a needy student, it can be extremely gratifying.

In summary, the "best faculty" are those whose academic interests and research activities are already internationalized. They are ready advocates for study abroad, willing to participate in a variety of committees to develop institutional policies and procedures, to seek scholarship support, and to develop new, exciting study abroad programs. On site they are devoted to the well-being of their students, aware that the demands of a program director can be twenty-four hours a day in times of crises. Such faculty have a passion for study abroad and greatly inspire their students.

DISINCENTIVES

For some faculty who have traveled extensively and/or studied abroad and/or conducted research abroad, involvement in study abroad is a natural extension of their interests. For others, however, it means breaking an inertia that has set in which simply hasn't included an additional time commitment to internationally oriented activities. Others assume an egocentric position and question, "What's in it for me?" Yet others complain that study abroad lures off campus the best and brightest students.

Depending on a faculty's particular area of specialization and research interest, s/he might not recognize any relevance between a student's study abroad experience and what faculty do. Nor is involvement in a study abroad program perceived as contributing to the work of the faculty. Senior faculty might readily engage in policy discussions and decision-making relative to the internationalization of the curriculum, but have no interest in playing "mother hen" to a flock of undergraduates abroad. And while younger, energetic faculty might relish such an opportunity, they are likely to receive discouragement, if not complete lack of support from their department chairs until they have secured tenure. From a purely practical perspective, it is not effortless to leave one's home and office for six weeks, a semester, or an academic year. Taking children out of school and asking a spouse to leave his/her work might be too difficult or impose too much of a hardship, particularly on a young family. If that is the case, the faculty should postpone participation in a study abroad program until it is more manageable.

Often faculty may be reluctant to teach abroad because of the logistical challenges of setting up such programs. Thus, it is important to have an administrator or graduate assistant who can lighten the burden of foreign-teaching faculty. Alternatively, an innovative model is to have MBA students or those students participating in the program design and propose study tours. If managed carefully, the students do the major organizational work, thereby lightening the faculty load. This can even be handled as a sort of student class project. Allowing students to be entrepreneurial in developing an appropriate program can prove to be a valuable learning experience.

INCENTIVES

Incentives for faculty involvement in study abroad programs must be provided by the administration and the experience must be regarded as an excellent means for faculty development. In the 1995 American Council on Education (ACE) report, *Educating Americans for a World in Flux: Ten Ground Rules for Internationalizing Higher Education*, suggestions relative to faculty support are cited:

> Among the key actions that an institution can take are the following: Encourage faculty to develop expertise in the global dimensions of their disciplines. Encourage interdisciplinary study. Give weight to international experience, skill, and foreign language competence as criteria in hiring new faculty. Provide faculty and staff with opportunities to develop their own international and language skills. Include international service or study among the criteria for tenure or promotion. Institutions have many ways to send a signal to faculty members about what is important (ACE Report, "Ground Rule Six").

Faculty are drawn to study abroad programs for a variety of reasons. Business faculty are often motivated by the desire to give students the international tools they need to work effectively in the new global marketplace of today. They recognize the value of providing students with their initial, international exposure in the structured, low-risk environment of a study abroad program before they graduate and enter the workforce.

Participation in a study abroad program is a definite faculty development option. It provides continuing education for the business faculty, keeping him/her in touch with the international business world and especially informed about the business climate of the host country. It provides an opportunity to develop and teach courses not usually taught on the home campus. And it can provide the opportunity to conduct research in a foreign setting. This might require additional time abroad, either before or after the study abroad program, to assure sufficient dedicated research time. Collaborations with foreign institutions and colleagues should be arranged in advance to make the most productive use of time abroad.

While faculty might appreciate the opportunity to be paid for the expenses of living and traveling abroad, compensation for teaching abroad and the administrative responsibilities of a study abroad program are not always that attractive. Extra compensation for teaching abroad might not be matched at the same rate that would be paid on the home campus. During the regular academic year, the faculty continues to receive his/her regular salary and the department is paid replacement salary so that an adjunct faculty can be hired to teach regularly offered courses. Or, faculty can be compensated via time release from teaching during the regular academic year. However, in the summer term, direct payment to the faculty for the additional course(s) taught abroad is usually the case.

Salaries in study abroad programs that offer liberal arts courses are typically lower than what a business faculty would make since a break-even budget on such programs is desired. The student participants pay for their real expenses, i.e. housing, meals, fieldtrips, airport transfers, orientation programs, etc., as well as a proportionate amount of the instructional costs. This would include the foreign faculty and the American accompanying professor and the latter's other real expenses. In low volume programs in expensive urban settings, for example, the challenge is to offer an affordable program within the reach of the average business student.

Institutional support is often necessary to bring monetary incentives to a normal level. If a department or college cannot provide the "rounding off" of a faculty's salary, a CIBER could make up the difference. Federal and other monies from various grant programs can assist with compensation, but significant fore-planning must take place to have sufficient compensation for business faculty.

A different approach is to pay faculty on a commission basis, in which they get paid more for attracting more students or other resources to the program. A dean or department chair would then have an additional management tool to parcel out money and other rewards. Other forms of institutional support could be administrative assistance with logistical arrangements and mentoring and encouragement, particularly for faculty who have little or no overseas teaching experience.

From the perspective of the home institution's administration, one incentive for faculty to participate in study abroad programs tends to be compensation. However, as previously discussed, this amount could be less than typically anticipated. The opportunity to go abroad can be seen as a perk and thereby very desirable. Another perk is the opportunity to do research abroad, possibly with foreign collaborators. Administrators can enhance this incentive by providing means for faculty to contact and interact with foreign research faculty in specific countries. A final incentive from the administration's perspective is faculty development. Numerous occasions abroad for self-improvement as a teacher/researcher are available. The ability to spend substantial time in a foreign setting, away from the demands and routines of the home campus, contributes to a renewing and a re-energizing of one's professional and personal lives. Many faculty report that they have gained new teaching insights, as well as research interests, from their experiences abroad.

Incentive structures are a function of the nature of the institution where they are developed. In instances where faculty take significant ownership of their program, they are likely to be satisfied with less compensation. For some faculty, study abroad programs can be regarded as a distraction from their home campus duties. In these cases, the institution must be proactive to develop frameworks within which faculty can continue to perform their usual duties, e.g. research, at the foreign location. Colleagues and administrators from the home institution can be of great assistance in this regard. Finally, faculty require the assurance that they will arrive in the foreign setting to find a good, safe, and positive situation for living, teaching, and conducting any other work-related activities. This will be especially important for faculty who don't speak the local language and are not familiar with the program site. If at all possible, faculty should be provided the opportunity to conduct a site visit prior the program's starting date. This time to become familiar with the local environment, amenities, and teaching facilities will not only orient the faculty, but also will enable him/her to speak knowledgeably about the program site to students and be seen as an authority.

In general, the incentive process to encourage faculty to participate in study abroad programs is likely to go more smoothly the greater the international orientation and vision of the home institution. In such institutions, innovative programs link research funding to participation in international program offerings in order to appeal to potential faculty who might want to both teach and research abroad. Another approach is to send pairs of faculty members abroad who are from different, yet complimentary, disciplines. For example, a business professor and a language/culture professor could go abroad together. Each can benefit from the other's expertise. The insights that emerge from such pairings are potentially invaluable. In particular, this can amount to personal mentoring for the business faculty.

Yet another approach is to encourage faculty to offer courses abroad that they might not be able to do at the home campus. Thus, many faculty might be attracted to teaching abroad if given the opportunity to offer coursework that they love, but can't necessarily teach at home. For example, business law courses are quite fascinating when taught in London in the context of the British legal system and traditional, common law-based commercial law.

A very different incentive approach is to charge the university with the responsibility of developing inter-institutional relationships with foreign universities. An aspect of the agreement would be to supply American faculty to teach at those institutions in areas where there is strong need. This could entail opening a course offered abroad initially to only American students to include native, as well as other international, students on the host campus. In a teaching exchange arrangement, the foreign university, in turn, would supply faculty to the American campus to replace the outgoing faculty and/or as the need arises to provide a particular expertise. At the extreme, a kind of virtual university approach, results in which faculty as free agents come and go as they are needed, depending on their specific core competencies.

Some international activities for faculty require no or minimal financial commitment on the part of the institution, such as participation in faculty teaching or research exchanges under the auspices of inter-institutional agreements. For the most part, however, some form of financial commitment must be secured to provide such opportunities to faculty as independent foreign travel and research, site visits to campus-sponsored or affiliated programs as part of the program evaluation process, or optimally their full participation in the home institution's own study abroad programs.

Even modest sums, i.e. $12,000–$20,000, to support a "study abroad faculty development fund" will provide encouragement to faculty members who are interested in developing a program abroad. Such a fund can support a site visit to a prospective program venue. It can also serve to extend the stay for a program director who would like to have additional time on site to conduct his/her own research after the program obligations have ended. The institutional investment is well spent. The study abroad program is administered by a responsible, institutional representative; the faculty has the multi-faceted experience of directing the program, experiencing the culture, and pursuing his/her own research interests. And at the conclusion of the international experience, the institution invariably receives back on the home campus a revitalized member of the faculty and an even stronger ally of study abroad.

PROMOTION AND RECRUITMENT

The ability to promote study abroad and attract students to such opportunities can be done effectively by faculty. They can take the lead in this area and significantly impact the rate of student participation. Although there is often a reluctance to use class time to discuss the value of study abroad, small commitments of time can yield impressive results. A faculty member can relate course matter to his/her own experience abroad. S/he can draw on other students' experiences abroad during class discussion and also invite international students and faculty to speak to the class.

The natural tendency is for faculty to support programs in which they are vested. These would be their own programs or those that they would like to lead. They might lean toward those programs that are managed by a committee on which they serve. Or faculty might have positive feelings about those places where they have visited or studied themselves.

In general, faculty should contribute to a campus "culture" that strives to foster interest in study abroad and provide a continuous validation of the study abroad experience. Faculty can help to create a positive atmosphere on campus that implicitly conveys to students that "study abroad is the thing to do", "just about everyone studies abroad", and "study abroad can really give you an edge in the job market after graduation".

PROGRAM DEVELOPMENT AND ADMINISTRATION

What should be the faculty member's role in developing study abroad programs? Should s/he be expected to create a program from start to finish, including logistics, or to what extent should the centralized international programs office/study abroad office participate? There are two primary models:

(1) Individual colleges and professors drive programs, and the central international programs office provides logistical and other support.
(2) The international programs office staff develops the programs, or a strong framework in which programs can be developed, and then goes out and recruits faculty by various means.

In the case of the latter model, there is a stronger role of the central office to educate faculty about the value of overseas programs, recruit them, nurture and mentor them. Given the typical faculty life cycle, faculty can be approached at various times during their career when the opportunity cost of getting involved in overseas programs is low. It is useful to instill young faculty with international values by giving them overseas experience early in their careers, but, on the other hand, older faculty are more likely to have the time to go abroad later in their careers.

Faculty involvement in overseas programs results, to a large extent, from leadership in the college. It is important to have deans and chairs who see the value of international experience and seek to have their faculty acquire it. One possibility is to require faculty to have foreign experiences in order to be promoted. At present, however, this is not a typical component of the tenure review process.

Another issue is consistency of succession in the faculty serving as directors of study abroad programs. Is it better to have the same faculty teaching abroad year after year, or to have a mix of faculty teaching abroad in succeeding years. There are advantages and disadvantages to each approach, and the best approach probably strikes a balance between these two options. Continuity of faculty tends to result in consistency, quality control, and program improvements, yet risks faculty burn-out. First-time faculty lack familiarity and experience and have difficulty in convincing students of their competence and knowledge when they are getting oriented at the same time as the program participants.

Many faculty simply do not have the temperament, inclination, or skills to deal with the vast amount of details that comprise a study abroad program. For those who do, however, study abroad program development and administration can be a very satisfying experience. By partnering with the central international programs/study abroad office, faculty can have direct involvement in the design and development of programs abroad. They can create curriculum for these programs and determine the credits offered.

Another essential consideration is the budgeting of the programs. An understanding of the financial constraints is critical in determining the possible components of a program. General logistics such as housing, meals, and fieldtrips must be decided. It will also make transparent the cost of the faculty's participation in the program in relation to the programs' total costs and the resultant fee charged to the students.

The student selection process is yet another activity that requires faculty participation. The academic preparedness of a student can be best determined by a faculty's review of the student's transcript and accompanying essay. Other academic issues are naturally the purview of the faculty.

Finally, faculty play an important role in the evaluation of programs offered by other American and foreign colleges and universities or third-party providers. In determining the academic worth of a program not administered by one's home institution, various academic considerations must be taken into account. Faculty are the optimal institutional representatives for this task.

For faculty who want the most involvement in study abroad, directing a program abroad on-site is the optimal experience. While programs can be year-long, semester-long, or a variety of lengths in the summer, the biggest growth has been in the short-term faculty-led programs. These can range from one- to two-week interim term programs to longer summer programs. Typically, faculty are engaged in the program development phase and also in many aspects of the administration of the program.

Institutional structures often determine the type of study abroad programs. Two major structural models can be identified:

(1) a central university-level study abroad infrastructure that serves as an umbrella to other, small scale programs within the university;
(2) more micro-level college- or department-based programs that are often less well structured and which may or may not be supported by a larger, university-level infrastructure.

There are advantages and disadvantages to each type of program. For example, university-based programs are less likely to duplicate key activities and can share resources. College-based programs are likely to be more flexible and attentive to specific faculty needs, and can have an easier time recruiting faculty. Where both types of structures are used, it is essential that the two work closely together, to optimally use scarce resources and maximize effectiveness.

A further question is what is the optimal structure to organize cooperation and collaboration between the two types of institutional units. To some extent, this depends on the history and organization of individual institutions. For example, some universities are large or have flat organizational structures and reflect a high degree of autonomy at the college levels. Where there is considerable separation between the colleges and the university, or where there are tensions based on territoriality, greater effort must be expended among the individual units to cooperate. In any case, the university umbrella should not overshadow the college units because it is ultimately the faculty who devise and drive the programs. It is important to foster the enthusiasm of the faculty so that they become the engines for study abroad programs.

The problems of structural relations for a business college within a university can be resolved in a variety of ways. One approach is to have a well laid-out division of responsibilities in which each unit understands its roles and performs accordingly. For example, the university-level international programs office can perform certain established functions that the business college understands and from which it can benefit. It is useful to delineate the roles that each of these units will play and then ensure effective means of communication between them. Additional suggestions include:

- Having a central administrator or coordinator at the business college who can interface with the university office of international programs/study abroad office. Accordingly, the coordinator can meet regularly with the university office to ensure good communications and coordination. Ideally, there ought to be two staff members for this purpose, one at an administrative level (e.g. Director of International Programs and Dean or Associate Dean of the College of Business) and one at the operations level to coordinate finer-grained issues. These staff can be recruited from existing faculty or those who have recently retired and may even do the job part-time.
- There can be a commission structure with "kickbacks" to the business college, depending on the numbers of students that each provides to the central university office. Revenues resulting to the college in this way serve as a strong incentive to the college and keep faculty interested.
- The central international programs office and the business college may share expenses associated with a given program, thereby reducing the resource expenditures of each.
- While the structure governing relations between the central university office and the business college is not always crystal clear, it is useful to have a common vision across the university. However, a key challenge is in translating this vision into ground-level strategy. Structures may lag behind the vision and are often embedded in traditional bureaucracies. Even within large bureaucracies, though, there is always room for entrepreneurial initiatives which the CIBER programs around the country make available.
- The most important component is the right team of people to build up the appropriate structure for study abroad programs. With a group of enthusiastic, cooperative colleagues, such programs can succeed even in the face of a substantial bureaucratic structure.
- Another important component is the right mix of study abroad programs in place that are appropriate to the specific circumstances of each university.
- Eventually, successful individual programs must be institutionalized, so they can continue and thrive. With time, a well-structured organization gives rise to a sense of ownership in the programs. This is healthy because ownership fosters stewardship and the development of a sound institutional structure.
- Good communication between the university's central office of international programs and the business college cannot be over-emphasized. Whenever important matters are discussed, it is critical to have representatives from each unit present for continued trust and maximum communication and outcomes.

- There are also advantages to developing integrated programs from two or more academic units from across campus, e.g. foreign languages and business.

An important benefit of the faculty's intense, thorough involvement in the development and administration of a study abroad program is that it tends to deepen his/her convictions about the value of study abroad. A faculty member becomes a stronger voice on campus, a more proactive ally of study abroad. The downside is that faculty often burn-out if they lead programs year after year. Optimally, more than one person would share in the responsibility of leading a program abroad, or this responsibility could be alternated year after year among several interested faculty.

A pre-program site visit or prior experience at the site is important preparation for the faculty. S/he should carefully review new program content, as well as current courses and activities. Familiarity with housing and meal options, field-trip destinations, transportation systems, banking establishments, and healthcare facilities, are all necessary.

Programs are often supported by a host national, a logistics organization, or the foreign student services office of a host university. The faculty should meet these contacts and establish good working relations with them well in advance of the students' arrival. This is essential to the smooth running of a program.

In working with program budgets, some business faculty might have particular expertise that could be applied to the development of a new budget and the evaluation of existing cost sheets. They could also consult on budget audits, plan for currency fluctuations, as well as contingencies and emergencies. Faculty can also bring a understanding of the relationship between tuition, financial aid and cash flow. Finally, they might have more experience managing considerable amounts of money that comprise the program's budget.

Faculty must understand that their on-site presence is likely to represent a range of responsibilities. They are the academic director of the program, as well as the administrative/resident director. They could be responsible for the on-site orientation of the students upon arrival. They have to manage the budget and advise on a number of academic and personal matters. Advising signifies a whole range of challenges, including mental health and cultural adjustment issues. They also serve as the health care and emergency response coordinator.

If leading a program abroad is more involved than an individual might want, then affiliated programs might offer the right amount of involvement. These are large consortial programs, i.e. the Council for International Educational Exchange (CIEE), the Institute for the International Education of Students (IES), the American Institute for Foreign Study (AIFS), etc., that welcome faculty participation on advisory councils, curriculum committees, on-site evaluations, etc. Faculty can have input in the selection of appropriate program sites, partners, and courses in such programs.

ACADEMIC ISSUES

In addition to the oversight of curriculum on study abroad programs, there are several other academic areas that are best served by faculty involvement. Program evaluation can utilize faculty expertise in a number of ways. Defining curricular goals and setting academic standards are mandated faculty responsibilities. The achievement of these goals and standards requires constant and consistent evaluation.

Another area is the pre-approval of programs offered by other American or foreign institutions. Faculty can determine course equivalencies, the degree of language acquisition, and credit transfer assurance. They can also monitor student performance in a variety of ways. A site visit is typically the optimal means of conducting a program evaluation.

The evaluation of transfer credit is nearly always a departmental decision that involves faculty. Initially, credit is considered on the basis of equivalency. Then courses that enrich or supplement the core curriculum are also reviewed. In addition, faculty can conduct interviews of returning students; this is often done to determine the extent of language acquisition. Faculty input is welcome in the evaluation of all types of educational experiences abroad including academic coursework, internships and service-learning for credit. Finally, faculty are the appropriate hosts for international faculty delegations whose task is to assess academic credentials and standards in a program.

Academic issues also engage faculty in the admissions process. Students going abroad should be assessed on academic preparedness, as well as maturity and ability to adapt to a new cultural environment. Once admitted, students can benefit from faculty involvement in the pre-departure orientation. Faculty can prepare them for the academic experience, as well as the cultural learning opportunity. And faculty can also participate in a re-entry program by advising students how to apply their new knowledge gained abroad in their academic and professional careers.

CONCLUSION

From campus advocate to on-site program director, there are many important roles that a faculty member can play. Business faculty, in particular, have a range of expertise that can be fruitfully applied to study abroad promotion and program development and administration. Working cooperatively with the institution's central office of international programs/study abroad office, faculty can contribute to a successful overseas program with high student satisfaction through the development of creative projects, challenging internships and interesting fieldtrips, as well as effective on-site administration. However, an institutional commitment must be made in order to offer the appropriate incentives to engage the "best faculty". Faculty involvement in study abroad can also be facilitated by the support of the CIBERs. Ultimately, faculty development through teaching and/or research abroad is a significant bonus to the overall experience.

INTERNATIONALIZING BUSINESS STUDENTS THROUGH THE STUDY ABROAD EXPERIENCE: OPPORTUNITIES AND CHALLENGES

Kenneth M. Holland and Ben L. Kedia

INTRODUCTION

Recruiting students to study abroad is a difficult challenge for American colleges and universities. Study abroad advisors and directors of international programs are searching for better ways of marketing the overseas academic experience. Approximately 3% of U.S. students who pursue a bachelor's degree study abroad at some point in their college career. In any given year, less than 1% (0.8%) of U.S. students take part in study abroad (Hayward, 2000, p. 9). American higher education falls far short of the Presidential Commission's target of 10% by 2000 set in 1979 (Strength Through Wisdom, 1979). The typical college student who participates in study abroad is an undergraduate liberal arts major who spends one semester in a country in Western Europe. In 1999–2000, 63% of American students studying abroad were in Europe (Snapshot of Report on Study Abroad Programs, 2000, p. 1). Almost one fourth go to one country – Great Britain. Fifteen percent of study abroad students travel to Latin America, 6% to Asia and 3% to Africa (Hayward, 2000, p. 10). The small number of U.S. students (129,770) who experienced foreign study in 1998–1999 compares unfavorably with the much larger number of foreign students (490,933) who enrolled in U.S. institutions (Hesel & Green, 2000, p. 5). Even more disheartening is the fact that nearly 50% of students

Study Abroad: Perspectives and Experiences from Business Schools
Advances in International Marketing, Volume 13, 115–139.
© 2003 Published by Elsevier Science Ltd.
ISSN: 1474-7979/PII: S1474797902130092

entering 4-year colleges say that they want to study abroad and that three out of four adults agree that students should study abroad (Hesel & Green, 2000, p. 1). When asked to choose which activity in college is most important to them, entering freshmen rank study abroad second only to internships (Hesel & Green, 2000, p. 3). There are obviously a number of barriers to student participation in foreign study.

Previous research has shown that students who enroll in pre-professional degree programs, such as engineering, education, nursing, or business, are less likely to spend a junior year abroad or even a semester in a foreign country than humanities and social science majors. One study found that the number of students from professional schools, such as architecture, engineering and business administration, was less than half of 1% of all professional students (McCormack, 1966, p. 369). In the European Union, by contrast, 22% of students who study abroad are majoring in management, 21% in foreign languages, 10% in engineering, 9% in social science and 8% in law (Jallade & Gordon, 1996, p. 5).

Since 1974, AACSB International: The Association to Advance Collegiate Schools of Business, formerly known as the American Assembly of Collegiate Schools of Business, has required business schools to address the international dimension in their curricula for purposes of accreditation (Kedia & Cornwell, 1994, p. 12). A 1991 roundtable on internationalizing business schools and faculty, hosted by Michigan State University's Center for International Business Education and Research, recommended international internships and individual and group trips overseas as a promising way of internationalizing business student life on campus (Cavusgil et al., 1992, p. 17). A 1998 study (Kedia & Harveston, 1998, p. 214) recommended that MBA programs replace the domestic with a global perspective, including foreign internship and study experiences for students. More and more business schools are recognizing that the managers they are training must be global managers, with international knowledge and experience and skills in managing cultural diversity (Kedia & Mukherji, 1999, p. 235). The effort to use study abroad as a tool to internationalize schools of business is having some success. The percentage of study abroad students majoring in business grew from 11% in 1985 to 16% in 1999. Humanities and social science majors represent 35% of the total.

Business schools are doing many things right. Our survey of study abroad advisors, conducted in the summer of 2001, revealed a much higher participation rate for business students than did earlier literature and, most surprisingly, a higher rate than that of students in other majors (see Table 1). Nearly half of the respondents reported that between 2 and 5% of business majors at their college studied abroad in 1999–2000. Only one-third of universities, by contrast, said that between two and 5% of students in all majors studied abroad. While 29% of respondents

Table 1.

What percentage of all majors studied abroad in the 12-month period, September 1999–August 2000?		What percentage of business majors studied abroad in the 12-month period, September 1999–August 2000?	
Less than 1%	43%	Less than 1%	29%
2–5%	35%	2–5%	46%
More than 5%	22%	More than 5%	24%
Total	100%	Total	99%

reported that less than 1% of business students took part in study abroad, a much higher percentage, 43%, indicated that less than 1% of all students had a foreign experience in 1999–2000. In response to an open-ended question, one study abroad advisor reported that business students studied abroad at a higher rate than any other major.

More than 40% of those who go overseas are from large, research institutions. Almost two-thirds of the participants are women, and 16% are minorities (Hayward, 2000, p. 10). Periods of study abroad are becoming shorter. Since 1985 the number of students spending more than a semester abroad has fallen from 18 to 10%. A recent poll of entering freshmen found that six out of ten students preferred a duration of one semester, 18% favored summer programs, 11% year-long programs and 9% short study abroad programs of a few weeks (Hesel & Green, 2000, p. 6).

Our survey of study abroad professionals, however, found that business students nearly equally prefer the very short experience (one month or less) and the long experience (at least one semester).

Our survey also found that students at larger universities have a stronger preference for short study abroad experiences than those at medium and small institutions (see Table 3). The larger institutions tend to be public and the smaller ones private. Public colleges attract students with lower incomes than their private counterparts. More affluent students can afford more easily to spend a semester or year abroad than students with fewer means.

Table 2.   The Overseas Component of the Study Abroad Program in 1999–2000 that Attracted the Most Business Students Lasted How Long?

4 weeks or less	35%
5 to 12 weeks	26%
More than 12 weeks	39%
Total	100%

Table 3. Percentage of Respondents Who Agreed That Students Prefer Short
Study Abroad Experiences (Less Than One Month), by Size of Institution
Measured by Number of Undergraduate Students.

Less than 5,000	34%
5,001 to 10,000	36%
More than 10,000	49%

Obviously business schools have made progress in recent years in the marketing of the study abroad experience, and in recruiting students to travel overseas
to participate in academic programs. Nevertheless, business schools still face a
number of challenges in recruiting students for foreign study. This paper examines
some of these barriers and offers some guidelines. A survey of the literature reveals
very little systematic study of what these challenges are and how institutions have
attempted to overcome them. To fill in these gaps and advance our understanding, the authors developed a survey instrument and mailed it to 304 institutions
of higher education in the United States with business programs accredited by the
AACSB. Rather than sending the questionnaire to the study abroad office at each
institution, the authors obtained a copy of the Section on U.S. Students Abroad
(SECUSSA) mailing list. SECUSSA is a subdivision of the National Association of Foreign Student Advisors (NAFSA). The questionnaire was addressed to a
SECUSSA member from each AACSB institution. When there was no SECUSSA
member, the instrument was addressed to "Study Abroad Director." The authors
received 127 completed questionnaires, for a return rate of 42%. The respondents
held a variety of positions. Nearly 40% were study abroad directors and one-quarter
were center for international programs directors, followed by the business school

Table 4. Position Title of Respondents (or Equivalent).

Title	Percentage
Director of Study Abroad	38%
Director of Center for International Programs	25%
Dean, College of Business (includes Assistant and Associate Dean)	10%
Director of Center for International Business	10%
Academic Advisor	4%
Professor of Business	4%
Director of Study Abroad for the College of Business Administration	3%
Assistant to Dean for Student Affairs	2%
Other	4%
Total	100%

dean and the center for international business director, at 10% each. In this paper, we will refer to those who completed the survey as "respondents," "advisors" or "study abroad professionals."

This is the appropriate pool to answer questions regarding marketing of overseas study and recruiting business students to study abroad. When asked who is primarily responsible for marketing study abroad to business students, 60% answered the study abroad director. Eighteen percent of the respondents indicated that the business school had its own study abroad director.

THE SURVEY INSTRUMENT

The instructions of the questionnaire informed the respondent that we are interested in examining the patterns of business students studying abroad. The purpose of the survey was to determine how to make studying in foreign countries more attractive to both undergraduate and graduate business students. The respondent was told that we are especially interested in learning what works and does not work on his or her campus. Following the instructions were sixty-five questions. Forty-three used a five-point Likert scale. The remaining questions either asked for information about the institution or provided for open-ended responses.

The Likert scale questions addressed three dimensions of the challenge of persuading business students to study abroad. The first dimension consists of the facilitating factors that students majoring in business face in taking the time to go to a foreign country, such as a rigid requirement of courses for the major. The second dimension encompasses all the challenges that universities face in inducing students to have a foreign experience, such as providing scholarships. The final dimension related to marketing, encompassing the best means of reaching business majors with the study abroad message. The data provide a profile of who studies abroad in business schools (Tables 1–8), identify potential challenges and facilitating factors (Tables 9–16) and indicate which marketing and communication techniques work best (Tables 17–20).

FACILITATING FACTORS

The survey points to a number of factors associated with a higher participation rate for business students in study abroad. As Table 5 reveals, offering scholarships is the most positive factor, followed by location of study abroad programs in English-speaking countries. Approximately 30% of American college students receive financial aid to study abroad, while 38% of foreign students receive financial aid

Table 5.   Factors that Facilitate Business Students Studying Abroad.

	Agree	Neutral	Disagree
Scholarships are an effective tool in recruiting business students to study abroad	79%	14%	7%
Students prefer study abroad programs in English-speaking countries	68%	18%	14%
Business students are more likely to study abroad if a business faculty member leads the program	61%	26%	13%
More business students would study abroad if the number of electives were increased	51%	33%	17%

to study in the United States (Hesel & Green, 2000, p. 5). A majority of respondents also agreed that having programs led by business faculty and increasing the number of electives would make it easier for business students to have a foreign experience.

In our sample, 19% of institutions offered four to nine study abroad programs led by business faculty in academic year 1999–2000, 50% offered one, two or three courses, and about one-third did not offer any. Either business faculty from the home institution or from the host country can teach study abroad courses. Business departments sometimes prefer the former structure because it is challenging for an American university with a business school to find a suitable institution overseas. Business schools and degrees in business administration are relatively new to foreign universities (McCormack, 1966, p. 371).

Other research of college student preferences shows that students are evenly divided on whether they prefer that study abroad courses be taught by faculty from U.S. colleges or by faculty from the host foreign country (Hesel & Green, 2000, p. 10). It is important to keep in mind that Hesel and Green surveyed high school students about to enter college, while we questioned university study abroad professionals.

Successful marketing strategies pay attention to product, place, pricing and promotion (Rodrigues, 1996, p. 115). Table 6 lists specific findings of our survey that can be used by study abroad professionals to improve marketing.

The lack of linguistic ability among students is supported by the fact that 74% of the institutions surveyed indicated that business students are not required to take a foreign language. The lack of a foreign language requirement in the business major stands in stark contrast to the fact that 57% of all college students plan to take a foreign language. A language requirement has a positive effect on participation in study abroad (Hesel & Green, 2000, p. 4). Universities, thus, can increase participation rates for business students by increasing the number of electives for

Table 6. What is Important in Marketing Study Abroad to Business Students.

Product

Students prefer almost equally short programs of one month or less or semester-long programs.

Students at smaller schools tend to prefer longer programs than those at larger universities.

Students prefer study abroad programs tailored for business students.

Business students are more likely to study abroad if a business faculty member leads the program.

Pricing

Scholarships are an effective tool in recruiting business students to study abroad.

Place

Students prefer programs in English-speaking countries.

Promotion

Show students that they can study abroad and graduate on schedule.

Demonstrate to students the career value of study abroad.

Make all business students aware of opportunities for foreign study.

Use faculty and students returning from overseas to market study abroad.

Train advisors in how to help students plan in advance for study abroad.

Hold study abroad information fairs where students can pick up brochures and talk to faculty involved in all study abroad opportunities on campus.

Provide web-based information to all students on study abroad opportunities over the Internet or campus Intranet.

Mail a comprehensive flyer to all business students, listing all study abroad opportunities especially tailored for them.

Place posters depicting study abroad opportunities in locations frequented by business students.

---

business majors, designing programs in English-speaking countries led by business faculty, providing more scholarships to participants and adding a foreign language requirement to the curriculum.

Having a full-time study abroad director is another facilitating feature (see Table 7). Fortunately, 70% of colleges and universities with an undergraduate business program have that position. Institutions that employ a full-time director differ in important ways from those that do not. Students at these institutions are more likely to value an experience in another country, and they are more likely to be required to take a foreign language and to study abroad. Universities that devote resources to study abroad staff and to scholarships obviously value the international student experience more highly than those that do not. It follows that faculty members at such institutions are more involved. Study abroad directors can devote time to arranging internships and to making arrangements for the transfer of credits earned at foreign institutions.

Another type of resource associated with relatively high participation rates is the presence of a recruitment budget. A majority of the responding institutions (61%), however, report that their institution, budgets nothing for specifically recruiting

Table 7.   Percentage of Respondents Who Agree to Statements Regarding Study
Abroad, by Whether the Institution Has a Full-Time Study Abroad Director.

	Agree (No Full-Time Director)	Agree (Full-Time Director)
Many business students do not recognize the value of studying abroad	86%	66%
There are study abroad programs led by business faculty	63%	79%
Study abroad credits are fully and easily transferable	53%	73%
Internships in foreign countries are available for business majors	51%	68%
Your institution regards the study abroad experience for business students as very important	42%	67%
Business students are required to take a foreign language as part of their major	14%	26%
There are sufficient scholarships for business students to study abroad	9%	21%
Business students are required to study abroad	3%	14%

business students to participate in study abroad programs. One-fifth of universities budget, less than one thousand dollars, while only 18% allocate more than $1,000 for this purpose. Three out of four respondents from schools that spend more than $1,000 on recruitment agree that their institution regards the study abroad experience for business students as very important, in contrast to only half at four-year institutions that budget nothing for recruitment. The survey also revealed a number of barriers to greater participation in study abroad by business majors.

CHALLENGES

Recent research identifies a number of barriers to study abroad. Students who do not want to study abroad (about half of all college students) give several reasons. The most frequently cited reason is unwillingness to leave the United States (34%), followed by cost (11%), delay in graduation (8%), interference with career goals (8%) and taking time away from academic goals (5%) (Hesel & Green, 2000, p. 5). Academic reasons, thus, are less important than fear and cost. Our survey of those concerned with study abroad for business majors supports the view that academic barriers are relatively low. The most frequent answers to the open-ended question, "Why many business students do not study abroad," were cost, inability

Table 8.   Reasons Respondents Give for Why Business Students Do Not Study Abroad.

Cost	21%
Could not complete major on time	14%
Do not recognize the career value of study abroad	13%
No interest in traveling outside the United States	12%
Lack of study abroad programs tailored for business students	10%
Lack of awareness of foreign study opportunities	8%
Lack of faculty encouragement	8%
Lack of advance planning	8%
Lack of language skills	4%

to complete the major on time, failure to see the career value of study abroad, no interest in foreign travel and lack of study abroad programs tailored for business students.

Business students face some disincentives in studying in a foreign country not shared equally by undergraduate liberal arts students. These barriers fall into five broad categories: academic, structural, financial, attitudinal and timing/duration.

Academic Challenges

Surprisingly, respondents pointed to relatively few academic hurdles (see Table 9). A successful study abroad program does not constitute an interruption of study but is an integral part of the student's four-year program (Durnall, 1967, p. 451). If the cost of going overseas is an additional semester or year of college, relatively few students will be willing to pay that price. Approximately two-thirds of the institutions surveyed, however, denied that either the number of required courses for the business major or their sequence is a barrier to overseas travel. It appears, moreover, that there are plenty of study abroad courses tailored for business students led by business faculty. Transfer of credits back to the home institution is not a problem.

Answers to open-ended questions, however, revealed that accounting majors at some institutions do face substantial academic obstacles to taking part in an overseas program. Advisors say that some accounting departments do not permit students to take required courses outside the United States and point to the rigidity of the curriculum and the number of required courses.

Table 9 does reveal some potential academic impediments. Business students are not required to study abroad, nor are they obliged to take a foreign language

Table 9.   Possible Academic Challenges to Business Students Studying Abroad.

	Agree	Neutral	Disagree
There are not enough study abroad programs tailored for business students	34%	13%	53%
The sequence of required courses for the business major penalizes students who study abroad, forcing them to take one or two additional semesters of course work in order to graduate	28%	8%	64%
The number of required courses for the business major does not leave enough room for study abroad courses	21%	10%	69%
Study abroad courses are not easily transferred back to the home institution	13%	16%	71%

at most universities. Studying a foreign language is one of the factors closely associated with student interest in foreign studies. Business students are not alone in shunning language study. The number of American college students studying a foreign language is falling. Foreign language study by college students in the United States has dropped from a high of 16% in the 1960s to 8% today (Wheeler, 2000, p. 2). Respondents divided almost evenly on the question whether the lack of a foreign language requirement discourages business students from study abroad. The lack of consensus on this issue may be related to the availability of foreign study in a number of English-speaking countries, including Great Britain, Canada, Australia, and New Zealand, and of English-language programs in non-English-speaking countries, such as the Benelux countries, Scandinavia and Japan.

Structural Challenges

Possible structural barriers include lack of study abroad courses of interest to business majors, difficulties in transfer of credits from a foreign institution, lack of foreign language facility by students and lack of a study abroad requirement. The survey points to the importance of having study abroad courses especially designed for business students led by business faculty. Business majors at larger universities are more likely to have study abroad programs tailored for them (see Table 10). While 89% of large institutions said that there are study abroad courses especially designed for business students, only 78% of small institutions offered them. Almost 70% of advisors at large schools say that students are more likely to study abroad if a business faculty member leads the

Table 10.   Percentage of Respondents Who Agree That There Are Not Enough Study Abroad Programs Tailored for Business Students, by Size of Institution Measured by the Number of Undergraduates.

Less than 5,000	47%
5,001 to 10,000	26%
More than 10,000	31%

program, while only 50% of respondents at smaller schools agree that that is the case.

Respondents report that nearly nine out of ten universities with business programs offer business students courses especially designed to meet their needs. Three-quarters of the respondents acknowledged that business faculty led at least one foreign study program. Two-thirds reported no difficulty with transfer of credits earned overseas. Working against greater participation by business students, however, is the fact, evident in Table 11, that business schools as a rule do not require their students to study a foreign language or to study abroad.

The results reported in Table 11 reveal, however, that business schools are doing the right things to internationalize their students through overseas trips. The vast majority of business schools are offering study abroad courses especially designed for their students and led by business school faculty. Students encounter few problems in transferring credits earned overseas to their home institution. Business schools have structured their overseas programs in such a way as to eliminate the lack of foreign language competence as a barrier. They either offer travel opportunities to English-speaking countries, or, in nations that speak a foreign tongue, they provide instruction in English.

Table 11.   Possible Structural Challenges to Business Students Studying Abroad.

	Agree	Neutral	Disagree
There are study abroad courses especially designed for business students	85%	6%	10%
There are study abroad programs led by business faculty	75%	12%	13%
Study abroad credits are fully and easily transferable	66%	15%	19%
The lack of a language requirement in the business curriculum discourages business students from studying abroad	45%	12%	43%
Business students are required to take a foreign language as part of their major	22%	4%	74%
Business students are required to study abroad	11%	3%	86%

Table 12. Possible Financial Challenges to Business Students Studying Abroad.

	Agree	Neutral	Disagree
Many business students would lose their part- or full-time jobs if they studied abroad	48%	29%	23%
Many business students cannot afford to lose the income they are earning from part- or full-time work	45%	34%	21%
There are sufficient scholarships for business students to study abroad	18%	15%	67%

Financial Challenges

Income-related problems, however, stand in the way of a foreign experience for many business students. Two-thirds of institutions agree that lack of scholarship assistance is a barrier. Those business students who are employed would have to give up their full- or part-time jobs. Monthly financial obligations may make this kind of sacrifice difficult. Approximately half of the respondents said that many business students would lose their jobs if they studied abroad and could not afford to lose that income (see Table 12). There is no data to indicate whether the financial disincentives faced by business majors are greater than those encountered by liberal arts students.

Attitudinal Challenges

To an even greater extent than academic, structural or financial hurdles, student and faculty attitudes block many students from taking part in foreign study. Liberal arts faculty, especially in foreign language and international studies, are likely to value foreign experiences for students and to encourage students to take advantage of these opportunities. Business faculty, on the other hand, traditionally have focused on the large American domestic market and have not recognized the value of sending students abroad. Business faculty sometimes point to the large number of foreign students pursuing professional degrees in the United States and then conclude that there is little American students can learn abroad. The accrediting body for business programs, AACSB, does require business schools to internationalize their faculty and students but does not promote study abroad for business students. Many business faculty contend that both overseas teaching and research lack rigor and resist partnerships with foreign institutions and discourage students and faculty from going abroad (Ivancevich & Duening, 1993, p. 30). They

Table 13.   Possible Attitudinal Challenges to Business Students
Studying Abroad.

	Agree	Neutral	Disagree
Many business students do not recognize the value of studying abroad	72%	9%	19%
Your institution regards the study abroad experience for business students as very important	59%	23%	18%
Many business faculty do not see the need for students to study abroad	43%	24%	33%

also argue that English has become the de facto language of business throughout the world and learning a foreign language makes little sense for native English speakers.

Our survey suggests that the attitudinal problem is greater among students than faculty (see Table 13). Nearly three quarters of respondents agreed that many business students do not recognize the value of studying abroad, while a plurality (43%) said that many business faculty fail to acknowledge the value for students of having a foreign experience. Only one-third of the respondents disagreed with the statement that many business faculty do not see the need for students to study abroad. There is a disjuncture between the attitudes of business students and faculty, on the one hand, and their institutions, on the other. Nearly six out of ten institutions regard the study abroad experience as very important for business students. Student indifference and fear are major challenges to expanding the percentage of business students who have a foreign academic experience. The answer to this problem is better marketing.

Durational and Timing Challenges

When and for how long study abroad experiences are offered influence their attractiveness to business students (see Table 14). The vast majority of universities offer programs in the summer. It is not as common, however, for them to be offered between semesters. There is a tendency to offer shorter experiences than the traditional junior-year or semester abroad. A plurality agrees that students prefer short study abroad experiences and that such brief programs are effective. Almost two-thirds of institutions report that foreign internships are available. In their survey of high school seniors, Hesel and Green found that the two most desired activities for college students are internships and study abroad.

Table 14.   Possible Durational and Timing Challenges to Business Students
Studying Abroad.

	Agree	Neutral	Disagree
Study abroad programs are offered in the summer	85%	3%	12%
Internships in foreign countries are available for business majors	64%	11%	26%
Short study abroad experiences of three weeks or less are effective	47%	20%	34%
Study abroad programs are offered between the fall and spring semesters or between quarters	44%	14%	42%
Students prefer short study abroad experiences (less than one month)	43%	26%	31%

Table 15 reveals some interesting differences between private and public colleges. Private and public schools schedule their study abroad programs somewhat differently, in part because of the income-levels of their students. Students at private institutions come from higher-income families and are not as dependent on employment or study abroad scholarships as are public university enrollees. It is more feasible, then, for private students to study abroad for the traditional year or for a full semester and to stay long enough to complete an internship. Many private institutions have a 4–1–4 calendar that is ideal for study abroad programs of one-month duration between the fall and spring semesters. There is less need, accordingly, to schedule overseas trips in the summer.

Private schools are paying more attention to study abroad and foreign internships than public institutions of higher education. These are experiences that private universities and colleges wish to offer their students and that contribute to the additional value that a diploma from a private institution brings to its recipients. The relative lack of attention paid by public universities is best revealed in the lower percentage of public institutions that employ full-time study abroad directors and internship coordinators.

Student-related Challenges

The final category of barriers centers around students (see Table 16). Minority students are less likely to enroll in overseas study than white students. There was no consensus on the question whether high-achieving business students are more likely to study abroad than other students. Other research suggests, however, that

Table 15. Percentage of Respondents Who Agree to Statements Regarding Study Abroad, by Whether the Institution is Public or Private.

	Agree (Public)	Agree (Private)
Duration and Timing Issues		
Students prefer short study abroad experiences (less than one month)	46%	33%
Study abroad programs are offered in the summer	88%	73%
Study abroad programs are offered between the fall and spring semesters or between quarters	38%	62%
Internships in foreign countries are available for business majors	58%	80%
Student-Related Issues		
Scholarships are an effective tool in recruiting business students to study abroad	80%	71%
Many business students cannot afford to lose the income they are earning from part- or full-time work	48%	36%
Business students of minority races are less likely to study abroad than white students	48%	67%
Academic Issues		
More business students would study abroad if the number of electives were increased	50%	54%
There are study abroad programs led by business faculty	74%	76%
Business students are more likely to study abroad if a business faculty member leads the program	69%	37%

there is a positive correlation between SAT and ACT scores and student interest in studying abroad (Hesel & Green, 2000, p. 5). The inability to bring one's spouse along on a foreign study tour does not appear to be a barrier.

Responses to the open-ended questions revealed that one of the biggest barriers to study abroad was that business students lacked information about foreign study or had misconceptions about it. The survey asked study abroad professionals to

Table 16. Potential Student-Related Challenges to Business Students Studying Abroad.

	Agree	Neutral	Disagree
Business students of minority races are less likely to study abroad than white students	53%	27%	20%
Business students enrolled in honors programs are more likely to study abroad than other business students	31%	46%	23%

assess the various means of communicating accurate information to students and their parents.

MARKETING

Students and their parents are much more interested in an institution's international offerings and programs than they were 15 years ago (Hesel & Green, 2000, p. 9). They are scouring universities' print and electronic publications for this information. There are a number of methods for communicating the study abroad message to business students. These media can be divided into two broad categories: direct and indirect communication.

Direct Communication

Direct communication includes faculty-student interaction, which could take place in the classroom, in the faculty member's office, or in an informational meeting or workshop. Many universities sponsor study abroad information fairs, where students can come to one place on a particular date and receive information on a variety of foreign study opportunities. Study abroad recruiters sometimes telephone students to inform them about opportunities. Students returning from a tour abroad will tell their friends and classmates about their experience. Table 17 reveals that faculty interaction is the most effective means of direct communication, followed closely by student word-of-mouth. Three out of four respondents said that information fairs are effective. Only one quarter of the institutions,

Table 17. Effectiveness of Direct Communication about Study Abroad.

	Agree	Neutral	Disagree
Faculty interaction with students is effective in recruiting business students to study abroad	97%	1%	3%
Student word-of-mouth is an effective technique in recruiting business students to study abroad	95%	2%	3%
Study abroad information fairs are an effective technique in communicating with business students about study abroad	74%	19%	7%
Telephoning business students is an effective technique in recruiting business students to study abroad	24%	60%	16%

however, thought the telephone was a good way of spreading the message (see Table 17).

The experience of the University of Houston College of Business Administration supports the finding that faculty commitment and involvement is critical to the recruitment of students to participate in an overseas program. Houston sought to internationalize itself through study abroad programs and formation of a partnership with a private business school in Spain (Ivancevich & Duening, 1993, p. 25). The University found that someone must be made responsible for attracting students and faculty to participate in study abroad programs. The administrator must then attract faculty who will act as advocates for study abroad in their classrooms. There must be mechanisms in place within the university for allocating rewards to faculty who recruit and assist business school students who elect to study abroad. They key to recruiting students is the identification of faculty members who value student study abroad (Ivancevich & Duening, 1993, p. 26).

Indirect Communication

Indirect communication includes electronic means, such as the Internet and videos, and printed media, including brochures, posters, newspaper advertisements and mailings. The respondents ranked highly flyers and brochures, the Internet and mailings to students (see Table 18). About half thought that postings to bulletin

Table 18. Effectiveness of Indirect Communication about Study Abroad.

	Agree	Neutral	Disagree
Flyers and brochures are an effective technique in communicating with business students about study abroad	72%	18%	11%
The Internet or Campus Intranet is an effective technique in communicating with business students about study abroad	68%	18%	14%
Mailings to students are an effective technique in communicating with business students about study abroad	58%	29%	14%
Bulletin board posters are an effective technique in communicating with business students about study abroad	55%	28%	17%
Campus newspaper advertisements or articles are an effective technique in communicating with business students about study abroad	54%	31%	15%
Videos are an effective technique in recruiting business students to study abroad	34%	53%	12%

Table 19. Percentage of Respondents Who Agreed that the Internet or Campus Intranet is an Effective Technique in Communicating With Business Students About Study Abroad, by Size of Institution Measured by the Number of Undergraduates.

Less than 5,000	59%
More than 10,000	80%

boards and newspaper advertisements were useful. Only one third, however, agreed that videos are an effective mode of communication.

The effectiveness of World Wide Web sites is related to the size of the university. It is less useful at smaller schools, where direct communication is especially valued (see Table 19).

When asked in an open-ended question to identify other techniques besides those listed in the survey instrument that are effective in communicating with business students about study abroad, respondents gave a variety of answers. Almost one-third mentioned presentations to students by faculty and study abroad advisors. The second most frequently mentioned means of communication was presentations to students by returning study abroad participants. Next was the Internet, including World Wide Web pages and electronic mail. E-mail messages promoting overseas study can be tailored to business majors and sent to specific distribution lists, such as all junior business majors. Several study abroad experts suggested including information about foreign study and internships at well-attended university functions, such as the president's welcoming address to

Table 20. Effective Communication Techniques Regarding Study Abroad, Identified by Study Abroad Advisors, by Frequency.

More Effective	
Presentations by faculty and study abroad advisors	32%
Presentations by former study abroad participants	18%
Internet (web sites and electronic mail)	16%
Less Effective	
Presentation of information at university functions	8%
Study abroad information fairs	5%
Presentations by local businesses and career advisors on importance of potential employees having study abroad experience	5%
Socials and club activities	3%
Presentations by foreign students studying in the United States	2%
Mailings to parents	2%
Campus television network	2%

new students. Study abroad information fairs and presentations by local business leaders about the career value of experience in a foreign country were mentioned by 5% of the respondents. Somewhat surprising was the fact that only 2% thought presentations by foreign students was effective in spreading information about study abroad.

Previous research suggests that presentations by foreign students studying in the United States about their culture, and business climate, can pique the interest of American students in study abroad. At the University of Rochester school of business, foreign students make such presentations eight times a year (Mangan, 1997, p. 6).

THE GOALS OF BUSINESS STUDENTS IN STUDYING ABROAD

Understanding the goals of students who study overseas is essential in effectively marketing the study abroad experience. Business students study abroad for a number of reasons. The desire to acquire foreign knowledge and experience that will give them an advantage in their careers is the strongest motive American students have in going abroad (Desruisseaux, 1999, p. 1). They expect to further their educational and professional development (Gullahorn & Gullahorn, 1958, p. 369). They desire to improve their skill in a foreign language and to gain a better understanding of a foreign culture. They seek adventure and the freedom that comes with being away from their home country. They wish to improve relations between the host country and the United States, including increased international trade. Some students who travel overseas for academic reasons believe that the experience will give them recognition at home and improve their employment possibilities. In a survey of high school students intending to study abroad in college, 47% cited as a reason expanding their cultural horizons, 24% "travel and seeing other parts of the world," and 11% "improving my job prospects." Only 3% mentioned "learning another language" or "studying things you cannot study in the United States," and 1% cited "promoting world peace" (Hesel & Green, 2000, p. 8). By combining language and cultural study with business study abroad, students can earn certificates and diplomas in business foreign languages offered by foreign educational, governmental and business organizations such as the Paris Chamber of Commerce and Industry, the Madrid Chamber of Commerce and Industry and the Goethe Institute (Voght & Schaub, 1992, p. 2). There are a number of initiatives that schools of business can take to overcome academic, structural, financial, attitudinal and durational barriers to study abroad.

INCENTIVES

In 1997–1998 Michigan State University sent more students abroad than any other institution of higher education in the United States. One of the chief reasons is that it offers a large number of study abroad programs, 140 in 50 countries, and develops approximately 10 new ones each year (Desruisseaux, 1999, p. 3). Universities can increase the opportunities for their students by joining consortia. In 1994–1995, 26% of students who went abroad participated in consortially-sponsored programs, compared to 6% in 1985 (Rubin, "Study-Abroad Programs," 1996, p. 2). Another important reason for Michigan State's success is that most of the new study abroad programs cost the same or less than what it would cost a student to stay on campus. Because Spanish is the most popular language studied in the United States, business schools should pay special attention to establishing new study abroad programs in Spain and Latin America. An effective marketing tool is to let students know that federal regulations require all institutions that receive U.S. funds to allow students to use their financial aid to study abroad.

Another incentive is scholarships especially for business students to study abroad. Students whose program of study does not make foreign travel in the fall or spring semesters feasible may find summer courses attractive. Students with employment or family responsibilities are more likely to travel overseas if short programs between one and three weeks are available. These short courses could be offered not only in the summer but also in the winter between semesters or during fall or spring breaks. Several graduate business programs now offer one- or two-week overseas study tours, many with no foreign-language component (Mangan, 1997, p. 1). In 1994–1995, more than half of the students who went overseas did so for a semester or less. Only 14% went for the entire academic year (Rubin, "Study-Abroad Programs," 1996, p. 2).

Study abroad can be made more attractive to business students by offering internships in addition to regular courses. Internships offer the potential for future employment, look good on a student's resume and appeal to students who prefer practical application to classroom learning. Some internships combine work in industry with classes at a foreign university (McCormack, 1966, p. 374).

A selling point is that studying overseas will provide at least informal education in the humanities and social sciences, areas of particular weakness in the curriculum of most business students. The language barrier can be lowered by offering intensive summer language institutes for business students planning to study abroad. The U.S. Army prepares its officers for foreign assignments this way in its language school in Monterey, California. Business students who enroll in any language class are prime recruits for study abroad. Most foreign language courses, however, emphasize grammar, syntax and reading rather than practical skills useful to business people. Special language courses with an emphasis on doing business in a foreign country will attract more business students. Universities could give students studying abroad a reduction in their tuition and fees. The U.S. Department of Education points out that studying abroad in many cases is cheaper than studying on campus because the students while overseas are not using the library, the gymnasium, the counseling center, the faculty or the staff (Burd, 2000, p. 1).

The University of Southern California's Marshall School of Business goes beyond just encouraging its MBA students to study overseas. It requires them to do so (Mangan, 1997, p. 3). Students who are forced overseas often develop an interest in international issues and travel that lead to longer trips in the future. The International MBA program at the University of Memphis requires its American students to spend a summer, and a regular semester abroad, to study and do an internship in a foreign country. The University of Wisconsin at Madison's five-year undergraduate major in international business requires students to be fluent in a foreign language and to spend a semester abroad. St. Norbert College in De Pere, Wisconsin, offers an undergraduate degree in international business, language and area studies that requires proficiency in a foreign language and at least one semester of study abroad (Giving an International Focus to Business Education, 1997, p. 2). The Monterey Institute of International Studies solves the elective problem by offering business courses in the language of the country or region with which the course deals, such as "German Business in the European Community" (Giving an International Focus to Business Education, 2000, p. 4).

Cost is one of the greatest barriers to student participation in study abroad. Worcester Polytechnic Institute offers a free passport to every undergraduate who is a U.S. citizen and operates 18 off-campus residential project sites, most of which are in foreign countries. Sixty percent of its management majors have some type of global experience (Importance of Studying Abroad, 2000, p. 2). In 1996, Lake Erie College announced that it would pay for a passport and a short trip abroad for all students during their junior year, on the condition that they take certain courses before traveling overseas (Rubin, "Colleges Offer Financial Help," 1996, p. 1). Arcadia University offers its students a week in London during spring break for $245 including airfare. More and more universities are paying the student's airfare. Linfield College and Webster University charge students who study abroad a fee equal to their regular tuition. Airfare is included (Rubin, "Colleges Offer Financial Help," 1996, p. 2). State universities, however, often do not have the financial ability to pay student airfare. Texas prohibits state funds from being used outside the country. Public universities, however, can often subsidize airfare and raise endowments to support student travel from private sources. Short trips overseas can be made part of a semester-long course. Airfare can be included in the tuition and fees for that particular course.

More students will participate if the home university, administers the study abroad program, than if it is offered by a consortium. Universities that have ongoing study abroad courses, offered every year, have a better chance of maintaining high enrollments. Ad hoc, unpredictable course offerings discourage students from considering a foreign experience (McCormack, 1966, p. 369). By signing formal exchange agreements with foreign universities, a university in the United States provides opportunities for its students to meet professors and students from foreign countries. This exposure may arouse their interest in foreign academic programs. Introducing international business components into regular business courses may also pique student interest in study abroad.

Because most business students are not proficient in a second language, broad-based study abroad programs whose curriculum is taught in English will be more appealing to business majors than those focusing on language (Durnall, 1967, p. 450). The traditional junior-year abroad was conceived for students seeking proficiency in a foreign language. If language acquisition is not the goal, programs can be shorter – a semester, a month or even a week. In non-language-based programs students do not typically enroll in a foreign university. A faculty member from an American university will accompany the students and see that in addition to academic requirements, their needs for food, shelter and transportation are taken care of. The selection criteria can be less stringent for non-language programs, since the participants will not be on their own.

RECOMMENDATIONS

Our survey of professionals responsible for marketing study abroad to business students allows us to make ten recommendations likely to increase the pool of students willing to leave the United States and the number who actually take advantage of foreign academic opportunities:

(1) Offer more English-language programs. Educate faculty on the value of such programs. A few weeks in any foreign country helps students overcome their fear of leaving the United States and whets their appetite for more adventurous foreign travel. Half of all American college students say they have no interest in foreign study, in large part because of fear.

(2) Establish more programs in Canada (both English and French language programs) and Mexico (both English and Spanish language programs) in order to reduce cost and to make it possible for more students to have an initial foreign experience.

(3) Certain business majors, especially accounting and management information systems (MIS), require that students complete a rigid sequence of courses and leave little room for electives. A study abroad experience, however, enhances the majors' cultural awareness and their employment prospects. Business schools need to give thought to how to make a foreign experience available to students majoring in such subjects. Two possible solutions are to develop summer programs for them or to identify overseas courses that can be transferred back and counted toward the accounting or MIS major.

(4) Offer more study abroad scholarships, especially at public, urban institutions. In addition to tapping university funds, approach local businesses that value international experience and linguistic ability to fund these scholarships.

(5) Provide incentives to business faculty to establish and lead study abroad programs, especially at public, urban institutions. Make it clear that such activity will count favorably toward tenure, promotion and merit raises.

(6) Provide forums for business faculty who have led overseas programs and their students to talk to prospective overseas participants about the benefits of study abroad for the business major.

(7) Require study abroad for undergraduate international business majors and international MBA students.

(8) Require students majoring in international business to take a foreign language at least through the intermediate level.

(9) Establish the position of study abroad director within the business school.

(10) Schedule presentations by corporate officers on the career value of study abroad.

CONCLUSION

As international trade accounts for an ever-larger percentage of America's gross domestic product, schools of business are placing a much higher value on the internationalization of their faculty and students. One of the principal means of internationalizing students is participation in a study abroad program. Business faculty, however, face many challenges in recruiting undergraduate and graduate students for such programs. These problems are greater in public universities. Although business schools have overcome many obstacles that long led to relatively low numbers of business students participating in study abroad opportunities, structural problems remain at many schools. The solution to lack of business student participation in study abroad lies, first, in greater faculty involvement and, second, in improved marketing of foreign academic experiences to students.

REFERENCES

Burd, S. (2000). Foreign study is named as a focus at Education Dept. Agenda-setting meeting. *The Chronicle of Higher Education Online Edition*, (May 3), 4 pp.

Cavusgil, S. T., Schechter, M. G., & Yaprak, A. (1992). *Internationalzing Business Education: Issues and Recommendations by Leading Educators.* East Lansing, MI: Report of the Michigan State University Center for International Business Education and Research 1991 Roundtable on Internationalizing Business Schools and Faculty.

Desruisseaux, P. (1999). Fifteen percent rise in American students abroad shows popularity of non-European destinations. *The Chronicle of Higher Education Online Edition*, (December 10), 6 pp.

Durnall, E. J. (1967). Study abroad programs: A critical survey. *Journal of Higher Education*, *38*(November), 450–453.

Giving an international focus to business education (1997). *The Chronicle of Higher Education Online Edition*, (October 24), 5 pp.

Gullahorn, J. T., & Gullahorn, J. E. (1958). American objectives in study abroad. *Journal of Higher Education*, *29*(October), 369–374.

Hayward, F. M. (2000). Internationalization of U.S. Higher Education: Preliminary Status Report 2000. Washington, DC: American Council on Education (www.acenet.edu/bookstore).

Hesel, R. A., & Green, M. F. (2000). College-bound Students' Strong Interest in International Education Contrasts with Actual College Experiences. *StudentPOLL*, *4*(3) (http://www.artsci.com/studentonline.cfm).

Importance of Studying Abroad (2000). *The Chronicle of Higher Education Online Edition*, (January 28), 2 pp.

Ivancevich, J. M., & Duening, T. N. (1993). Internationalizing a business school: A partnership-development strategy. *Selections*, *10*(Autumn), 23–37.

Jallade, J.-P., & Gordon, J. (1996). Student mobility within the European Union: A statistical analysis (vol. 1). *European Institute of Educational and Social Policy* (May).

Kedia, B. L., & Cornwell, T. B. (1994). Mission based strategies for internationalizing U.S. business schools. *Journal of Teaching in International Business*, *5*, 11–29.

Kedia, B. L., & Harveston, P.D. (1998). Transformation of MBA programs: Meeting the challenge of international competition. *Journal of World Business*, *33*(2), 203–217.

Kedia, B.L., & Mukherji, A. (1999). Global managers: Developing a mindset for global competitiveness. *Journal of World Business*, *34*(3), 230–251.

Mangan, K. S. (1997). Business Schools Promote International Focus, but Critics See More Hype Than Substance. *The Chronicle of Higher Education Online Edition*, (September 12), 6 pp.

McCormack, W. (1966). New directions in study abroad: Opportunities for students in the professional schools. *Journal of Higher Education*, *37*(October), 369–376.

Rodrigues, C. (1996). *International Management: A Cultural Approach.* Minneapolis/St. Paul, MN: West Publishing Co.

Rubin, A. M. (1996). Colleges offer financial help to encourage foreign travel. *The Chronicle of Higher Education Online Edition*, (November 1), 5 pp.

Rubin, A. M. (1996). Study-abroad programs for Americans had boom years in 1994–1995. *The Chronicle of Higher Education Online Edition*, (December 6), 6 pp.

Snapshot of Report on Study-Abroad Programs (2000). *The Chronicle of Higher Education Online Edition*, (November 17), 2 pp.

Strength Through Wisdom: A Critique of U.S. Capability (1979). Washington, D.C.: U.S. Printing Office.

Voght, G. M., & Schaub, R. (1992). Foreign languages and international business. *ERIC Digest* (ERIC NO: ED347851).

Wheeler, D. L. (2000). More students study abroad, but their stays are shorter. *The Chronicle of Higher Education Online Edition*, (November 17), 3 pp.

World Class Learning (1998). *Black Enterprise*, (May), 86–89.

HIGH QUALITY STUDY ABROAD PROGRAMMING: THE ROLE OF THE CENTRAL STUDY ABROAD OFFICE

Cindy Felbeck Chalou and Inge Ellen Steglitz

INTRODUCTION

Certain administrative structures and processes need to be in place on the home campus to provide high quality study abroad experiences for students. They provide the support needed to make study abroad programs successful and effective. To this end, they need to be based on criteria that ensure the best possible quality in these arrangements as they relate to stated program outcomes.

As do most study abroad offices, the MSU *Office of Study Abroad* works with a set of desired study abroad learning outcomes. The goal is to motivate students to participate in study abroad because it can help them develop important skills and attitudes they will need for living and working in the increasingly interconnected environments of the twenty-first century. MSU study abroad programs are designed to:

- facilitate students' academic development and intellectual growth;
- contribute to students' professional development;
- accelerate students' personal growth;
- develop students' skills for relating to as well as communicating and working with culturally different others.

Study Abroad: Perspectives and Experiences from Business Schools
Advances in International Marketing, Volume 13, 141–157.
© 2003 Published by Elsevier Science Ltd.
ISSN: 1474-7979/PII: S1474797902130109

Aiming to facilitate student learning in these outcome categories, the MSU study abroad office provides support and expertise in the areas of:

(a) program development;
(b) program marketing;
(c) program advising;
(d) program management and services;
(e) program evaluation.

FUNCTIONS OF THE CENTRAL STUDY ABROAD OFFICE

Study Abroad Program Development

It is desirable that new study abroad programs be initiated from academic departments and colleges rather than study abroad offices. In this way, the departments have ownership from the beginning and take a more active role in and responsibility for the recruitment, effective implementation, monitoring of academic quality, and overall evaluation of the program. To assist the departments and colleges in this role, the MSU Office of Study Abroad has developed a well-established development, approval, and review process for new study abroad programs.

Faculty members who wish to develop a new study abroad program may apply for an optional Study Abroad Program Development Grant. The MSU Office of Study Abroad provides matching funds that cover part of the costs of an exploratory visit to a site, or sites, where a new program will be developed. Grants are limited to travel and per diem expenses, and the college(s) and department(s) provide matching funds of varying amounts. The Office of Study Abroad may provide as much as two-thirds, and as little as one-quarter, of the funding, with the appropriate college or colleges providing the remaining funding. Such shared funding arrangements assist in establishing a partnership from the earliest program development stage.

The funding amounts and priorities for new programs need to be established to effectively communicate the strategic plan of the office; and these amounts and priorities will change as the program types and office mission changes. All MSU study abroad programs are expected to address the learning outcomes previously mentioned. Priority in funding is currently given to proposed programs that are designed, among other things: to be a semester (or more) in length; to be cost effective; to be integrated into MSU's curriculum; to include credited foreign language instruction (unless in an English-speaking country); to provide students structured opportunities for developing inter-culturally; and to rely on host-university faculty for instruction.

In many cases a faculty member proposing the new program may have conducted research abroad or established a significant relationship with international colleagues. However, it is not uncommon for faculty members to have limited experience with the complexity and details involved in establishing a new study abroad program. For this reason, it is helpful to provide written guidance to questions to ask or elements to look for while conducting a site visit. A detailed list of site visit questions, and issues, can be a tool for obtaining information. It is preferable that this list be more detailed than necessary with the expectation that not all questions will be answered; in this way, certain minor questions may bring up critical issues and thereby provide important information to move the process to the next level of development. This list should include questions related to: academics, curriculum, teaching style and methodology; health and safety; student services such as counseling, advising, and orientation; logistical arrangements such as housing, food, computer access, trips/activities, and facilities, including accessibility; fees and any other financial implications such as exchange arrangements; staff (resident directors, instructors, advisers); access to local culture; and pre-departure information such as visa requirements and application process.

If a faculty member returns from a site visit with plans to develop a new program, he or she should be required to discuss the proposal with appropriate administrators in the department(s) and college(s). This will ensure buy-in at all levels and eliminate the possibility of a program based solely on the passion and commitment of one faculty member.

Evaluation of new program proposals should focus on a number of key elements, including program subject matter, learning objectives and instructional models, and the following issues:

- the relationship to other institutional or consortia study abroad programs in the host country and/or in the subject matter area;
- the extent to which the field trips, host-institution faculty, and aspects of the host culture and environment are woven into the program and courses;
- plans for incorporating foreign language coursework into the program;
- the program environment and logistical arrangements that address issues of health, welfare and security of students;
- a review of the efficiency and viability of logistical arrangements, including student housing and meals, classrooms, and educational excursions;
- the minimum, as well as desirable, student qualifications for participation in the program;

- the likely student enrollment initially and in subsequent years (cite evidence or basis for estimates);
- the minimum enrollments needed to cover costs and contingency plans to cover financial losses;
- a detailed plan to be used for recruitment.

Once a program has been approved and implemented, a formal evaluation should take place (see section (e)) at frequent intervals during the early stages of the program and less frequently after establishment. Although several MSU colleges conduct informal evaluations, there is currently only one college that conducts a formal three-year peer-review of all the college's programs. In addition to these academic and administrative reviews and evaluations, it is absolutely critical that safety be continuously addressed. MSU strives to keep its study abroad programs as safe as possible through regular monitoring of programs. See section (d) for policies and procedures that MSU has designed to assist in safeguarding the safety and well being of study abroad participants.

Study Abroad Marketing

Effective study abroad marketing requires a holistic view of marketing, an understanding of what it is we are trying to promote through out marketing efforts,[1] an understanding of who the target audiences are, and an assessment of each audience's information and service needs as well as their program interests. While students are the obvious primary target audience, parents and other significant family members constitute immediate secondary audiences. However, a successful study abroad marketing effort must include tertiary audiences who will not participate in study abroad but will carry the message to students about the importance and validity of study abroad as an integrated part of the college experience. Such tertiary audiences are faculty members, academic advisers, residence hall staff, and others. At MSU, a study abroad marketing team (consisting of an assistant director, two program coordinators and the Office of Study Abroad editor) is charged with the coordination of the various promotional activities, including the creation of publications, on and off campus. This includes the coordination of the study abroad resource room and the Peer Adviser Program.[2] Over the years, the team has developed a variety of marketing strategies, some of which are described below.

Students and Parents
Both students and their parents will be at varying levels of awareness of, and sophistication about, study abroad. Large segments of both populations need to *be*

informed at very basic levels about the existence of study abroad as an academic option in the undergraduate college experience. At MSU, this basic information need is addressed by including study abroad information in university-wide promotional materials as well as by the study abroad office's participation in the Academic Orientation Program for incoming freshmen. Once a fundamental understanding has been achieved of what study abroad is, students and their families need to *be educated* about various program options and features. At MSU, this need is met primarily by way of semi-annual study abroad fairs and comprehensive publications, such as the study abroad program catalog. Finally, students who know what study abroad is and are aware of their options, need to *be motivated* to commit to participation in a program that best meets their needs. At MSU, the goal is to motivate students through program-specific information meetings, individual program brochures, and individual advising sessions with program faculty leaders, academic advisers, and study abroad program coordinators. Ideally, the various advisers a student will see during the decision-making process will be able to not only provide detailed program information, but to also help students see how individual program features are linked to students' desired learning outcomes.

The MSU study abroad marketing team has been working with the "I-E-M" (inform, educate, motivate) approach successfully for a number of years. The individual components of the approach are obviously interconnected and must take place continuously (as cohorts of new students enter the institution) and simultaneously (as, at any given time, there are students on campus who need to be informed, educated, and motivated about study abroad). Central to the "I-E-M" marketing approach at MSU have been regular publications audits aimed at identifying 'holes' in the chain of publications and to eliminate inconsistency, inaccuracy and unnecessary redundancies. A thorough publications audit also aims to create publications that, at each stage in the decision-making process, give students the information they need *at that point*, rather than inundating them with information that, because it is presented too early in the process, confuses them or is simply disregarded.

A holistic marketing approach also keeps an eye on retention; that is, strategies must be developed to reduce attrition (i.e. lower the number of students who cancel from programs at various points during the application and acceptance process). The MSU marketing team has only begun to focus on this aspect; suggested approaches include newsletters to accepted students and regular e-mail messages from the coordinator in charge of the program.

The immediate institutional end-goal is to motivate and enable as many students as possible to participate in study abroad. From the students' perspective, though, participation in study abroad is one of many possible activities competing for their attention and cannot be seen as a *terminal* goal. Rather, for students, study abroad participation must be conceptualized as an *instrumental* outcome. The MSU study abroad marketing effort, therefore, focuses on study abroad participation not as a stand-alone end-goal, but rather as one of the many activities students will engage in during the course of their college career to prepare themselves for their future professional and personal lives. In other words, study abroad is presented as one possible activity that can help students develop skills deemed important by employers.[3] Positioning study abroad into students' overall college life-cycle and in relationship to their personal, professional, and academic goals, helps the study abroad marketing effort by allowing a certain amount of 'piggy-backing' on other units' activities and events such as career fairs and residence life programs.

University Faculty and Staff
No amount of direct marketing to students and their parents by the study abroad office will be ultimately successful if the study abroad message is not simultaneously carried by the larger university community, including faculty members, academic advisers, student life staff, and, very importantly, the university leadership. The MSU marketing team has begun to develop strategies aimed to increase the degree of active support given the study abroad initiative in units across campus. These strategies are again based on the "I-E-M" approach, assuming that the larger university community, just as the students and their parents, consist of individuals who are unaware and uninformed about study abroad and/or who need to be motivated to bring the study abroad message to their students. In other words, a high quality study abroad marketing effort must ensure that the larger academic community know enough about study abroad and individual programs so that its members can accurately, consistently, and enthusiastically speak to their various audiences about them. One of the ways in which MSU attempts to achieve this, for at least a segment of that larger population, is through Academic Adviser Site Visit Grants. Other initiatives, such as study abroad workshops for faculty and academic advisers and articles in various campus publications, are being developed. Connections are also forged with various Student Life departments and other service units on campus.

Marketing as a Central Function in the Study Abroad Office
Effective study abroad marketing must view marketing as a central function in the office. Connections must be made among staff members in charge of marketing and those in charge of, for example, advising, so that the advisers are aware of their crucial role in completing the marketing cycle by helping students become excited and committed to a particular program. Efforts must be made to make the information gathering and application process as easy and transparent as possible to students (and their parents). Therefore, the marketing team needs to work closely

with colleagues in charge of administering the application/admissions process and ensure that there is a seamless transition for the student from informational materials to application information and acceptance packets.

Clearly, the primary function of study abroad marketing is to inform students, parents, and others of an institution's high quality study abroad offerings, and to motivate them to participate. A holistic approach to marketing, however, also contributes to the quality of the overall study abroad effort by paying attention to issues of customer satisfaction and the office's image. For example, it is within the purview of the MSU study abroad marketing team to design and implement training of front-line staff (including peer advisers) so they can more professionally serve those visiting the study abroad office. Including the numerous application forms and informational handouts in a publications audit to ensure that they are user-friendly is one way in which marketing can directly influence the quality of the overall study abroad experience.

Study Abroad Advising

Every college and university has its own philosophy, policies and approach to study abroad that will greatly influence the commitment, style, and level of advising on each campus. Advising is an integral part of the "inform, educate and motivate" approach and is commonly done by faculty members, academic advisers, peer advisers, and study abroad staff. The expertise of each of these groups can complement one another and eliminate the need for one individual or group to have all the answers.

There are many approaches to successful advising. What works with one student may not work with another, and what worked this year may not work next year. What is clear is that advising is a very complex and dynamic interpersonal process that cannot be reduced to easy formulas or universal answers.

Before providing basic program information, advisers need to establish an open and honest relationship with a student to assist in defining his or her personal abilities, goals, and perceptions. Obtaining background information from the student lays the foundation for the most important question of all: "What are your reasons for wanting to study abroad?" Some students may have a clear idea of what they hope to accomplish, while others simply want to experience another culture. Helping to clarify their objectives will force students to explore what they hope to accomplish by participating in a study abroad program. Just as there is no single reason for studying abroad, there is no single "perfect" program: the "right" program is that which is appropriate for a particular student and meets the home institutional standards and mission. Various forms of advising can be done by an academic adviser, a returned student, an informational video, a web page, a faculty member, a study abroad professional, or an interactive computer program. Since it is the student who must take responsibility for making a success of his or her international experience, it is in the student's best interest to use all the available resources and become familiar with as many programs as possible. The more the student knows about the foreign country, culture, and the educational system and its expectations, the better he or she can make an informed choice. Such information can be obtained from area study centers, faculty with international experience, study abroad staff members, the web, international newspapers, and international students from that country/region, etc.

Students often know the location and optimal timing of their desired program but have given little consideration to the best type of program for their individual background preparation and learning styles. More independent students, or students with sufficient foreign language skills, prior area studies coursework, or prior experiences abroad are well prepared for direct enrollment immersion programs; whereas, less independent students, or those students without prior experience abroad or study of the language and culture, may prefer short-term faculty-led programs. Study abroad programs vary along many dimensions, among them location, duration, types of courses offered, foreign language requirements, type of housing, and whether or not courses are taught by home or host country faculty.

Students should be encouraged to discuss and share their plans and information with relevant others, such as parents, family or significant others. In some cases it is critical to have the support of these individuals in order for a student to have a successful experience. If so, students should be encouraged to involve them from the beginning of the planning process. Additionally, students must take a realistic look at finances. Even if finances are not a major concern, students should realistically look at all costs associated with participation.

Students should be reminded that a successful study abroad experience requires four to twelve months of careful planning. Longer lead-time is needed for longer programs. Planning time is needed for all aspects, including the initiation of discussion with the student's academic department to determine what effect study abroad might have on degree credit, time of graduation, and advantage in the job market after graduation.

With proper training, returned study abroad students can serve as effective peer advisers and the best recruiters. It is crucial to provide complete training so peer advisers are thoroughly informed of programs and procedures and gain skills in effective advising. The selection of peer advisers is critical since some students have difficulty generalizing about their experience to make it relevant to others. Interested and committed students who made the most of their opportunities abroad, and who have a real desire to use what they have learned to assist others, can be very effective adjuncts in the advisory process.

When students return to campus, they are likely to experience another period of adjustment, with sometimes unexpected difficulties. It is not unusual for students to feel very different from their peers precisely because of their study abroad experiences. Advisers can be a good audience to students reflecting back on their experiences abroad. Organizing meetings and social gatherings for returning study abroad students to meet each other can help students forge new friendships with study abroad in common. For those students who leave their off-campus study sites early due to illness or other unplanned circumstances, advisers can be the most important link to the home campus, collaborating with appropriate university offices and representatives to provide the student with an appropriate path back to campus.

Due to the critical role that academic advisers play in promoting and advising on study abroad at MSU, the Office of Study Abroad (OSA) has made a concerted effort to work closely with this group. The *Academic Adviser Focus Group* consists of representative advisers from all study abroad colleges. This group provides a consultative role to OSA, suggesting needed materials, information and workshops, and serves as a liaison body between OSA and advisers, helping to enhance the communication, advising, and understanding of study abroad. Members of this focus group have been influential in the development of workshops to address concerns such as the advising of transfer credits, internships, and funding for study abroad. A workshop covering the basics of advising of study abroad is offered regularly for new advisers and serves as a refresher to continuing advisers.

OSA offers up to six annual grants for advisers to visit MSU study abroad programs. The travel grants allow individual advisers to better understand the design and functioning of particular programs, and be exposed to, and experience the local culture. More broadly, these grants provide advisers insights into the sorts of skills and perceptions that students gain when they study abroad. Adviser grants cover the cost of airfare, ground transportation, and reasonable per diem expenses (food and lodging) for a one-week site visit to an MSU study abroad program. Once the site visit is completed, the adviser is required to submit a report that describes the site visit activities and impressions, lists the positive program features and those that need improvement, and identifies possible specific strategies and activities that will increase study abroad participation in his or her college/unit. The recipient is expected to play an active role as an advocate in his or her college/unit for all MSU study abroad programs.

The advising process helps students develop effective strategies that shape their future careers. The skills required to write an effective essay of intent, a component of nearly every study abroad application, are applicable to job applications and to applications for graduate or professional study. The language and cultural learning that occur through study abroad are more effective with good preparatory training, and can be valuable credentials for some future career paths. The advising process thus provides an opportunity to encourage students to make mature assessments of the relevance of study abroad to their future goals and to make their study abroad not only a productive learning experience but a significant episode in their professional development.

Study Abroad Program Management and Services

Application and Admissions Process
Most standard applications include: personal information; academic information and transcripts of all university-level work; letters of recommendation; evaluation of foreign language ability; information about medical and special needs; emergency contacts; agreement to participate; personal essay(s); and acknowledgment of receipt of billing and refund information. It is best to include as much information as possible in the initial application so that complete information is obtained at one time and does not require follow-up. The application form not only serves the purpose of evaluation, but as the most reliable permanent and accessible profile on each student. Carefully worded agreements and policies can help avoid future problems with disgruntled students or those with behavioral problems. Special sensitivity also needs to be given to certain types of information such as mental and physical health, special needs, judicial records, etc. To ensure maximum fairness and legality in the application process, legal counsel should review all forms.

Likewise, the admissions criteria need to be clearly communicated, followed by a fair and equitable admissions process. At MSU there are three simultaneous review processes: academic review of transcripts and essays by the faculty responsible for the program; review of the health form by medical personnel; and faculty review of judicial reports.

Awareness and understanding of student medical concerns can make the difference between a successful smooth program and a tragic one. The MSU Occupational Health/Travel staff review all health forms for possible concerns and either contact the student to discuss basic information related to traveling with certain health conditions, or refer the student to a physician. If the student is referred to a physician, a letter from the physician is required before the student can participate in the program. If the student does not provide this letter, he/she will be required to sign a waiver. The faculty leader receives from the health clinic a list of the students with information related their specific health concerns.

Knowledge of behavioral problems should be utilized during the admissions process and communicated with the student prior to departure. After obtaining a list of applicants with on-campus judicial records from the Office of Judicial Affairs, the MSU Office of Study Abroad notifies faculty leaders of students with judicial violations and recommends that faculty meet with the student to discuss the violation(s). Students are also informed that an acceptance decision may be reversed if, following acceptance and prior to departure, their conduct raises doubt that they should be allowed to participate.

File Management
With large numbers of study abroad students, file management can be a monumental task. Therefore, all processes should be clarified for the entire staff and streamlined as efficiently as possible. Whether submitted on paper or electronically, application data should be available in two locations to ensure no crucial information is lost. Incomplete applications should not be accepted. If outside units or faculty are involved in the application and admissions process, required information must be distributed to those units in a timely manner.

An electronic or paper check-off system for individual files or programs, particularly those with supplementary materials or peculiar processes, and a visual "flagging" system may aid in streamlining the process to avoid excessive handling of files. A procedural manual with steps for file management serves as a valuable tool for reference and a training resource for future staff members.

Program Logistic
One of the key functions of a central study abroad office consists of providing support in the areas of housing and classroom arrangements, program group flights, and the organization of field trips and excursions. The degree of involvement in each of these depends on the program type and will generally be greater for short-term faculty-led programs than for semester-length direct-enrollment programs. A key criterion in deciding on the type of living arrangements set up for students is the degree of cultural immersion desired in a program. Field trips and excursions should primarily be designed to supplement and enrich the academic curriculum. An important criterion, of course, in making on-site arrangements of any kind are health and safety concerns.

Group flights are usually arranged for programs with large numbers of participants (20+) and/or when simultaneous arrival of all students is highly desirable. Concerns in arranging group flights are the possible loss of required deposits when a group flight doesn't fill up by a specified time, as well as the potential for tragedy and legal ramifications in the case of a disaster. At MSU, students are never *required* to take the group flight, even though they might be strongly encouraged to join the group.

Collaboration with Units Across Campus

Study abroad programs cannot be run successfully without intense collaboration with academic and administrative units across campus. A recent count at MSU showed that the study abroad office has close ties with nearly 100 other offices, not counting the individual academic departments involved in study abroad. On the administrative side, centrally important are good relationships and jointly developed procedures with, for example, the registrar's office, the financial aid office, central billing, risk management, judicial affairs, and credit evaluation. On the academic side, good working relationships must be established with faculty members, academic advisers, department chairs, and representatives from the deans' offices. At MSU, the Deans' Designees Committee consists of a dean-appointed representative from each of the colleges involved in study abroad. It serves in an advisory function to the study abroad director, with a mandate ranging from policy setting to review of newly proposed programs. Study abroad, by its academic nature, absolutely requires very close ties with sponsoring colleges and departments.

Orientation Programming

In a high quality study abroad program, the pre-departure, on-site, and reentry phases are considered integrated parts of students' international education experience. Ideally, in a pre-departure program, students will be given information on program logistics, health and safety issues, the host culture, culture shock and adjustment, and, of course, on the academic program itself. A high-quality pre-departure program aims to equip students with the cognitive, affective, and behavioral tools they need in order to gain the most from their international experience academically, personally, and interculturally. Students will also be given a 'preview' of the on-site and reentry orientation activities and are encouraged to take responsibility for their own preparation and continued learning during and after the experience. The focus of such programs is on providing the practical information students need to participate in a program successfully and safely *and* on showing them how to ask meaningful questions that will help them learn about the host culture and themselves.

The latter is best accomplished once students are on site. A thorough arrival orientation should be followed by an on-going series of group meetings during which assigned reflective journal entries, cultural observations, and reactions to cultural difference are discussed. Students participating in direct-enrollment programs in locations where they may be the only U.S. student on campus can participate in such activities through work-books and/or via web-based activities. While it is relatively easy to convince students of the need for pre-departure orientation, and, for the most part, of the value of continuing orientation on site, motivating students to participate in re-entry activities is notoriously difficult. This is primarily due to the fact that students react differently to the experience of re-entering their home cultures. Individual reactions depend on length of stay, location, degree of immersion in the host culture, and a range of personal characteristics. One way of ensuring that students have the opportunity to participate in re-entry orientation when they need it, is to offer regular re-entry sessions throughout the academic year. At MSU an initiative has been proposed to add a practical component to re-entry orientation by offering a workshop (in conjunction with representatives from career services and placement) on how students can best incorporate their international experience into their résumés and job interviews.

Depending on how large an institution's study abroad program is, it can be nearly impossible to offer this kind of thorough pre-departure, on site, and re-entry orientation to all students on all programs. Decisions on how to allocate resources for the best possible impact must be made based on the type of program.[4] However, an effort should be made to give *all* students the opportunity to participate in such activities if they so choose, even if a full-blown orientation program is not part of their study abroad program. One effective way of providing students with relevant conceptual frameworks and basic cultural information is through university-wide for-credit courses on cross-cultural communication, cultural learning, and culture-specific information. Such a course is currently being offered through the MSU College of Arts and Letters.

Faculty Workshops
Group orientations for new study abroad faculty are an efficient and effective way to introduce new leaders to the policies and procedures related to study abroad. Previous faculty leaders and returned students can provide anecdotal descriptions of various steps and techniques for a successful program, and distribution of a informational handbook can complement these verbal presentations. Due to the limited faculty time, additional workshops need to address significant issues that are directly applicable to their leadership roles. MSU has led a successful faculty workshop titled *Dealing with Difficult Study Abroad Situations* to assist faculty with challenging situations associated with the study abroad experience. This workshop involves a panel of on-campus experts to address specific topics and answer questions related to real situations. The panelists include the University Physician, the Risk/Insurance Manager, the Assistant General Counsel, and representatives from Residence Life, Counseling Center, and Judicial Affairs. Each panelist highlights how their area of expertise impacts the study abroad application and admissions process, on-site behavioral problems, and liability. Workshops such as these provide tools for faculty leaders, establish uniform responses to certain issues and procedures, and aid in providing high quality experiences for both students and faculty.

Financial Issues

Finances play an integral part in the administration of study abroad programs as well as a key influence on student participation. Careful consideration begins at the program development stage when thought should be given to the on-site costs as well as the potential student participation that impacts the distribution of costs. Standard budget policies must be developed for across-the-board expenses such as faculty salary and expenses, office expenses, communication costs (faxes, phones, mailings, etc.), and contingency funds.

Informing students of costs must be done in a transparent manner so that they are fully aware of estimated expenses and whether such items are included in the program fee. A statement indicating that fees may be subject to change due to unexpected circumstances will protect the institution from dramatically fluctuating exchange rates and unexpected pricing changes.

One of the most common barriers to studying abroad is limited finances. For this reason, it is critical to establish a strong and supportive relationship with the financial aid office. Using all types of federal financial aid for study abroad is legal as long as the student is eligible and the home institution has approved the courses taken abroad for credit. Knowledge of what federal, institutional and private support is available and how it is awarded is necessary to understand how study abroad students might use aid. Communication with several offices, including financial aid, the registrar, and academic departments, is needed to coordinate special policies and procedures for awarding aid to study abroad students. Cooperation is required to properly award aid, to verify its use, and to avoid violating federal and state law.

A good general resource for financial aid is The Financial Aid Information Page (http://www.finaid.org). This free resource on financial aid for higher education lists information about aid, advice about finding aid, and even financial aid for study abroad. Other sources of funding are the general grants, loans, or fellowships awarded by private organizations, businesses, churches, and others. MSU has developed a brochure titled "You Can't Afford NOT to Go!" to assist students in financing their study abroad experience (http://www.studyabroad.msu.edu/shared/afford.pdf).

Safety Concerns

The health and safety of study abroad participants must be the primary concern of institutions. In study abroad, as in other settings, participants have a major influence on their own health and safety abroad through the decisions they make before, during, and sometimes even after the program and by their day-to-day choices and behaviors. Participants should read and carefully consider all materials related to safety, health, legal, environmental, political, cultural, and religious conditions in host countries. They should provide the study abroad office accurate and complete physical and mental health information and any other personal data that is necessary in planning for a safe and healthy study abroad experience. They should comply with the terms of participation, codes of conduct, and emergency procedures of the program, obey host-country laws, and be aware of local conditions and customs that may present health or safety risks when making daily choices and decisions.

Likewise, there are steps that the institution should take to assist in safeguarding the safety and well being of participants. While acknowledging that no single plan can address all contingencies, MSU has adopted the following procedures to keep its study abroad programs as safe as possible:

(1) The Office of Study Abroad daily monitors safety issues in countries and locations for all MSU programs by reviewing State Department advisories and other reports to learn of any emerging safety concerns;
(2) A university-wide committee analyzes safety concerns and security conditions of all programs. This committee has ultimate authority for approving programs and sites with regard to safety issues, including canceling programs or requiring revisions to programs to ensure safety and security;
(3) Students are automatically enrolled in and billed for appropriate health and accident insurance;
(4) Each participating student and faculty member is provided a study abroad handbook that outlines, amongst other things, safety and security issues including what to do in cases of illness, accidents, assaults, violent political situations, etc.; and
(5) Emergency procedures are in place, including medical and general emergency evacuation procedures.

Study Abroad Program Evaluation

What constitutes effective program evaluation depends on the type of program being evaluated and the institutional and administrative context in which the program takes place. At a minimum, programs need to be evaluated by their participants, the students. The MSU study abroad office offers this opportunity to all study abroad students by providing them with comprehensive evaluation questionnaires that consist of a quantitative and a qualitative portion. The quantitative portion is in scantron format and allows students to evaluate programs in terms of pre-departure, on-site, and return issues in several categories (logistical arrangements, academic program, field support, cultural learning, overall evaluation). Separate questionnaires exist for long-term and short-term programs, both reflecting peculiarities specific to each type of program. The qualitative portion of the questionnaires allows students to write open-ended responses to questions that are of particular interest to prospective students interested in learning more about a particular program. For example, program participants are asked about the biggest cultural differences they encountered on their program, what the primary benefit was that they derived from their participation, what the best ways were to meet locals, and how much spending money they recommend a student budget for the program. Both the quantitative and qualitative information is made available not only to program faculty leaders, department heads, and college representatives, but also to students researching program options.[5]

In addition to structured feedback from students, the MSU study abroad office also collects information from faculty members (by way of faculty program reports for which a template is provided), on-site personnel (where applicable), and MSU staff returning from site visits to programs. Processes are currently being developed to allow a systematic and integrated analysis of these various types of information so that a comprehensive understanding can be gained of what works and doesn't work in a particular program. Crucial for the ultimate success of this data gathering and analysis will be the establishment of effective feedback loops. This entails dissemination of relevant information to stakeholders and procedures that detail what the consequences will be for programs that are judged to be sub-standard (as well as for programs whose overall rating is 'good' or 'very good'). Both of these processes can be established successfully only if there is close cooperation between the central study abroad office and the colleges sponsoring study abroad programs. At MSU, some steps in this direction have been taken with at least one college that has developed its own internal evaluation procedures, which are designed to avoid redundancy and to allow information to flow between the involved units. A project is also underway at MSU for the development of a web-compliant database that will allow easy access to custom-tailored program information for broader audiences on and off campus. Here, too, the close relationship between evaluation, marketing, and, to a lesser degree, orientation is evident.

In sum, effective study abroad program evaluation is based in desired program features and learning outcomes and allows the feeding back of information to relevant function areas in the study abroad office as well as other administrative and academic campus units.

CONCLUSION

Quality cannot be achieved through a single procedure nor can it be accomplished in a fixed time period: rather, it is a continuous process that requires regular monitoring and alteration. This paper has outlined those administrative structures and processes needed to provide high quality study abroad experiences for students. Implementing these suggested procedures will aid in making successful and effective study abroad programs.

NOTES

1. We are, in effect, trying to promote study abroad in the larger context of international education; that is, in the context of the idea that a high quality college education must include an international component. In our marketing efforts, we argue that studying abroad is an effective way to add such an international components to one's curriculum. Promotion of individual programs, finally, is done on the basis of the idea that a particular program will help a student achieve his or her goals and desired learning outcomes.

2. Peer advisers are returned study abroad participants who serve as first contact advisers in the study abroad resource room and who are trained to speak about study abroad to various campus groups.

3. See, for example, *MSU survey shows labor market strong for grads*. MSU New Bulletin, Dec. 9, 1999.

4. For example, a semester-length program in India will require more effort in the way of orientation than a five-week, faculty-led program in Western Europe.

5. The function of these qualitative answers obviously crosses into the study abroad office function areas of orientation and marketing, in addition to providing valuable information for comprehensive evaluation.

ADMINISTRATIVE ARRANGEMENTS FOR STUDY ABROAD

Ivy McQuiddy and Jerry Wilcox

ADMINISTRATIVE ARRANGEMENTS FROM A BROAD UNIVERSITY PERSPECTIVE FOR STUDY ABROAD

The adage, "Think globally but act locally," defines success for study abroad. As we examine this from the broad university perspective, this means placing educational and research activities in an international rather than a national or local dimension. To accomplish these objectives requires special handling of many of the institutional policies and procedures. Presidential priorities, institutional mission, and strategic plans must encourage collaboration within the campus community, the state and around the globe. These are some of the conditions necessary for the development of international opportunities. Other papers presented during this "International Roundtable on Study Abroad Programs in Schools of Business" address special issues that concern specific study abroad developments. They will address administrative arrangements from the program perspective. In this section, we will discuss the administrative matters from the institutional side which create the environment that allows faculty to develop study abroad programs for their students.

In an effort to appreciate how administrative arrangements facilitate the development of study abroad opportunities, this paper looks at the following areas: institutional policies and procedures, university infrastructure and stake-holders, collaborative agreements, stages of an agreement, and finally the role of information technology.

Study Abroad: Perspectives and Experiences from Business Schools
Advances in International Marketing, Volume 13, 159–189.
© 2003 Published by Elsevier Science Ltd.
ISSN: 1474-7979/PII: S1474797902130110

INSTITUTIONAL POLICIES AND PROCEDURES

We shall now examine existing procedures, accountability procedures, and maintenance of standards. To do this we will need to set forth a set of questions to direct us. What special considerations have to be made to enable study abroad programs to become an integral part of the curriculum? How do administrative arrangements on the home campus influence study abroad programming, identify participants, and define institutional support? As study abroad is integrated into the institution's academic offerings, this new dimension contradicts many of the established policies and procedures. New programs such as study abroad are often forced to fit into the existing rules and regulations. Sometimes the fit can be made satisfactorily, but many times, it's more effective and efficient to recognize the differences and create new policies and procedures. The institution must acknowledge and accept education abroad into the system.

Beginning with the academic units, students are expected to take courses across disciplines at their home institution. They want the same flexibility abroad. Most institutions believe that this is a valid point. Other academic disciplines may provide substance or context relevant to the student's success and enhance the international experience. Who determines the credit for such curriculum issues? That will depend on home institution policies. Other experiences such as internships are sometimes considered outside the purview of academics, although experiential learning has gained value. This aspect of education brings in the private sector and its relationship to campuses, not only in the U.S., but abroad as well. Other relevant policies affecting students who study abroad include dual degree program requirements, credit and grade equivalencies, and full course load to name a few. All these policies need to be reviewed.

If study abroad programs are to be considered within the offerings of the home school, and students are considered to be in enrolled status, institutional policies and procedures must be followed.

In addition, services provided by the university, such as admissions, financial aid, immigration assistance, and registration, should be available to all students for study abroad. The expertise developed in these specific areas can be utilized, thus saving resources for the business school faculty to develop programs and concentrate on internationalization strategies.

INSTITUTIONAL INFRASTRUCTURE AND CAMPUS STAKEHOLDERS

The various units within the university which are stakeholders in making the appropriate arrangements for a successful study abroad program, and who can enhance collaboration and sustainability for study abroad activities, are the areas of international affairs, academic affairs, financial aid, the registrar, dean of students, health center, crisis management, information technology, alumni relations, distance learning, admissions, and study abroad; in addition, of course, to the colleges, academic departments, area studies centers, language studies departments, and career center. As Toyne & Martinez mention in their chapter, "Winning Collegial Support," in *A Field Guide to Internationalizing Business Education* (edited by Scherer et al., 2000), the academic links between various departments across campus not only enrich programs but also are becoming essential because of "the rapid changes in technology, political boundaries, and economic regionalization." Likewise, the intra-campus sharing of services extends the collaborative efforts to offer the best approach to sustained international programs.

Before investigating more thoroughly the specific administrative arrangements, the campus infrastructure should be examined. A strong central administration supporting international activities is crucial. Whatever the activity, approval from the highest university officials and governing board is required. Usually this is pro forma, if the procedures have been accepted as protocol. Agreements should be developed with the involvement of as many of the stakeholders as possible. For example, offices dealing specifically with international students and scholars and with international activities, including study abroad, plus the highest level of administration, should be central to establishing the policies and agreements for international alliances. This will ensure a commitment to facilitate efforts with immigration documents, registration, funding, and other services. More specifics on the process of preparing agreements and examples of actual agreements appear later in this paper.

Regarding the optimum arrangement for the promotion of international activities on campus, it is recommended that an individual or office, assisted by an advisory board or council mandated to deal specifically with linkages and program development be created. In any case, policies are necessary which complement the mission and objectives of the university relating to international activities.

The entity overseeing international activities needs a direct link with the office administering the documents for international students and staff and the study abroad programs for home students. These offices must work closely with the offices disbursing financial aid, keeping track of credit and grades, providing health care and counseling and links to health and safety networks.

Each institution will determine the best procedure to establish good lines of communication among the designated units. From the many modes of operation, each institution must decide which is most effective for its culture. Effective organizational structures might involve faculty/staff committees within colleges and departments dedicated to reviewing globalization opportunities; evaluating options, discussing developments, and examining procedures. The outcomes influence activities not only within the college, but also throughout the institution. A member of each of the possible college committees could then represent that college at a general university council or board on international issues.

COLLABORATIVE AGREEMENTS

The mechanism to make linkages and incorporate programs overseas into the educational structure at home is found in the form of contractual agreements. Such an agreement is at the core of all administrative arrangements. This contract discloses the relationships and establishes roles and responsibilities for each party.

In an effort to guarantee that programs are integrated into the system, to receive the fullest institutional support and to become central to the university's mission, agreements and or contracts should be signed by the president, approved by the body overseeing university affairs, and for state institutions, follow the state's mandated code of education. Having legal coverage and involvement of the different units of the university is exigent to any extension outside the boundaries of the campus. This aegis provides credibility, protection, legitimacy and visibility for student, faculty and staff mobility and international education. The administration assumes a significant coordinating role in setting priorities for exchange activities in institutions of higher education and mobility choices of faculty, staff and students. (For an example of the Legal Foundations for exchange agreements, see Appendix A.) In addition, for examples of exchange agreements, consult Chapter 4 of the publication Cooperation with a University in the United States: NAFSA's Guide to Interuniversity Linkages, NAFSA: Association of International Educators, Washington, D.C., 1997.

The legal agreement is the cornerstone for a university's involvement in an ongoing partnership with an agency or institution for the purposes of specifically described overseas activities. These documents signed by the president or designated official endorse the implementation of the desired collaboration.

Two types of agreements subsume most study abroad activity. The provider or affiliation study abroad agreement allows students from the home campus to travel to another country to participate in activities generally designed for visiting students. This type allows the provider to offer a study abroad program to students with the full support and knowledge of the home campus. Students generally have to go through an application or selection process on campus. Students going to these programs are guaranteed credit, registration, financial aid, and their status at their home campus. The agreement describes what is expected by each of the parties. (See Appendix B for an example of an Affiliation Agreement.)

The exchange agreement involves much more of the home institution. This type of agreement can be made between two or more parties. If more than two parties are involved the agreement is often called a consortial agreement. For a two party or bilateral agreement, normally there is a general agreement of cooperation and a specific, supplemental addendum describing the exact project or type of exchange. Without the second agreement little action occurs. The general agreement simply outlines the general areas for exploration, such as student exchange, faculty exchange, exchange of library and other materials, etc. (Examples of both the general and program agreements are contained in the NAFSA publication mentioned above, and also in Appendices C, D & E, which contains copies of The University of Texas at Austin agreement templates.)

In either case, the relevant units mentioned above must all work in concert and therefore, they must understand their respective roles for agreements to be realized. With a broad base of the university community and interested parties abroad, the support is in place to accommodate procedures. The university community should have access to the procedures for the sake of consistency and time. The involvement of faculty and staff is key to the success of any program. The necessity for buy-in by many players on campus, prohibits an agreement being signed and sealed without first being accepted by a broad and appropriate group of supporters. The method of disseminating the information most effectively will depend on each institution's organization.

Outside the realm of the agreements mentioned above is another type of collaboration which may require a contract or legal document. This would be used to guarantee the needs off-campus for faculty-led programs. When programs intend to use faculties and facilities out of the country and/or the personnel from other agencies for excursions or accommodations, the responsibilities and commitments need to be documented to some extent. These arrangements do not need the endorsement of the university, but the program, itself, needs to go through the approval process from department through the college level, especially if university funds are to be used.

STAGES OF AN AGREEMENT

What stages constitute the formation of an agreement? The following stages have been generally identified as most significant.

It is important for the institution to develop procedures to enable interested parties to easily follow the steps to bring a partnership into existence and to gather the support from the college communities. First is the initiating stage followed by approving and endorsing, then document drafting, program monitoring, finalizing, and reviewing the agreement.

Step 1: Initiating

The initiator is expected to provide a rationale for the agreement, stating the benefits to both institutions to gain the broadest base of support. Sometimes the realm will be limited to a single department, but at other times the agreement will consist of departments in a college, several colleges or inclusive of the entire university, perhaps organized by disciplines or projects. Gathering information and determining shared interest is the first step. Some of the significant information to be requested follows: the contacts at the host and relevant program descriptions which are associated with each of them is imperative; the different types of exchange or study that will be carried out; who the authorized officials are to sign the agreement. But that's not all, and many times that's all that is available when an agreement is signed. To implement the exchange, the staff who will provide assistance to the faculty, staff or students participating is crucial. Practical information is essential to the success of the program, but many times is not available. (See Appendix F for an example of a Worksheet used to gather rationale and background information necessary for an effective exchange agreement, in addition to providing an opportunity to gather campus wide support.)

Step 2: Approving and Endorsing

After the rationale is presented, the approval process begins. The proposal should first gain support within the department. When this is accomplished, routing for additional endorsements is necessary. This step allows other departments within a college to be informed of initiatives and to voice interest or concerns. Other units within the system can simultaneously consider the options as well. The process enables the possibility of greater involvement and recruitment.

Step 3: Finalizing the Document

The agreements themselves will be finalized by the international affairs office and examined by the legal department or system unless a template has already been accepted. Then the agreement is sent to the president or other official signator for signature. (See Appendix G for an example of the stages of formulating an exchange agreement.)

Step 4: Reviewing the Agreement

Provisions for reviewing agreements warrant a place in the procedures. Regular evaluation of the exchange activities offers insights into the practicalities of running a successful exchange and allow for adjustments to be made. A termination date on the agreement document serves to enforce a timely review of program activities. Evaluation criteria are determined by the program activities. Each program therefore should have its own set of criteria, reflecting the objectives.

ROLE OF TECHNOLOGY

Along with the expanded use of campus resources, technology constitutes a revolutionary force in exchanges, academic mobility and delivery of educational services worldwide. We can be in closer communication with partner institutions and at home. We can communicate in our own timeframe as they can without disturbing normal schedules. In cases of emergency, we can get immediate information. We can use the power of the web and e-mail to gather campus support for participation in exchange activities. The Internet is reshaping knowledge dissemination. Library resources are potentially available online. Web sites provide information that is more accessible to everyone. In fact, now that web sites are available, the information for administrative arrangements for exchanges and affiliations can be made public both at home and abroad.

Communication has become instantaneous. This reality has had mixed reviews. It's wonderful when news and responses are forthcoming. However, it's quite a different matter when hundreds of messages are received daily. Some in international education are concerned that this technology diminished the influence of the study abroad experience because students remain too tied to home.

This newfound information technology is both a challenge and an asset. Nevertheless, the impact of new technology has affected the delivery of educational programs. It is yet to be determined how these new tools will interface with study abroad. The potential to combine elements visually, orally and aurally means that people all over the globe can conference easily and opens a new frontier. At this time, students commonly take a course at home with a professor, research a paper accessing information from all over the world, and communicate daily with faculty and staff on site and at home while on a program out of the country. This is extremely positive on the one hand, and very complex and problematic on the other. Web sites allow students all over the world access to program information which can mislead them without proper advising. Quality control is also a problem when information is obtained so freely.

In closing, let us continue to examine the impact of technological advances on our globalization endeavors. It's too soon to judge, but societies are changing rapidly and we must be prepared to weigh both the positive and negative effects on study abroad. One thing is definite: in our administrative arrangements, we will need to consider these advances and react to incorporate and evaluate them as we develop new policies and procedures, infrastructures and stakeholders, and the methods by which we establish and maintain agreements.

APPENDIX A

Academic and Scientific Cooperation and Exchange Agreements

The Legal Foundation

Exchange agreements by the University of Texas at Austin and foreign universities are governed by a combination Texas State law, Texas Higher Education Coordinating Board Rules, and University of Texas at Austin policies. The format of the exchange agreement has been prescribed by the UT System Board of Regents and is located on the web site of the Associate Vice President for International Programs: http://www.utexas.edu/ogs/international/.

Texas Education Code

In brief, the Texas Education Code § 54.060. *Resident of Bordering State or Nation or Participant in Student Exchange Program: Tuition*, states "(c) The coordinating board by rule shall establish a program with the United Mexican States and with Canada for the exchange of students and shall establish programs with other nations for the exchange of students to the extent practicable. . ."

Texas Higher Education Coordinating Board Rules

After that legislation was passed, THECB rules were written to govern the exchange of students. The following is an edited version of those rules (full set is available at http://www.thecb.state.tx.us/rules/rulemain.htm):

THE TEXAS HIGHER EDUCATION COORDINATING BOARD RULES: CHAPTER 21, SUBCHAPTER AA RECIPROCAL EDUCATIONAL EXCHANGE PROGRAM SECTIONS 21.901-11.

Purpose: The purpose of the reciprocal educational exchange program is to enable Texas students of participating institutions to afford to participate in exchange programs with foreign institutions in order to help them better understand the culture, language, needs, and expectations of other nations of the world and the State of Texas.

Definitions: (4) Full-time Enrollment or Study – For undergraduates, the equivalent of at least 12 semester credit hours per semester or as defined by the institution. For graduates, the equivalent of at least 9 semester credit hours per semester or as defined by the institution.

Eligible Institutions: An institution eligible to participate in the exchange program must:

(1) be a public or private degree-granting institution of higher education located in a nation other than the United States whose programs have recognition of official validity; or
(2) be a public institution of higher education in Texas; and
(3) designate a program officer who will be responsible for all transactions relating to the exchange program.

Eligible Participants: A person is eligible to participate in the exchange program if he/she:

(1) has been enrolled for one or more semesters at the originating institution;
(2) is a citizen or permanent resident of a participating nation or an individual enrolled in a public institution of higher education in Texas;
(3) is nominated by his/her originating institution;
(4) meets the admissions requirements and any restrictive enrollment criteria of the receiving institution;
(5) enrolls or studies on a full-time basis at the receiving institution; and
(6) has not participated in the exchange program for more than 12 months.

Tuition Rate to be Paid: UT reciprocal agreements state that the outgoing student pays the relevant tuition at his or her own institution. In coming students do not have to pay tuition, but may need to pay nominal fees; plus they are required to carry approved health insurance.

Reciprocity: The number of units of instruction exchanged would ideally be equal in any given year. If balance is not attained in any one year and more students from other nations are participating in the program than are students from Texas, parity is to be established within a five year period.

Formula Funding: When a Reciprocal Educational Exchange Program exchange takes place, the Texas institution may request formula funding for the hours taken by foreign students attending classes in Texas. They may not request formula funding for their students who go abroad under this reciprocal exchange program.

THE PROVISIONS OF THIS CHAPTER 21, SUBCHAPTER AA, SECTION 21.906, AMENDED TO BE EFFECTIVE NOVEMBER 23, 2000 (25 TexReg 11387)

University of Texas at Austin Policies and Procedures

All *incoming* reciprocal exchange students apply directly to the Graduate and International Admissions Center like other international students. They must pay the application fee, other nominal fees that may be required, and have adequate health insurance. The maximum length of their stay as an enrolled student is 12 months, although typically, two terms is the longest, while many students en- roll for only one term. The following paragraph is from the General Information catalog:

Exchange students: A student who is admitted to the University through a reciprocal exchange program is classified as a non-degree student. An exchange student may not register for more than two long-session semesters and one summer semester. . . .

Outgoing reciprocal exchange students pay their UT tuition and fees for 12 credit hours. This remains at UT for the incoming exchange student. The outgoing student also must register with UT as a reciprocal exchange student and pay a fee. This keeps them enrolled at UT during their study abroad, and allows them to access their normal financial aid package. Courses taken on reciprocal exchange programs count as in-residence credit and grades will be figured into the UT GPA.

Reciprocal exchange students from abroad who complete their time at UT may want to apply for regular UT degree program status. There are strict limitations on the amount of credit an international student is allowed to transfer to a UT de- gree program, if admitted. Check with the Graduate and International Admissions Center to verify the rules governing such an application.

APPENDIX B

AFFILIATION AGREEMENT

between

THE UNIVERSITY OF TEXAS-AUSTIN

and

(insert affiliate name here)

THE UNIVERSITY OF TEXAS AT AUSTIN (hereinafter referred to as UT-Austin) and affiliate name, a study abroad organization, having its principal office located at official affiliate address (hereinafter referred to as X), enter into an agreement of affiliation to establish opportunities for students to study in other countries during their UT education.

A.

The purposes of affiliation between UT-Austin and X are as follows:

- to provide quality overseas study abroad programs for summer, semester and academic year sessions to the students who attend The University of Texas-Austin;
- to promote student interest in the educational programs and services of X programs in Europe (see attached Memorandum of Understanding);
- to facilitate enrollment of students in these programs;
- to provide services to students that are in compliance with relevant federal and state laws.

B.

To achieve the goals stated in Section A above, The University of Texas-Austin will, insofar as its means and the laws and the Constitution of the State of Texas allow:

- advise eligible students (proficiency statement to insert here if applicable) of the opportunities available through this affiliation;
- assist interested students with enrollment, course selection, advising, and related services;
- verify enrollment of student(s) in the program(s) involved and inform each student about the applicability of courses to that student's degree program;

- evaluate the academic performance and course credit for each student upon successful completion of his/her academic program(s).

C.

To achieve the goals stated in Section A above, X will:

- provide academic courses of quality, duration, and content appropriate to the curricula of participating students seeking to complete The University of Texas-Austin courses;
- guarantee that all university courses will be taught by native instructors employed by the accredited universities;
- provide an on-site two week intensive language acquisition course for each program that will be continued once a week for the duration of each study term;
- assist students selected for the program with enrollment in the university courses;
- monitor student participation and progress in the courses and inform The University of Texas-Austin if student participation is unsatisfactory or if a student has withdrawn;
- provide an official transcript issued by the accredited overseas university for each student;
- provide participating students with housing, and assist with their other local logistical needs or problems they may encounter while abroad;
- provide a resident director upon arrival;
- provide cultural excursions;
- provide ground transportation to and from the host city;
- provide medical and life insurance for each student;
- provide academic advising and tutoring;
- provide a program orientation prior to departure and on site;
- provide for a designated representative/s from The University of Texas-Austin to evaluate and monitor the programs on site as necessary (see attached Memorandum of Understanding);
- as the programs permit, provide for designated faculty, instructors, or assistant instructors to assist with the programs during the summer sessions (see attached Memorandum of Understanding);
- award scholarship funds for X programs to The University of Texas-Austin on an annual basis (see attached Memorandum of Understanding).

D.

The University of Texas-Austin and X agree to designate the following individuals to oversee and facilitate implementation of this affiliation agreement in cooperation with other appropriate administrators within The University of Texas-Austin and X:

Program Coordinators:

For UT-Austin:

Dr. Ivy McQuiddy
Director of Study Abroad
Assistant Director, International Office
The University of Texas-Austin
Drawer A
Austin, Texas 78713-7206
Telephone: 512-471-6490
Fax: 512-232-4363

For X:

contact name
title
affiliate name
street address
city, state zip
Telephone:
Fax:

The University of Texas-Austin Program Coordinator will represent the policies of The University of Texas-Austin to X. The Program Coordinator for X will be responsible for representing the policies of X to The University of Texas-Austin. The Coordinators will periodically review and evaluate the academic program and services offered by X.

E.

Participating students shall be subject to the rules and regulations of X while abroad.

F.

The scope of the activities under this Affiliation Agreement shall be determined by the funds regularly available at both institutions. Each party to this agreement shall be responsible for expenses incurred by its employees.

G.

Termination of this Affiliation Agreement can be initiated by either party and shall be effective by giving the other party at least six (6) months advance written notice of its intention to terminate, provided that all students enrolled in the programs at the time notice of termination is given shall be permitted to finish their course of study. Termination shall be without penalty. If this agreement is terminated, neither The University of Texas-Austin nor X shall be liable to the other for any monetary or other losses that may result.

ATTEST:

FOR THE UNIVERSITY OF TEXAS-AUSTIN

Larry R. Faulkner   Date
President

FOR affiliate name

---

president's name   Date
President

MEMORANDUM OF UNDERSTANDING

AFFILIATION AGREEMENT

between

THE UNIVERSITY OF TEXAS-AUSTIN

and

affiliate name (X)

Conditions and Additional Information:

1. This agreement includes the following X programs:
(list multiple site locations is applicable here)
2. X will provide the director for The University of Texas-Austin all program information, including, but not limited to, program changes, prices, descriptions, and locations in a timely manner.
3. X will provide for, and pay for, representative/s from The University of Texas-Austin to travel to country and evaluate the program every two to three years, or as deemed necessary by both parties.
4. X will hire, as appropriate, designated faculty, instructors, or assistant instructors to assist with the programs in Spain during the summer sessions. The location

of the sites in the summer include: _____ . There is a total of seven sessions during the summer months. Once any given summer program reaches the enrollment of twenty students or more, the opportunity to serve as an assistant X director at said location in Spain will be given to a representative of The University of Texas-Austin. Compensation for the assistant director will include airfare, living accommodations, and a salary. The request for the assistant director will be made to the Department of Spanish and Portuguese. X will make these requests by the second week in April of each program year.

5. X will award scholarship monies on an annual basis to The University of Texas-Austin to award to the University of Texas-Austin students based on financial need. Students must have a 3.00 GPA and demonstrate the need for financial assistance.

This Memorandum can be modified at anytime with the joint approval of both X and The University of Texas-Austin.

FOR THE UNIVERSITY OF TEXAS-AUSTIN

Ivy McQuiddy, Director
  Date

FOR affiliate name

---

president's name, President   Date

APPENDIX C

Academic And Scientific Cooperation And Exchange Agreement

between *(Partner Institution)*

and *The University of Texas at Austin*

This agreement is made and entered into between *(Partner Institution)* and The University of Texas at Austin (UT).

Whereas, the participating parties believe that international understanding, the educational opportunities for their students and the professional opportunities for their academic staff, would be enhanced by an international academic and scientific cooperation and agreement; and

Whereas, the purpose of this agreement is to establish a framework within which academic and scientific cooperation may develop between the institutions. This agreement shall be identified as the parent document of any specific Program Agreement between the parties;

Now, therefore, the parties agree as follows:

SECTION 1: *Types of Cooperation*

1.1   The parties to this Agreement indicate their willingness in principle to cooperate in the promotion of teaching and research activities. Under this agreement, the types of cooperation may include:

- reciprocal exchange of students,
- reciprocal exchange of staff and faculty,
- collaborative research projects,
- exchange of publications, reports and other academic information,
- collaborative professional development, and
- other activities as mutually agreed.

1.2   Each type of cooperation shall proceed as mutually agreed upon in a specific program agreement identifying the governing conditions of that activity. The Program Agreement shall provide details concerning the specific commitments made by each party and shall not become effective until they have been reduced to writing, executed by the duly authorized representatives of the parties, and approved.

1.3   The scope of the activities under this agreement shall be determined by the funds regularly available at both institutions for the types of collaboration specified in the supplemental agreements, and by the amount of financial assistance obtained by either institution from external sources. Each institution shall be responsible for expenses incurred by its employees under this agreement, except as may be stipulated in any supplemental agreement.

SECTION 2: *Commencement, Term, Renewal, Amendment and Termination*

This agreement shall become effective on the date of its signing by both parties, continue thereafter for five (5) years subject to revision or modification by mutual written agreement and shall terminate automatically at the end of such period unless thirty (30) days prior to termination, The University of Texas at Austin provides written notice to [partner institution] of its intention to renew the agreement for an additional five (5) year term. Either party may terminate this agreement at any time, without penalty subject to the following notice provision. Termination by one institution shall be effected by giving the other institution at least ninety (90) days advance written notice of its intention to terminate, but any students who have commenced at either university at the date of termination may complete their courses of study. Termination shall be without penalty. Any amendment to this agreement shall be made with acknowledgement in writing from both institutions.

Executed by *(The Foreign Institution or Organization)* and the University of Texas at Austin in duplicate copies, each of which shall be deemed an original.

The University of Texas at Austin   *Partner Institution*
_____   _____

(Signature)   (Date)   (Signature)   (Date)

Larry R. Faulkner

President

APPENDIX D

Program Agreement/Student Exchange

between *(Partner Institution)*

and *The University of Texas at Austin*

This program agreement is made pursuant to and is subject to the terms and conditions of the Academic and Scientific Cooperation and Exchange Agreement between the insert Name of Partner Institution and the University of Texas at Austin. This Program Agreement is between the following schools/colleges, department, or centers:
(Insert specific Partner Institution and specific academic units at UT.)

❑ *Purpose*
   The primary purpose of this Agreement is to institute an exchange of students that will provide student participants with an opportunity to study and benefit from the academic and cultural environment of the other.

❏ *Academic Coordination*
   The individuals designated to coordinate the student exchange programs are listed on an attachment to this agreement. Their responsibilities entail the following:

   • *oversee the selection of students to participate in the exchange,*
   • *facilitate academic matters for the students received by the host institution,*
   • *provide assistance to enrolling incoming students, and*
   • *serve as liaison between the two institutions:*

❏ *Numbers, Level, Selection and Balance*
❏ *The exchange shall be limited to the equivalent of up to _____ full year students per academic year from each institution during the term of the Agreement. Both institutions will review the exchange program on a regular basis for any imbalances in the number of students exchanged and will adjust the numbers as necessary to maintain a well-balanced program.*
❏ *The overall balance of incoming and outgoing students must be maintained over the period of the agreement. Each institution has the right to approve the number of students it will receive in any given year.*
❏ *This exchange includes graduate and/or undergraduate students, who have completed at least one year of undergraduate study.*
❏ *The home institution will nominate students for the exchange on the basis of academic merit and other factors as may be agreed upon by both institutions. The host institution reserves the right to make final judgment on the admissibility of each student nominated for the exchange 4.0.*
❏ *Academic Program*
❏ *Each participating student will take courses regularly offered at the host university, with the understanding that the host institution reserves the right to exclude students from restricted enrollment programs.*
❏ At the end of the period of study, the host institution will provide the sending institution with a report of the courses and grades received by each exchange student.
❏ Transfer of academic credit will be determined by the home institution.
❏ Student Status and Responsibilities
❏ Exchange students will register for a full course load and pay applicable tuition and fees to their respective home institutions and such nominal fees as may be required by the host institution for exchange students.
❏ Students participating in the program will be subject to and must abide by all the rules and regulations of the host institution.
❏ Participating students shall be responsible for housing, travel, medical insurance, and subsistence costs, and neither university shall be held liable for such charges.

❑ Exchange students will be required to purchase comprehensive health insurance, including medical evacuation and repatriation benefits.
❑ Housing and Other Assistance

- The respective international offices will provide exchange students with university documents required for the student to obtain a visa, housing information, and on-site orientation. General assistance will be provided on arrival at the host institution to help students locate living accommodations.

❑ Amendment, Term, Termination, and Renewal
❑ This agreement shall become effective on the date of its signing by both parties, continue thereafter for five (5) years subject to revision or modification by mutual written agreement and shall terminate automatically at the end of such period unless thirty (30) days prior to termination, The University of Texas at Austin provides written notice to [partner institution] of its intention to renew the agreement for an additional five(5) year term. Either party may terminate this agreement at any time, without penalty subject to the notice provision below. Any amendment to this agreement shall be made with acknowledgement in writing from both institutions.
❑ Termination by one institution shall be effected by giving the other institution at least ninety (90) days advance written notice of its intention to terminate. Further, this agreement will automatically terminate upon termination of the parent Academic and Scientific Cooperation and Exchange Agreement but any students who have commenced at either university at the date of termination may complete their courses of study. Termination shall be without penalty.

Executed by (*The Foreign Institution or Organization*) and The University of Texas at Austin in duplicate copies, each of which shall be deemed an original.

The University of Texas at Austin   **Partner Institution**
_____   _____

(Signature)   (Date)   (Signature)   (Date)

Larry R. Faulkner   Name

President   Title

APPENDIX E

Program Agreement/Faculty And Staff Exchange

between [*Cooperating Institution*]

and **The University of Texas at Austin**

This program agreement is made pursuant to and is subject to the terms and conditions of the Academic and Scientific Cooperation and Exchange Agreement between the [insert Name of Cooperating Institution] *and the University of Texas at Austin. This Program Agreement is between the following schools/colleges, department, or centers:*
(Insert specific Cooperating Institution and specific academic units at UT.)

This agreement provides the specific framework for the following activities:

- collaborative research projects,
- reciprocal exchange of staff and faculty,
- exchange of publications, reports and other academic information,
- collaborative professional development, and
- other activities such as conferences, symposia, and workshops as mutually agreed.

Collaborative Research

Insert description of the collaborative research that will be conducted.

Specify resources needed and who will pay for costs associated with the research i.e. employee salary, computer resources, lab equipment.

Faculty/Staff Exchange

Insert detailed terms and conditions of the exchange e.g. how many faculty/staff will be exchanged and what activities will take place.

All matters related to the rights and responsibilities of employment, including the salaries and benefits of exchange faculty and staff, are the sole responsibility of the home institution.

The period of the exchange visit of any faculty/staff member of the home institution shall not exceed *(insert maximum length of time period for each individual).*

Exchange Faculty/Staff shall be subject to the host institution's rules, regulations, and policies. The host institution will orient exchange faculty and staff to pertinent rules. The home institution will withdraw the faculty/staff member from the exchange assignment upon the request of the host institution.

The host institution will, on request, provide information to assist exchange faculty/staff in locating living accommodations and information and assistance required to obtain a visa, work permit, or other documents necessary to enter and stay in the host country. However, the ultimate responsibility for making the appropriate arrangements and meeting the legal requirements to enter, live and work in the host country is the responsibility of the exchange faculty/staff and the home institution shall communicate this responsibility to exchange faculty/staff.

If teaching is involved in an exchange, the arrangement must be reciprocal so that neither participating institution suffers any hardships in maintaining required teaching loads.

Information Exchange and Exchange of Materials

The institutions agree to exchange information on the current state of their studies in the areas of collaborative work. Similarly, they will make available to each other well before their publication or the filing of patent applications any manuscripts and notices of invention in these areas that fall within the terms of the agreement and are not subject to restrictions in other grants or contracts.

In order to promote the joint work and carry out this exchange on a noncommercial basis, the parties also agree to make available to one another research materials and/or samples within the terms of this agreement and not subject to restrictions in other grants or contracts.

Publications

The parties shall publish the results of their collaboration under the titles of the two institutions. The results of the joint work on a subject where both research groups have had original results and ideas already shall be published under the authorship of all investigators who made substantial contributions and under the titles of both UT Austin and the cooperating institution, regardless of where the final experiments or research were performed.

Intellectual Property

All publications resulting from the collaboration between the two institutions under the terms and conditions of this Agreement must give recognition to this

Agreement therein. Likewise, this Agreement must also be mentioned in all courses and formal presentations which result from collaboration under the terms hereof.

Both parties agree to the exchange of publications, such as books, academic journals, and other official publications, and research information generated by either of the parties in connection with this Agreement.

Inventions made jointly by members of the two research groups will be jointly owned by the cooperating institution and UT Austin in accordance with UT Austin policy on intellectual property.

Academic and Disciplinary Rules

The parties agree that the academic requirements of both educational institutions shall be respected and that all current, applicable policies covering matters of academic responsibility and social discipline will be distributed to the other party and carefully followed.

Funding

Resources for the implementation of this Agreement are dependant upon budgetary availability. Neither party is obligated to expend any resources in connection with this Agreement. Should either party not have the funding necessary to carry out any obligations under this agreement, it shall immediately notify the other Institution of such fact and of such portions of this Agreement that may be deemed terminated or modified.

Should a joint grant or contract be awarded, the institution to whom the prime award is made shall be responsible for allocating funds according to the budgets approved by the granting agency, both institutions, and the Principal Investigators for support of the two groups, including salaries, supplies, equipment, travel, and indirect expenses.

Relationship of the Parties

This Agreement shall not be construed to create a relationship of partners, employees, servants or agents as between the parties. The parties to this Agreement are acting as independent contractors. With respect to employee compensation for services provided in connection with this Agreement, each party shall indemnify the other for their own employees' salaries, withholding taxes, workers' compensation, and other employment related obligations.

Use of Institutions' Name

Neither party shall use the other institution's name, or any name or trademark in any form, including advertising, promotion or sales literature without first obtaining the written consent of the other institution.

Governing Law

This agreement shall be governed by and construed under the laws of the State of Texas, which shall be the forum for any lawsuits arising from and incident to this Agreement.

Non-Assignment

This Agreement may not be assigned by either party without the advance written consent of the other.

Notice

Any notice to either party hereunder must be in writing signed by the party giving it, and shall be served either personally or by U.S. First Class, registered or certified mail, or by overnight or expedited delivery service, addressed as follows or to such other addressee as may be hereafter designated by written notice. All such notices shall be effective only when received by the addressee.

Amendment, Term, Termination, and Renewal

This agreement shall become effective on the date of its signing by both parties, continue thereafter until _____ (not to exceed five (5) years) subject to revision or modification by mutual written agreement and shall terminate automatically at the end of such period unless thirty (30) days prior to termination, The University of Texas at Austin provides written notice to [*partner institution*] of its intention to renew the agreement for an additional term. Either party may terminate this agreement at any time, without penalty subject to the notice provision below. Any amendment to this agreement shall be made with acknowledgement in writing from both institutions.

Termination by one institution shall be effected by giving the other institution at least ninety (90) days advance written notice of its intention to terminate. Further, this agreement will automatically terminate upon termination of the parent Academic and Scientific Cooperation and Exchange Agreement. Termination shall be without penalty.

Executed by (*The Foreign Institution or Organization*) and the University of Texas at Austin in duplicate copies, each of which shall be deemed an original.

The University of Texas at Austin   *Cooperating Institution*
_____   _____
(Signature)   (Date)   (Signature)   (Date)

Larry R. Faulkner   Name

President   Title

APPENDIX F

Academic And Scientific Cooperation And Exchange Agreements

With Foreign Universities

Worksheet

Approval process and legal authority: *The Office of the Associate Vice President for International Programs is responsible for overseeing the exchange agreement approval process. This office will not normally have responsibility for the administration or implementation of agreements; nor will it be responsible for the allocation of any resources in support of agreements. Exchange agreements between the University of Texas at Austin and foreign universities are governed by a combination of Texas State law, Texas Higher Education Coordinating Board Rules, and University of Texas at Austin policies. The format of exchange agreements has been prescribed by the UT System Board of Regents. Sample formats for the general and program agreements are located on the web site of the Associate Vice President for International Programs http://www.utexas.edu/ogs/international. Agreements not using these formats would normally have to be approved by the UT Board of Regents.*

Duration: Agreements normally are valid for five (5) years; therefore, when considering an exchange relationship with a foreign partner institution, sustained faculty involvement for any kind of exchange remains the most critical ingredient in a successful relationship. Faculty must serve as the academic coordinators and student recruiters when applicable, plus help monitor the balance and quality of the exchange.

Current Active Agreements: Before completing this Worksheet, check the web site of the Associate Vice-President for International Programs for the current list of Academic and Scientific Cooperation and Exchange Agreements. http://www.128.83.84.48/default2.htm For additional information, call 232-3609.

This questionnaire is used to obtain the information needed by the Office of the AssociateVice President for International Programs to prepare the Academic and Scientific Cooperation and Exchange Agreement and the Program Agreement. Please answer the following questions:

Part 1 Information about the foreign institution (exchange partner):

1.1 Complete name of foreign institution (to be entered on all exchange agreement documents):

1.2 Institutional Web site URL:

1.3 *Proposed types of exchange with the foreign partner institution (check all that apply):*

— Reciprocal exchange of students
— Reciprocal exchange of staff and faculty

(Include detailed terms and conditions of the exchange e.g. how many faculty/staff will be exchanged and what activities will take place and he maximum length of time period for each individual).

— Collaborative research projects

(Include a description of the collaborative research that will be conducted and Specify resources needed and who will pay for costs associated with the research i.e. employee salary, computer resources, lab equipment.)

— Exchange of publications, reports, and other academic information
— Professional development
— Other activities such as conference, symposia, and workshops, as mutually agreed.

1.4 List any specific sub-unit(s) (schools, colleges, faculties, departments, centers, institutes, etc.) in the foreign institution with which the agreement is to be made, unless the exchange applies to the entire overseas institution. Please include any relevant web sites for those units:

1.5 *Name and title of chief executive officer authorized to sign the exchange agreement on behalf of the cooperating institution:*

1.6 Cooperating institution contact information:

Exchange Program Coordinator:
Name
Title
Mailing Address

Telephone
Fax
E-mail address
Web address

In the case of a program agreement that includes student exchange:

Advisor for Outgoing Students, i.e. students coming to UT::	*Advisor for Incoming Students i.e. students enrolling at the cooperating institution:*
Name	Name
Title	Title
Mailing Address	Mailing Address
Telephone	Telephone
Fax	Fax
E-mail address	E-mail address
Web address	Web address

For program agreements related to other exchanges activities, list appropriate contact individuals; for example, exchange of faculty and staff, collaborative research projects, exchange of publications, collaborative professional development, other activities as mutually agreed (add extra sheets if necessary):

Name
Title
Mailing Address

Telephone
Fax
E-mail address
Web address

Part 2 Information about the University of Texas at Austin endorsement and support for the proposed exchange agreement:

The UT faculty initiating this proposed agreement is to consult with the appropriate UT departments/schools/colleges and the UT area or language studies directors when appropriate. In the case of agreements related to the exchange of materials such as books and films, the faculty member should discuss the agreement with the Director of General Libraries.

- Rationale for the proposed exchange agreement. (e.g. How is the activity with the proposed partner of mutual benefit to both institutions? For student exchanges, how does this benefit out UT students, and what is the probability of attaining an appropriate level of reciprocity? If UT already has agreements to provide students an opportunity to study in the proposed country or site, what new possibilities does this partnership offer? What are the enhancements/attractions within the broader UT community?) Attach extra pages if necessary:

2.2 UT Exchange Academic Coordinator, i.e. faculty member responsible for administering the proposed agreement:

Name
Title
Mailing Address
Telephone
Fax
E-mail address
Web address

- Approval of the head of the campus unit responsible for administering the proposed agreement
  (e.g. college or school dean, department chair, center director, etc.)

  (Signature)
  Name
  Title

- UT academic units in support of the proposed agreement:

  If the proposed exchange includes student exchange, consult with the head of the UT Study Abroad Office, tel. 471-6490. Consult the web site of the Associate Vice President for International Programs for contact information on the study abroad/student exchange committees of the various UT colleges and schools. Otherwise, contact the head of the campus unit that may be interested in supporting the exchange agreement. Feel free to use e-mail endorsements, please attach.

UT Campus units   Name

Date student exchange agreement reviewed by the head of the Study Abroad Office:
• Initiator(s) of the proposed agreement:

Name   Department

Date submitted

Send the completed Exchange Agreement Worksheet to:

Office of Associate Vice President for International Programs

APPENDIX G

Procedures For Establishing Student Exchange Linkages With Foreign Institutions

Rationale for Establishing a Reciprocal Exchange Agreement

A series of important steps must be in order to create and maintain an on-going exchange of opportunities and cooperation with a foreign institution. Collaboration can be achieved in several ways: Faculty or student exchange, exchange of materials, research participation and involvement, and shared conference planning are only some of the possibilities. Both the cooperating institution and UT should be able to gain from the relationship. Sometimes these goals are achieved through bilateral agreements and at other times through networks of participating institutions. In any event, a linkage requires a substantial commitment of time and energy.

This document focuses on the establishment of a linkage with a foreign cooperating institution involving the exchange of students.

The Office of the Associate Vice-President for International Programs is responsible for overseeing the process of establishing reciprocal exchange agreements.

Currently, UT has nearly 100 active agreements that provided opportunities for over 300 UT students to study abroad for the academic year 1999–2000.

Agreements normally are valid for five (5) years; therefore, when considering an exchange relationship, please note that faculty involvement is the most critical ingredient in sustaining a successful exchange. Faculty must serve as the academic coordinators, student recruiters, and help monitor the balance and quality of the exchange.

Identify Appropriate Cooperating Institutions and Complete the Worksheet

The following list outlines areas of inquiry that should be investigated when a linkage with a foreign institution is under consideration.

1. Check the web site of the Associate Vice-President for International Programs to see if an Academic and Scientific Cooperation and Exchange Agreement exists. http://www.utexas/ogs/international/links. You may find that UT already has an agreement with the prospective partner institution. If so, you may only need to develop the Program Agreement.
2. In preparation for completing the Academic and Scientific Cooperation and Exchange Agreement Worksheet for UT Faculty (see worksheet template on web site of Associate Vice President for International Programs), consider this issues outlined below to identify the mutual strengths of the cooperating institution and UT.

   - Identify strong academic programs and departments
   - Gather student and faculty statistics
   - Investigate academic institutes and libraries
   - Compare university structures
   - Exchange and review catalogs
   - Review web sites
   - Describe types of academic programs most beneficial to each institution that could be complemented by a study abroad component
   - List faculty and administrators who are interested and committed to the proposed exchange.

1. Describe possible living arrangements at the host institution for faculty and/or students.
2. Outline anticipated costs and funds available.
3. Examine the probability of attaining an appropriate level of reciprocity.
4. Identify relevant policies and possible limitations at each institution.

5. List enhancements/attractions within the broader UT community.

Secure Endorsements & Provide Information for the Student Exchange Program Agreement

The initiating UT unit must consult with and secure a written endorsement/letter of intent to enter into the agreement or have the Academic and Scientific Cooperation and Exchange Worksheet counter-signed by the following:

6. *The Dean of the college/school or their designee, such as the college/school study abroad committee, of the UT unit initiating the agreement and,*
7. *Any other college/school, department or academic program, or student service unit that will participate in the agreement and,*
8. *The Study Abroad Coordinator, International Office (SHC/Campus code A7000)*

Following the above, the UT faculty proposing the agreement should send the following information to the Office of the Associate Vice President for International Programs, MAI 101.

✓ The Academic and Scientific Cooperation and Exchange Agreement Worksheet for UT Faculty, which includes a description of the expected benefits of the proposed linkage, a brief overview of the partner institution, and contact information of faculty and academic coordinators at UT and the proposed partner institution.
✓ Copies of any relevant correspondence between the initiating department or other UT Austin personnel concerning the proposed linkage, including any brochures or other general information about the cooperating institution.

Review the UT International Exchange Agreements Format

International exchange agreements involving student exchange normally are for a five year term and consist of the *Academic and Scientific Cooperation and Exchange Agreement* and the *Program Agreement for Student Exchange*. Final copies of the agreements are prepared by the staff of the Office of International Programs. Both agreements are required to have been signed by all parties before any student exchange activity can proceed. The templates are located at: http://www.utexas/ogs/international/links/.

Approval and Presidential Endorsement of the Agreement

After receiving the proposed Worksheet, the staff of the Associate Vice President for International Programs will send the agreement for the approval of the President. As soon as the president signs the agreement, two original sets will be sent to the initiating UT unit to be forwarded to the foreign institution for endorsement. One original set must then be returned to the Office of the Associate Vice President for International Programs. When both sets of the agreement have been signed and one set returned to the Office of the Associate Vice President for International Programs, this office will:

❑ send copies to appropriate representatives on our campus, including the International Office, the initiating UT unit, other endorsers of the agreement, appropriate research center directors and other UT units that should be aware of the agreement, and
❑ add the agreement to the official UT web site of International Agreements of Academic and Student Exchange.

Evaluation and Renewal/Termination of the Agreement

Designated academic coordinators at UT, in collaboration with the Coordinator and/or staff of the Study Abroad Office, will monitor the various aspects of the exchange including the balance of the students coming and going. Before the agreement expires, faculty and staff at UT will review the activities of the exchange and make recommendations to the Associate Vice President for International Programs as to whether or not the agreement should be extended. After consideration of this recommendation, it will be the Associate Vice President's task to communicate the final decision to the cooperating institution.

CHOOSING PARTNERS AND STRUCTURING RELATIONSHIPS – LESSONS LEARNED

Andrea Poehling and R. D. Nair

INTRODUCTION

Offering study abroad and exchange programs in partnership with Schools of Business around the world is a cost-effective way of providing a meaningful international academic opportunity for students. They also help lay the foundation for wider collaborations on other dimensions, such as faculty exchanges, with partner institutions. However, structuring and administering these programs requires a clear guiding vision of the overall objectives of the program as well as a firm grasp of the administrative details involved. In this paper, we describe some of the key ingredients involved in choosing partners and structuring successful international education partnerships.

The experience our office – in the School of Business at the University of Wisconsin–Madison – gained as we developed overseas programs can be applied to other business schools that seek to expand their international portfolio. In the four years since our office's inception, we have increased the number of semester programs from 3 to 17 and the number of short-term programs from 2 to 10. Over this time period, the total number of students receiving credit for overseas business programs has risen from 54 to 198 per year. International programs at the University of Wisconsin–Madison are housed within each school or college (business, engineering, agriculture, etc.). The university monitors the programs at a

Study Abroad: Perspectives and Experiences from Business Schools
Advances in International Marketing, Volume 13, 191–207.

central level, but a *laissez-faire* attitude exists. Central administration understands that each school has its own needs, knows its own academic structure, fosters its own overseas relationships, and thus is best suited to run its own international programs. In writing this paper, we understand that not all readers will be administering business study abroad programs from an international office within the school of business, but the lessons we have learned . . . and outline below . . . can be applied to centralized as well as decentralized operations.

TYPES OF PARTNERSHIPS

A *bilateral exchange agreement* forms a partnership between two universities. A given number of students are exchanged on a short-term basis: a summer, semester or academic year. For every outgoing student that a university sends, an incoming student from the partner university is accepted. Students are visitors at the host university – participation is based on the understanding that the exchange program enhances one's studies at home rather than leading to a degree at the host university. Financially, students pay tuition to the home university, although they are considered students at the host university for the term. In an exchange program, students typically attend classes and live with students from the host country and from other countries around the world. Students navigate the educational system and life abroad much as a local student would, but with the added assistance of an international office. Exchange programs allow students to live abroad for a time while attending a business school of equal caliber to their home university.

Exchange programs are typically considered the most desirable type of partnership. Since agreements limit the number of students that are exchanged, the "ghettoization" of students from one university does not occur. Students have an authentic international experience, as they must maneuver the host university's systems, which are intended to serve students from the host country and around the world, not just Americans. Students learn in the host country's academic system rather than an American classroom placed in a different country. By partnering with peer institutions around the world, universities ensure that students receive a comparable education to what they would at home. Hosting students from the partner university brings diversity to U.S. classrooms and allows outgoing students to meet students from the host university even while they are on the home campus. For all the benefits of an exchange program, however, one cannot overlook the fact that such arrangements are commonly recognized as complex and difficult. Reciprocal exchanges are labor intensive, as they entail a two-way flow of students, require additional assistance to mainstream visiting students into an existing system, and necessitate detailed bookkeeping to ensure that a balance of students is maintained.

Because suitable exchange partners are not always available in desired locations, many schools consider a different type of partnership. In an *affiliated partnership* the flow of students is one way: The U.S. university sends students to the host institution without receiving incoming students in exchange. The host institution is either a degree-granting institution that also accepts students on a study abroad basis or it is an independent organization only serving study abroad participants. Financial arrangements are different than in an exchange program. In one affiliated financial model, students pay tuition directly to the host institution, at their rates, rather than paying tuition to the home university. In a variation on this model, the partner institution charges the U.S. university a fee for each student. In turn, the home university charges the students, maintaining a fee differential between in-state and out-of-state students (although not necessarily identical to on-campus tuition differentials) in order to keep costs down for in-state students.

Some *degree-granting institutions abroad* offer such arrangements because they lack outgoing students for an exchange, but they have the resources to accept incoming students on a study abroad basis. In this case, students may have an experience similar to what they would have if they were participating in an exchange program.

The more common situation is either an *institution that has a special study abroad division* within it or *one that is exclusively dedicated to serving international students*. In these cases, the participants tend to be non-natives (often Americans) and most often English is used as the language of instruction. Academics and student services tend to be a hybrid between an American system and that of the host country. For example, a program may have certain aspects of American scheduling but use a European style of lecturing. From this point forward, discussion of affiliated partnerships assumes this latter version. Although affiliated programs often result in ghettos of American students who do not fully experience the host country's academic system, the benefits are not to be overlooked. In some locations it is impossible to find a suitable exchange partner, either because of a market saturated by American students (e.g. London) or because courses are taught in a language that the students do not speak fluently (e.g. Spain). Some students, especially those who are not experienced travelers, prefer to experience life overseas within the context of an American system; they might not participate in an international program otherwise. Finally, it is possible that a university's exchange programs cannot accommodate all interested and qualified students. Since affiliated programs accept any student who meets their minimum qualifications, a large number of students can be sent abroad.

A third type of model, *partnerships with administrative agencies*, augments services provided by an exchange partner or are the basis of faculty-led study abroad programs. Two examples illustrate this type of partnership, the University of Wisconsin–Madison's semester program in Paris and short-term winter break program in London and Paris. Our program in Paris is rather complex, as it allows students to participate in either an exchange at a leading business school or a hybrid business exchange at the same university and language program (affiliated program) at a separate institution. To complicate matters, the exchange partner is accustomed to working with graduate students who are quite independent and who speak French well; we tend to send undergraduate students with varying levels of French. To create a more student-friendly program, we have found an administrative partner that centralizes our partnerships and provides services that our partners do not. Apartments are arranged, orientation is geared specifically to our students, and a social program includes weekend trips and excursions around the city. While many of our students certainly could (and do) manage in Paris by only interacting with the exchange partner, the program appeals to a larger audience of students because of the added benefits provided by the administrative partner.

The same administrative partner takes on an even larger role during our faculty-led short-term study abroad program in Paris and London. A faculty member from our university teaches our students, but our international programs office simply does not have the on-site resources or knowledge of these European cities to fully support the program overseas. Instead, we contract the administrative partner to provide classroom space and audio/visual support, housing for both faculty and students, airport reception, orientation, social programs, pre-departure information, and on-site staff and support. Under this arrangement, our university maintains control over the academic program while relying on one trusted overseas partner to organize all logistical details. This type of arrangement could be expanded to a longer program. Administrative partners are contracted to provide a tailor-made program for the home university, so it is essential to communicate exactly what your university needs.

ASSESSING YOUR NEEDS

Assessing your institution's needs will give you direction in the search for partners. Your students and their priorities should be the primary consideration in the needs assessment. Without student participation, the programs will fail. Students base their decisions on a number of factors, including geographic location, cost, course compatibility and accessibility, duration, and prestige of the partner institution.

Geographic location is often students' primary consideration. Life in a big city appeals to some, while others want small, comfortable, or easy access to outdoor splendors. Some students wish to fulfill a life-long dream of living in London, others want to live in Asia so they can take long weekends to places that from the U.S. would chew up most of their vacation time later in life. Simultaneously improving Spanish and learning about NAFTA while living in Mexico, or studying in a developing market instead of a more "mainstream" country appeal to the career-minded student. Family heritage can also be a factor; currently we have a student studying in Stockholm who travels throughout Sweden visiting his grandparents and other relatives during university holidays. Despite the many reasons students have for choosing particular locations, we have found that they do not frequently match the recommendations of our advisory board. The board prefers that we establish programs in developing economies both for strategic reasons for the School of Business and with the desire of employing persons experienced in these economies, but this recommendation does not necessarily fit well with our students' intended destinations.

Costs are prohibitive to some students and will be a factor in their decision of where ... or even *if* ... to study overseas. Include both affiliated and exchange programs in your portfolio, as costs can differ dramatically between the two. Be cognizant of the cost of living at various sites and of the airfare expense to get there. A more in-depth discussion of finances is included in the section on implementing and maintaining the partnership.

Even beyond location and cost, students are concerned about *course compatibility and accessibility.* No matter how fabulous the program, students will not participate if they cannot make progress toward the degree. You *must* be certain that courses offered at the partner university will fulfill your students' foundation, major or elective requirements. Prior to entering an agreement, obtain syllabi of the potential partners' courses, have faculty at your university equate them, and determine if the list of equivalent classes will attract your students. While courses should generally include the same content, avoid being overly rigid when comparing classes. Assess whether the host university's credit system is compatible with yours; if the number of contact hours per class is significantly lower than your institution's standards, you have a problem that must be addressed.

Access to classes is as important as determining compatibility. Discuss enrollment limitations with the partner and, if they exist, the enrollment priority for visiting international students. Review past semesters' timetables to find out how frequently courses are offered. Ask how far in advance course offerings are published, and when international students register. Some students wish to supplement their overseas curriculum by taking non-business courses; determine if the partner university offers such courses and if your students are permitted to attend.

It is crucial to partner with universities that have academic systems that fit well with yours.

Language of instruction relates to course accessibility; if students can't speak the language in which the class is taught, they won't attend the program. The ideal partner offers courses for students of all language abilities: Business courses taught in English; business courses taught in the local language to non-native speakers; business courses taught to local students in the local language; and courses specifically aimed to teach or improve language skills. Assess whether your students have the capacity and the desire to take business courses in a foreign language. While we certainly advocate programs taught in another language, the unfortunate reality is that many students do not have the ability to attend such courses. As well, students who do have language skills are often reluctant to risk taking a course in another language and obtaining lower grades. Several of our partnerships have been terminated ... or not begun in the first place ... because of a classroom language barrier.

Your partner's *academic calendar* will impact students' participation. Choosing a partner that offers semester, academic year and summer programs provides greater options for your students and efficiency for your institution. Summer programs provide an international experience to students who cannot spend a semester or year abroad for financial or academic reasons. If your partner offers semester, year and summer programs, you have the advantage of learning and operating within only one system. Determine if the host university's calendar will fit within your academic calendar. The fall semester of many of our European partners extend into February, well beyond when our spring semester begins. Some partners make concessions for exchange students to finish early, ensuring that students can attend spring semester courses back home. If you choose to partner with a university that requires students to stay until February, you are essentially offering a spring- or academic year-only program, as very few students will choose a program that requires them to take spring semester off.

Reputation of the partner university is something that many students will consider, but usually only after weighing the factors listed above. Students assume they will receive a good education at whatever university they attend because it has the endorsement of your university. Despite this, reputation is a critical factor in selecting universities, not only to address the concerns of students who *do* care about it but also to gain faculty support and to emphasize your institution's prominence on an international scale. Faculty support, or at least the absence of faculty resistance, is crucial. Faculty members are vital to having courses equated, encouraging student participation, and developing new programs, among other things. By partnering with top-notch business schools around the world, your school shines by association.

Consider whether your overseas programs will serve undergraduate or graduate students. The University of Wisconsin–Madison's semester and year programs are geared toward undergraduate students, as demand is strong among that population. Few graduate students elect to spend a semester abroad due to a variety of reasons including financial constraints, family obligations, the short duration of the MBA program, and the desire to enter the work force quickly. Study tours, in which students earn three credits during a three-week period over winter break or just after spring semester, are much more popular than longer programs among graduate students. Although most students we send abroad for a semester are undergraduates, we do allow our overseas partners to send us graduate students in exchange.

When first establishing an international portfolio, distribute questionnaires in classes. Ask about preferred locations, language ability, cost expectations and likelihood of attending. When analyzing the data, know that what students say and what they do may often conflict. Even the student with the best intentions may encounter a roadblock or change of heart that prevents overseas study. Once you have established a portfolio, consider where students want to go (or are already going) when thinking of where to expand. To assess this, make note of the locations they request that your office does not currently have in its portfolio. Request data from other study abroad offices on campus and the admissions office about business students who are going abroad on programs other than those sponsored by your office.

FINDING GOOD PARTNERS

Partnering with appropriate and reliable partners is essential to the success of an international portfolio. Start by reviewing rankings in reputable publications, such as *The Financial Times*. Look to other international offices on your campus to determine if their partners abroad have business schools. Consult your faculty. Not only can faculty provide contacts at institutions abroad, but they can also provide advice as you establish and implement a program. Consider the overseas partners of your peer institutions in the U.S. Chances are your peers abroad are partners with your peers at home. Similarly, once you have established a number of agreements, assess with whom your current partners are partnering. Many of the University of Wisconsin–Madison's successful "expansion universities" appeared as a result of strong recommendations from our existing partners. Talk with your colleagues at these universities about the positive aspects of the overseas partner and what drawbacks they perceive. As you are establishing the agreement, consult with these colleagues as necessary.

One note of caution: Be wary of the faculty member who wishes to start exchanges based on a personal relationship at a university abroad. Such friendly offers from faculty can be awkward. While such offers may end up to be perfectly fine agreements, more than often they are not. Be sure to scrutinize the potential partner abroad as you would any other university. To avoid such partnerships, thank the faculty member for his or her interest and cite your office's strategic plan for developing new programs, which includes student demand, geographical and linguistic requirements, and other points listed in the "Assessing your needs" section of this chapter.

Once you have generated a list of potential partners, determine if they will fit well with your business school and the requirements you have for overseas partners. Assess print and on-line materials. Often a cursory screening can tell you that the partnership won't work, either because of incompatibility of curriculum, language of instruction, or the focus on graduate or undergraduate programs. If the relationship looks viable, contact the overseas university with specific questions, express an interest in partnering with them and conduct a site visit. As well, offer to host the potential partner at your campus.

Site visits are essential for getting a sense of the host university and for building relationships with colleagues abroad. Meet with faculty and staff. Tour facilities your students will use. Check out the city. The visit permits you to assess whether the school is a good fit for your students and your institution, and to present your university and its policies for incoming exchange students (which can be very different than those for international degree-seeking students). Having firsthand experience at the host university will help immensely when writing materials and advising both incoming and outgoing students. Ideally, the director of the international office (who will ultimately decide whether this university will become your partner or not) as well as the person managing the international office on a day-to-day basis (who advises students and acts as the contact to the host university) will both participate in the site visit. Not only are two perspectives better than one, but both play important roles in creating successful partnerships.

By visiting a campus, you will build relationships with staff and faculty abroad, the benefits of which will pay off tremendously when communicating across great distances, particularly when a problem occurs. Talking with faculty and administrators will give you a sense of the academic system and the commitment to internationalization. Now is the time to clarify access to classes, grading procedures, academic catalogs, pre-requisites, student selection and application to the host university. Talk with students from the host country and with other international exchange students to get their perspective on academics and social life.

Tour the university, including places your students will frequent: libraries, computer labs, classrooms, student organization area, social areas and the international office. Visit housing facilities. Sit in on classes, even if they are conducted in another language. By observing the students and the instructor, you will get a sense of the academic environment.

Assess student services provided by the international office and the campus at large. The ideal partner will provide airport reception upon your students' arrival, a buddy program through which they are linked with a student at the host university, orientation that thoroughly introduces academics and life in the host country, and events throughout the semester. Housing will be arranged. International office staff will be accessible throughout the workweek and will provide instructions on what to do in an after-hours emergency.

TAKING THE PLUNGE. WHAT TO DISCUSS BEFORE SIGNING AN AGREEMENT

A written agreement, which delineates the terms of the partnership, ensures that both parties are certain of expectations for both hosting and sending students. Some universities require that a written agreement be established before exchange of students begins, and many have a template. Contact your university's legal department when drafting the agreement. In addition to addressing the needs of your students, address the needs of incoming exchange students.

The agreement should address the following:

- *The length of the agreement.* Three years is reasonable, as this gives ample time for partners to become accustomed to one another's systems, but also means that the partnership can be terminated without great delay if something goes awry. In subsequent editions of the agreement, once both parties have gained confidence in the partnership, the length might be extended to five years or more.
- *Number of students to exchange.* Anticipate demand from your students and assess how many incoming students your institution can handle when establishing the number. Be conservative at the beginning, as you and your partner can increase the number of students in future years, despite what the agreement says. Specify the length of time that students can spend at each university, and whether you will account for them on a semester or academic year basis. For example, if you count students on a semester basis but will accept students for the academic year, the student who spends an academic year will count as two semester students. If balance is an issue for either institution, state that the number of students exchanged must be equal within a given time period. In addition to including

this provision in the agreement, every year you and your partner should confirm the number of students each institution will accept. Despite what was written in an agreement, one year our office had to temporarily stop accepting incoming students from one of our partners because of a gross imbalance. In another instance, the partnership worked so well that in the second year we doubled the number of students exchanged. Check your university's policies and procedures for balancing the number of students prior to drafting the agreement. For example, the university may allow you to sustain an imbalance on a yearly basis as long as it the program balances over a certain number of years. Or, the university may allow you to apply the surplus of one program to the deficit of another.

- *Level.* Delineate whether you will exchange undergraduate or graduate students or both.
- *Access.* This section explicitly states access and limitations to classes and services. Address prerequisites, enrollment limitations, course load and access to business and non-business classes. We recommend that students have the same privileges as degree-seeking students to the extent possible, in addition to services geared specifically to exchange students, such as an orientation program and access to international office staff. Special services for incoming international exchange students, separate from international degree-seeking students, are essential. Exchange students will need more guidance, as they attend the host university for a relatively short period of time.
- *Participant responsibilities.* State that students are subject to the rules and regulations of the host university, must comply with the instructions of their advisors, and are responsible for procuring their own passport and visa.
- *Language ability.* When courses are conducted in different languages at each university, language ability is an issue. When a universal test is not available for language assessment, agree to an alternate method, such as having a foreign language faculty member assess students' abilities. The Test of English as a Foreign Language (TOEFL) is an instrument available worldwide and is the easiest way to assess incoming students' English abilities. Clarify your institution's minimum TOEFL score.
- *Selection of participants.* The home university typically selects students based on their own criteria as well as minimum qualifications set by the host university, which should be stated in this section. Officially, the host university offers acceptance, and in some cases must deny students because the partner did not select students based on the host university's minimum eligibility requirements.
- *Tuition and fees.* If this is an exchange agreement, state that tuition and fees will be charged by the home university and not by the host university. If this is a study abroad or administrative partnership, tuition and fees will be paid to the host institution. Establish billing and payment procedures, including whether

the students will pay the host institution directly or whether the home university will collect fees from students and pass them along to the partner.

- *Housing, food and travel.* Students are typically responsible for their own non-academic concerns, although in some cases the host university will arrange or assist with arranging housing.
- *Medical costs.* Describe the health services available to students. Insurance is a hot topic, as students are legally required to prove coverage in many countries. Specify the insurance requirement and any procedures. In any case, students should be advised by the home and host universities to have insurance for routine and emergency care while abroad. Some home universities require students to show proof of insurance, while others require all students to purchase one university-sanctioned policy. Even if your university requires a specific policy, be certain to advise students to scrutinize it and buy supplemental insurance if their particular medical situation requires.
- *Exchange of information.* Agree that partners will update one another with new information as it becomes available. Also, specify when promotional materials, application forms and transcripts will be sent. Outline the application process and deadlines. Identify a contact person at each university.
- *Internships.* State whether students have access to career services at the host university. Regardless of whether or not your university assists with finding internships, include a clause in the agreement stating that internships are permissible. By including such verbiage, extending the student visa is much easier if in fact a student does obtain an internship.
- *Faculty mobility and exchange of educational materials.* Including a section on exploring short-term faculty exchanges and joint academic projects sets the stage for deepening the exchange in future years.
- *General terms and conditions.* Designate the officers of the exchange, outlines policies for approval, review and termination of the project, and state any limitations of the resources committed, and set the duration of the agreement. The agreement should be signed and dated by responsible officers of each institution.

IMPLEMENTING THE AGREEMENT

Once the agreement has been signed, the next step is implementation. Select well informed, qualified students to send to your partner. Create efficient and informative systems for incoming students. From this point, maintenance defines the relationship between you and your partner.

Doing an excellent job in recruitment, selection, and predeparture preparation of your students going abroad benefits not only your students and your office, but also the partner university. Your overseas colleagues will greatly appreciate hosting students who have a clear understanding of life abroad and of the host university in particular. While recruiting, give students as much information as you can, and be accurate; students should have information that allows them to select a program befitting their particular needs and that starts preparing them for life overseas from the moment they start researching their program. Program summaries, cost estimates, and lists of classes for which students will receive credit, as well as the host university's catalogs and materials should be available in hard copy in your office's resource area and posted to the web. Information meetings provide a forum for you to explain policies and sell particular programs. Individual advising allows students to discuss specific concerns. Past participants are among the most valuable resources you have; they quickly become the experts on the program after having lived it. Their enthusiasm speaks volumes to future participants. Collect evaluations and reports from participants at the end of the study abroad program; in addition to asking evaluative questions, get factual information. Incorporate responses into program-specific handbooks. Ask students' permission to distribute their names and email addresses so that future participants may talk with them. Ask past participants and international exchange students to lead program-specific breakout sessions following the general information meeting. If your office employs student help, consider hiring past participants. Use a variety of tools to recruit students to international programs.

A discussion on costs is merited, as this is a primary concern for many students. Be accurate with cost estimates, and include this information in recruiting. Although some offices charge an all-inclusive fee, the School of Business at the University of Wisconsin–Madison does not. Tuition is charged by the university for exchange programs or by the provider for study abroad programs. We also include estimates for housing, meals, local transportation, fees charged by the host university, visa processing fee, International Student ID card, and international airfare, if they are not included in fees charged by the study abroad or administrative provider. We do not include estimates for passport, as many students already have one, or for entertainment or vacation travel, as these costs vary widely among individuals. We also list the $250 administrative fee charged by our office on the cost estimate sheet. Indicate if any of the costs are based on local currency and if so, indicate the rate used in calculating the cost to U.S. dollars.

In addition to including the total cost for a particular program, we have found it instructive to include a chart comparing the cost per month (excluding tuition) of each program on the cost estimate sheet. To establish a baseline comparison, we also include the cost per month of the home university. Programs can vary in length by several months, and the cost per month may be much less on a longer program even though the total cost is the same as a shorter program. Excluding home university tuition from an all-inclusive study abroad fee demonstrates that study abroad programs are often extremely expensive for students paying in-state tuition but a good deal for students accustomed to paying out-of-state tuition.

Scholarships are awarded to alleviate some of the additional expenses associated with overseas study. The University of Wisconsin–Madison School of Business' scholarship model awards two types of scholarships: Incentive scholarships and need-based scholarships. Because maintaining a steady number of students on exchange programs is essential to sustaining our partnerships with overseas universities, we grant $500 to any business major who participates in an exchange. We also realize that for some students, $500 is not enough to make overseas study affordable. As a result, we work with our student financial services office to identify students who demonstrate financial need. We then award up to $2,000 based on the individual's amount of need. By providing both types of scholarships, we are able to fill our exchange programs and assist students who might not otherwise afford overseas study.

In addition to providing financial incentives and clearly describing costs, explaining application requirements and procedures should be part of recruitment. Establish minimum requirements, create an application form, and set deadlines. In establishing minimum requirements, consider setting a minimum grade point average, number of credits earned, and whether you will accept non-business majors as well as business majors. Incorporate the host university's requirements in your selection process. The minimum requirements set by your office may actually be more strict than those of the host institution. Partner with foreign language departments to assess students' language abilities for programs that require fluency. If a program will accept an unlimited number of your students, you can adopt minimum requirements and admit all students who meet those requirements. For programs with a limited number of spaces, determine how you will select students. Our office reviews applications, admitting students with the highest grade point averages and shows a commitment to the host country's culture by previous coursework. If we are unsure of who to admit at that point, we interview the applicants in question. We aim to select mature students who are committed to living and studying abroad, will represent our university well and will benefit from the exchange. Especially at the beginning of a partnership, it is critical to send top quality students, both for the impression they will make on the host university, and what they can contribute back to your university while abroad and upon their return.

The University of Wisconsin–Madison's application form both explains the selection process and collects data. In addition to the application form, we require students to submit a transcript and the university-wide waiver for participation in overseas programs, the $250 program fee and (for unlimited-space programs) the host university's application forms. We use the transcript to verify students'

GPA, major, number of credits earned, and prior courses. The program fee is refunded if students are denied. The application form outlines the program fee refund policy, and we require applicants to sign a statement saying they understand and agree to it. We also require students to sign a statement committing them to our mandatory pre-departure class and orientation program. On the application, we tell students that their names and email addresses will be made available to their peers on the program and to future participants unless they indicate that this information be withheld. We collect demographic information on the applicants to ensure we have it for our university's data collection and for the national Open Doors report, coordinated by the Institute for International Education. We ask for emergency contact information, and we allow students to indicate whether they want information about the program mailed to this person (usually a parent). Although many of this information could be collected later, we try to create an efficient system that requires students to submit information to us only a limited number of times. Students appreciate this parsimony and it makes our office run more smoothly.

Due to the volume of applicants and to the limited numbers of students we can accept into exchange programs, the main application period for our fall and spring semester programs is early spring semester of the previous academic year. If space remains for spring programs, we re-open the application process in early fall semester. Each application period opens with an information meeting and closes with the application deadline of the second Thursday in March or October, respectively. By collecting all applications in March, all applicants for limited-space programs are considered equally regardless of whether they prefer to go overseas in fall or spring. Logistical benefits arise from this arrangement also. Spring participants are guaranteed their acceptance nearly a year in advance and thus can arrange fall-only housing, plan fall classes based on the fact that they will go abroad in spring, obtain a passport in a timely manner, and begin researching their host country. The international office has ample time to work with these students prior to their departure. However, early in fall semester the international office should review academic progress of these students to ensure they have not hit an academic or personal crisis that would preclude them from going abroad. We send admissions decisions to students via email.

After admitting students, our focus is on preparing them to go abroad. We distribute an acceptance packet to each student, which includes both a general and site-specific handbook, a pre-departure checklist, the U.S. State Department's consular information sheet, a course selection worksheet to aid in discussions with their academic advisor, reports from past participants and acceptance and medical assessment forms that must be returned to our office. A copy of the acceptance packet, along with a letter introducing the international office's role in the student's overseas experience, is mailed to parents if the student requested this on the application form. As information and applications from the host university are available, we send them to our students and return completed applications to the host university. The semester prior to going abroad, we require students to participate in a pre-departure course called International Perspectives. International Perspectives has three goals: First, to provide students with general background on international business and current events; second, to provide students with knowledge specific to their host country; finally, to give students the tools necessary to adapt to a culture different from their own. To achieve these goals, we require students to complete independent work, including weekly summaries of news articles about their host country, a series of worksheets about different aspects of the host university, and a final report. Class sessions, covering culture shock, guest lectures that address different regions of the world, and a traditional orientation program are also components of International Perspectives. Outgoing students talk with past participants and exchange students from the host university throughout the course, either to get information for homework or as part of the orientation program. In addition to structured programs, the international office should provide assistance via email and individual advising prior to a student's departure.

E-mail is the primary mode of communication once students are abroad. Send an e-mail within a few days of students' arrival reminding them of your office's most important policies and encouraging them to contact you if they have questions. Throughout the semester, forward updates from your university, assist with registration for the following semester, and reply promptly to students' questions. At the end of the term, ask students to evaluate the program either via an on-line evaluation form or a report about their experiences. Use feedback to make changes to your office's systems if necessary and tactfully provide feedback to the host university if you think it will be useful. Keep reports and evaluations available in your resource room or on your web site for other students' use.

In addition to serving outbound students well, it is essential to have systems in place that address the needs of incoming students. Provide accurate pre-departure information, a clear application process, access to courses, a buddy program, orientation programs, events and assistance throughout the semester, and an evaluation through which students can provide feedback. Word travels fast; the degree to which exchange students are satisfied with your university will impact the number of students attending in future years; the more students you host, the more students your partner university will accept from you.

Fostering strong relationships with the central and other international offices on campus is a crucial part of internationalizing the School of Business and has clear benefits to both outgoing and incoming students. At our campus, exchange coordinators from across campus meet monthly. Incoming students benefit from our cooperation to create pre-departure materials, orientation programs, and social programs throughout the semester. For outgoing students, sharing information about common partners makes equating courses, advising students, and creating handbooks much easier and more accurate. The University of Wisconsin–Madison's business students in Chile benefit from the fact that we partner with the same university in Santiago that our College of Letters and Sciences does. Our publicity and site-specific information is based on their office's materials. Many courses had already been equated. As well, Letters and Sciences had already set up an on-site orientation program and contracted a housing coordinator for their students, which our students are able to pay for and participate in as well.

Another cooperative measure is linking students with one another. Establish a buddy program, which pairs students from your university with incoming exchange students. Host an international reception at the beginning of each semester and invite newly arrived incoming students, students from your university who have studied overseas in the past, representatives of internationally focused student organizations, students already selected to go abroad, and those with an interest in international programs. Continue linking students via recruiting and orientation meetings as well as social events throughout the semester, such as an international potluck dinner.

WHEN THINGS GO BAD

Despite the best-laid plans, not every partnership will function as you hope. The key is to recognize this in advance. Determine if your students will adapt well to the academic system and want to attend the university, and if you are comfortable endorsing the program. Unfortunately, you may not find out that a program is one you wish you would have avoided until after the partnership has begun. You may need to make adjustments or even end the partnership.

Be creative. Our office inherited an exchange agreement with a university in Beijing, and we quickly realized that most of our students would not have the language skills to live in Beijing for a semester. As such, we made special arrangements with our Chinese partner university for them to host a two-week program in English, complete with lectures, company visits, and cultural attractions for 25 of our students in exchange for four Chinese scholars to do research at our university for four months.

Another adjustment we have made was in response to lack of academic rigor. Students on our London program reported that certain classes are extremely easy. Clearly, we do not want to lower our academic standards in the process of sending students abroad. On a recent site visit, we learned that the overseas instructors were frustrated at having our third-year students in the classes, which are intended for their second-year students. Therefore, the partner university and our university agreed that these courses would no longer be available to our students.

Unfortunately, not all relationships can be fixed. Our office has terminated two agreements (both inherited from a previous administration of our office). One partnership ended because the overseas international office left students to fend for themselves in a very difficult culture for our students to navigate. A number of reasons contributed to the demise of the second agreement: The overseas partner offered only economics courses, which were not always relevant to our business students, an academic calendar that did not fit well with ours, and an atypical agreement that permitted overseas students to receive an MBA at our university, which was not supported by our MBA program.

CONCLUSION

A portfolio of strong and active exchange partnerships is an excellent way of complementing the international business curriculum of a School, and to enrich the educational experiences of students in a cost-effective manner. Properly nurtured, it can serve as a foundation for other forms of collaboration, and also serve as a useful network for the exchange of ideas and the mutual improvement of practices.

STUDY ABROAD CONSORTIA: COLLABORATIVE VENTURES AMONG SCHOOLS

Sally Innis-Klitz and Janice E. Clark

INTRODUCTION

During the past decade there has been a growing consensus that study abroad experiences are valuable not only for students majoring in the language of the country in which they intend to study, but that they also provide vital experiences for students enrolled in business programs. This is a change from the early 1980s when it was rare to find a business program offering study abroad experiences for its students. The increasingly global nature of commerce and the need for business professionals to effectively interact with people in a work force growing more diverse are strong arguments for students to study abroad. In addition to exposing students to different cultures and peoples, the study abroad experience challenges students to function in unknown environments and situations, teaches students about themselves, and forces them to look critically at their own resources and values. It is the ultimate "Problem-Based Learning" experience (PBL).

On many campuses, study abroad programs were traditionally run through language departments. The programs usually required students to have a proficiency in the language of the country in which they planned to study prior to going abroad and the curriculum focused on disciplines related to the arts, social sciences, and humanities. While some limited programs existed earlier, it wasn't until the early to mid-1980s that business programs began to develop and promote

Study Abroad: Perspectives and Experiences from Business Schools
Advances in International Marketing, Volume 13, 209–226.
© 2003 Published by Elsevier Science Ltd.
ISSN: 1474-7979/PII: S1474797902130134

study abroad programs specifically designed for their students. These programs differed from traditional study abroad programs in two key areas; the curriculum included business courses and the courses were often taught in English, regardless of the language of the host country.

The success of study abroad programs for business students since the concept took hold almost twenty years ago has been mixed. While the number of programs has grown, the percentage of students studying abroad is less than the goals set by government offices and national educational organizations. Rapid growth in the globalization of business, fueled in large part by the even more rapid growth in technology, has propelled the need for people entering business today to have a perspective beyond their own national boundaries. Recognition of the need for international education has reached the highest levels of government. In 1998, amendments were made to the Higher Education Act of 1965 that included direct reference to, and support for, Undergraduate International Studies. In recent years, various U.S. government officials have emphasized the value of international education, going so far in some pronouncements as to state that it directly contributes to national security.

It is neither plausible nor necessary for colleges and universities to offer study abroad programs in every country. What is possible, however, is for colleges and universities to work together through consortia agreements to expand the number of quality study abroad experiences available to their students. This paper will review some of the background related to the increased national visibility of and support for study abroad programs for students in all disciplines and will address, from the perspective the University of Connecticut, various consortia models and aspects of implementation.

RECENT DEVELOPMENTS IN NATIONAL SUPPORT FOR STUDY ABROAD PROGRAMS

1998: Amendments to the Higher Education Act of 1965

The 1998 Amendments to the Higher Education Act of 1965 included Section 604, which dealt directly with Undergraduate International Studies. Within Section 604 are statements that encourage the formation of study abroad program linkages among the private, government and academic sectors. While this act relates specifically to government action and funding, the items and philosophy embodied in the Amendment lend strong support to those striving to increase the Study Abroad options on their campuses. To illustrate the tenor of the Act, selected edited sections follow:

SECTION 604. UNDERGRADUATE INTERNATIONAL STUDIES AND FOREIGN LANGUAGE PROGRAMS.

(1) AUTHORITY – The Secretary is authorized to make grants to institutions of higher education, combinations of such institutions, or partnerships between non-profit educational organizations and institutions of higher education, to assist such institutions, combinations or partnerships in planning, developing, and carrying out programs to improve undergraduate instruction in international studies and foreign languages.

(2) USE OF FUNDS – Grants may be used for projects and activities such as –

   (A) planning for the development and expansion of undergraduate programs in international studies and foreign languages; . . .

   (E) programs designed to develop or enhance linkages between 2- and 4-year institutions of higher education, or baccalaureate and post-baccalaureate programs or institutions; . . .

   (F) the development of undergraduate educational programs in locations abroad where such opportunities are not otherwise available or that serve students for whom such opportunities are not otherwise available . . .

   (G) the integration of new and continuing education abroad opportunities for undergraduate students into curricula of specific degree programs;[1]

2000–2001: Statements of Support at the Federal Level

On April 19, 2000, President William Clinton issued an Executive Memorandum on International Education stating, "It is the policy of the federal government to support international education." Among the commitments stated in the Memorandum which was designed to promote and facilitate international education is the commitment to "promoting study abroad by U.S. students."[2]

President George W. Bush's transition team received a White Paper, *Toward An International Education Policy for the United States,* from the Alliance for International and Cultural Exchange and NAFSA: Association of International Educators (NAFSA), which maps out a strategy for making international education integral to higher education. One of the goals outlined in the paper is to increase the number of U.S. students studying abroad. While the number of American students going on study abroad has reached record numbers, 100,000[3] in 1997–1998 rising to 129,770 in 1998–1999 academic year, these students represent less than 1% of the approximate 15 million undergraduates in the U.S.[4] This percentage increases to 3.4% if one were to use a base figure of one quarter of the total undergraduate population which is a more realistic pool. The objective as stated in the paper is "that 20% of American students receiving college degrees will have studied abroad for credit by 2010, and 50% by 2040". The report also cites as an objective the increase of study abroad programs to nontraditional locations outside the United Kingdom and Western Europe.

Congress is also voicing its support for international education. Senators John Kerry (D-MA) and Richard G. Lugar (R-IN) introduced a concurrent resolution in the U.S. Senate on February 1, 2001, calling for the United States to establish an international education policy. One of the outcomes of the policy should be to "significantly increase the number of U.S. students participating in study abroad."[5]

The increased support and recognition for international education is clearly a step in the right direction. However, the increased recognition for study abroad programs creates a mixed set of opportunities and challenges in institutions where resources and support may not be keeping pace with the expanded role for international education envisioned in the initiatives cited above. How do those involved with offering study abroad programs address the following goals and issues:

- More students are studying abroad but the numbers are still not close to the goal articulated by NAFSA of 20% by 2010 and 50% by 2040.
- Students are looking for more options in location and types of programs, but the majority of programs are still focused on traditional locations. The ten top countries in which U.S. students studied in the 1999–2000 academic year were, in descending order, the United Kingdom, Spain, Italy, France, Mexico, Australia, Germany, Costa Rica, Israel, and Ireland.[6] How do institutions offer a sufficient variety of locations, including an increased number of non-traditional locations, and encourage students to consider these additional locations?
- It is necessary to match the growth in student participation with a growth in the number of staff with the expertise to administer, develop, promote, monitor, and assess programs. Increased support is essential for international education to gain recognition and credibility on campuses. If the increase in support in terms of both resources and policy does not materialize, how can a study abroad unit maximize its programming and offerings?

CONSORTIA – A WAY TO EXPAND OPTIONS

One way for an institution to broaden the number of options available to its students is to join consortia or co-sponsor study abroad programs so that the administration for these programs is shared or fully handled by another institution. This allows schools to have a measure of control over a study abroad program without having the responsibility of the totality of the administrative duties. The extended offerings available through consortia also have the potential benefits of:

- Allowing institutions to offer programs in non-traditional locations where they otherwise would not have enough student interest to maintain a partnership.
- Encouraging more students to study abroad because they are more likely to find a program to meet their objectives and interests.
- Assigning academic credibility to a program by partnering with institutions that are respected by your institution.

NAFSA recognizes consortia as a viable way to "encourage study abroad or broaden options" for students and gives guidance on the implementation of consortia in its "Principles for U.S. Study Abroad" by the following statement:

> *Co-sponsoring Study Abroad Programs Administered by Other Institutions:* In order to encourage study abroad or broaden the options readily available to its students, a number of institutions have elected to join consortia or co-sponsor study abroad programs in which another institution handles program administration. A consortium or co-sponsorship arrangement for study abroad should provide opportunities that are consistent with the institution's overall academic objectives, requirements, and standards; the program should be administered in accordance with the principles for study abroad program administration; . . . and the home campus role in the co-sponsorship should be evaluated periodically by faculty, staff, and students to determine if the objectives are being met.[7]

Consortia Models

There are multiple models for consortia depending on the academic and administrative goals of an institution. While every consortium is different, varying in size, goals, and profile of members, there are three typical models of administration:

(1) *Model 1* – Professional Administration: consortium administration is handled by a professional unit outside of an academic institution which acts under the guidance of the consortium members.
(2) *Model 2* – Point Institution: one of the consortium member institutions is primarily responsible for program administration and student enrollment.
(3) *Model 3* – Shared Administration: one consortium member institution takes a larger role in some aspects of administration but all consortium members

enroll their own students and are actively involved in program development and assessment.

Students are unaware of the management differences between these models and, as the costs are similar in the three models, their program selection is not influenced by the type of consortial arrangement. Students are most interested in courses, credits and destination.

The University of Connecticut has long been a proponent of study abroad programs for business students. One of the University's longest-running study abroad programs designed specifically for business students is a Model 3 consortium. The following will briefly describe UConn's experiences with Model 1 and Model 2 type consortia. The focus, however, will be on the third model, where UConn's experience might be most beneficial to those institutions wishing to develop consortial relationships.

Model 1 – Professional Administration

There are several professional organizations outside of academic institutions that administer study abroad programs, but perhaps the most widely recognized is CIEE: Council on International Educational Exchange. For over 50 years, CIEE has been involved with students and international activities. CIEE is comprised of almost 800 professionals and support staff working in more than 30 countries that administer programs that annually serve approximately one million students and one thousand educational institutions.[8]

Educational institutions may become members of the Council by application, paying a membership fee, and committing to the Academic Consortium Membership Agreement. All member colleges and universities who sponsor study abroad programs managed by the Council's Division of International Study Programs are members of the Academic Consortium. It is this Academic Consortium that determines the accreditation of Council Programs. The Academic Consortium meets annually to evaluate academic quality and discuss academic issues.

The Academic Consortium Board (ACB) is the governing body of the Consortium and is comprised of members elected from the Consortium member institutions. Those eligible for election include the official representatives from the member institutions, and faculty members or administrators who have the approval of the institution's official representative. This Board is charged with quality assessment and direction for the Council study abroad programs.

Each Consortium member institution is asked to designate people to serve in several capacities related to the Consortium. In some institutions the same person may hold several responsibilities. The official representative to the Consortium has the key responsibility of voting on Consortium issues and is usually the person who signs the Consortium agreement. This individual is assumed to be the correct contact for all purposes unless other representatives are named.

An administrative contact must be selected by the member institution. This person is responsible for the processing of applications and, in many cases, is the study abroad advisor. Also critical are the campus contacts for billing and grades. The billing contact is responsible for receiving invoices for participant fees and for Consortium dues. The grades contact receives grades for each participant from their institution once the program is finished and is responsible for seeing that the courses and grades are properly recorded on the official school record. If the study abroad administration is centralized, it is usually the Study Abroad Office that assumes responsibility for all of the above.

Model 2 – Point Institution

Institutions of higher education need not rely on a professional organizational structure to create and administer a study abroad consortium. Often a consortium is created because a school has a Study Abroad program in place and would like to expand the number of students participating in that program by inviting students from other institutions to participate. The question becomes how much of the administrative activity remains centralized with the originating institution. In this model, one school largely controls the administrative functions. Each consortium member advertises the program and processes the conversion of courses and grades to their institution's transcript, but one key distinction between this model and Model 3 is that students usually enroll and register through the point institution rather than through the home institution. This arrangement does not, however, preclude the option of the home institution maintaining registration of its students in order to process financial aid.

The Consortium of Universities for International Business Studies in Paderno, Italy, is this type of consortium (http://www.bschool.ukans.edu/Programs/ItalyProgram/). Twenty-nine schools are members of the consortium with the rights to have input into the program details, such as academic offerings and student life issues as well as priority enrollment should the program reach capacity. Students, however, send all applications to the point institution, the University of Kansas, and are enrolled as University of Kansas students upon program admission. Faculty to teach in Paderno are recruited from among the consortium members.

One advantage of Models 1 and 2 is the ease of sending students to a wide variety of destinations that do not require any program management on the part of the member institutions.

Model 3 – Shared Administration

In this model, schools enter into an agreement where the governance of the program is more equally distributed throughout the consortium members. The members in this type of consortium maintain a high level of autonomy. While there is a lead school with general responsibilities for administering the program under the agreed upon policies, each consortium school is responsible for enrolling its own students. The ability to maintain enrollment for students at their home institution is one of the most positive aspects of consortium membership. By maintaining continuous enrollment at their home institution, students are usually eligible for their full financial aid packages and, in public institutions, their in-state/out-of-state standings may not be impacted. The students apply directly to their own school and admission decisions are made at the home institution with the names, applications, and payments of those accepted are forwarded to the lead school.

Member institutions have two other key responsibilities: to recruit students and to see that students' courses and grades are properly recorded. Because one lead school usually handles the major administrative, financial, and logistical details, the consortium member schools must agree to some type of management fee-either an overall membership fee or a per capita fee included in the student program cost. For example, for the two consortia programs that it manages, the University of Connecticut includes a $200 per student management fee in the individual student program charges.

It is the responsibility of the lead school to be the primary contact with the international host institution. The lead school must set up all the arrangements with the host school including drawing up the contracts and ensuring that the expectations of both sides are clearly articulated.

Getting Started: The "Why's" and "How To's" of a Model 3 Consortium

Consortia, like study abroad programs themselves, usually have their origin with an individual, department, or administrator of one university or college. Once an idea is formed and the rough outline of the curriculum and the budget are developed, it is often apparent that one university or college may not be able to generate enough students on its own to operate a cost-effective program abroad. The idea of organizing a consortium becomes attractive.

Benefits of Forming a Model 3 Consortium
• *Cost of offering the program.* Obviously, it's easier for five universities to work together to produce the critical mass needed to offer a cost effective program

than it is for an institution to do it alone. Cost effective study abroad programs make it possible for a wider variety of students to participate. Also, the creation of a consortium program among public universities and colleges in a region would eliminate the need for students to pay out-of-state tuition to the program organizer.

- *Resident director.* If the program requires the presence of an on-site resident director who often also teaches a course, it is less of a burden to the home universities if the directors are assigned on a rotational basis. This is especially important in at this time as many institutions are experiencing cutbacks in resources.
- *Regional cooperation.* Instead of competing with programs offered by schools in the same geographic area, consortium agreements would encourage more efficient use of higher education resources and would help to eliminate duplication of effort within the region.
- *Developing a regional network.* Consortium programs provide faculty with the means to meet and work with colleagues from other institutions. Through the Consortium, students are also provided with a way to develop their own associations and network among the partner schools.
- *Sharing information.* The existence of a consortium for one program abroad will often lead to the sharing of information about other study abroad opportunities which may be available to students of consortium members.

Picking your partners. A Consortium designed to offer extended Study Abroad opportunities for students need not be large. Consortium organizers generally would agree that universities/colleges with similar profiles create the most effective partnerships. It is key that the institutions agree on criteria and goals for the program. Also critical is the need for one school to have the interest and ability to coordinate and administer the program. When identifying potential compatible partners, you may wish to consider:

(1) *Institutions that have a perceived need for the program you are proposing, and an interest in establishing a study abroad program in the targeted country.* Before inviting institutions to join the consortium, find out what programs they already operate themselves or offer through other consortia or organizations. The Internet, Peterson's Guide for Study Abroad and faculty networks can be a good source for this information. Find out as much information as possible about your potential partners.
(2) *Institutions located in the same geographical location in the U.S.* Consortia organized on a regional basis make it easier for members to get together. Once a year, members should meet to evaluate the program, fine tune the curriculum

(if necessary); establish a rotation of resident directors with each partner; examine and adjust the budget; etc. Regions may have umbrella academic organizations that host meetings or support a regional consortium in other ways.

(3) *Institutions with similar curricula at their home campuses.* Identify a university or college with similar programs at home, i.e. a major in Italian if you are trying to organize a consortium for Italian Studies in Italy.

(4) *Institutions with similar program goals and institutional level of commitment.* Use faculty networks to determine if sponsoring departments would have the same overall goals for their faculty and students. This impacts the overseas curriculum as well as the commitment each partner university or college is willing and able to make to provide staff and/or faculty as campus coordinators or overseas resident directors.

(5) *Whether the institution is private or public.* Ascertain potential partners' fee policies for study abroad programs. While it may be philosophically appealing to send a diversified student group abroad, fee structures at private universities and colleges may create an awkward situation when their students realize that participants from the public institutions are paying half of what they've been charged for the same program. Many private institutions charge students going abroad the normal home fees, while public universities and colleges frequently charge actual costs of sending the student abroad.

(6) *Institutions with similar institutional ranking, accreditation, student profile.* The consortium organizers might select partners based on the academic compatibility of the participants. For example, an AASCB-accredited business school may feel that it's important for all members of the consortium to be AACSB accredited, assuring a certain consistency of curricular needs and student criteria.

(7) *The organization of study abroad administration at each institution.* While study abroad administration should not be the deciding factor in the selection of partners, it is essential to know how each consortium member handles its administrative and logistical tasks, such as:
- Recruiting;
- enrolling students;
- billing students;
- paying the institution that is responsible for organizing the program;
- handling credits;
- appointing resident directors on a rotating basis;
- interacting with their financial aid office.

Ideally, students enrolling in a consortium program abroad should remain fully integrated at their home university/college, giving them access to all of the institutional support they would normally receive on the home campus. Also, the lead partner needs to know how and when it will receive the program fees from the other consortium partners.

CONSIDERATIONS FOR THE LEAD PARTNER (PROGRAM ORGANIZER)

We can't stress strongly enough the importance of establishing good relationships with the academic department(s) that sponsor the overseas programs, and with the offices on the home campus that provide the administrative, student, and financial support that make it possible to send students abroad. These may include, but are not limited to:

- Faculty, deans, and department heads on campus who provide the overseas programs with
  - their academic credibility. (This is extremely critical. Programs cannot flourish without the backing of the sponsoring academic unit.)
- Academic advisory services.
- Bursar or Billing Office.
- Registrar for registration of participants, posting of grade reports from abroad, and re-entry.
- Financial Aid Office.
- Budget and Accounting Offices.

Additionally, good working relations with the consortium representatives in the U.S. and with host institutions abroad are key to the success of the endeavor. Without the cooperation of all of the above, it would be difficult to manage programs abroad. Finally, there are certain background principles to keep in mind when setting up a study abroad program, whether the program is a consortium or an individual venture. They are articulated well by NAFSA in its *Principles for U.S. Study Abroad*.

SAMPLE MODEL 3: CONSORTIUM FOR BUSINESS STUDENTS ABROAD/THE NEW ENGLAND CONSORTIUM

The Consortium for Business Students Abroad is an example of a small, regional consortium that has worked to the advantage of all the schools that participate. The

Consortium for Business Students Abroad (CBSA) is comprised of the University of Connecticut (UConn), the University of Maine, the University of New Hampshire (UNH), the University of Rhode Island (URI), and the University of Vermont. Representatives from both the business schools and study abroad offices of these schools met in 1984 and determined that they wanted to offer a study abroad experience for business students. Collaboration among these schools formed a logical partnership. The schools are all the flagship public institution in their state and their business programs are accredited by AACSB International – the Association to Advance Collegiate Schools of Business. Three of the schools, UConn, UNH, and URI had prior experience working together as consortium partners in another, more traditional Spanish language program in Granada, Spain. A copy of the Consortium Agreement for Grenoble and a sample budget for Grenada are included in the appendix.

While the demand for business programs at these schools was at capacity, the schools did not individually have enrollments large enough to sponsor a study abroad program that could provide a critical mass of students. By uniting, the schools could provide enough students to be able to attract potential partnerships with institutions abroad.

After much discussion, research, and review the Consortium chose the University of Grenoble, France, as the partner school. Key considerations in making the location decision were: the reputation of the University of Grenoble; a willingness on the part of the University of Grenoble to accept students and devote resources to ensuring a quality experience; a willingness to offer experiential opportunities such as study tours; quality of student living issues; and an interest in that particular region by Consortium faculty members.

At the time of its inception, the CBSA program required a resident director as part of the Grenoble program agreement. The necessity for a resident director varies with the desires and commitments of the schools involved. The resident director is usually a faculty member from one of the consortium schools who spends the semester (or year, depending on the program) on site with the students. The resident director usually teaches a course, supervises any educational site visits or tours, and is available to "trouble-shoot" academic or personal concerns. While the concept of a resident director is generally positive, it is also expensive. The director's salary and housing may be built into the budget and passed on to the students, or the academic department may continue to pay the salary. The latter is becoming increasingly difficult for departments due to budget cuts and faculty shortages. Even by rotating the responsibility for sending a resident director among the consortium members, the expense is such that it may be prohibitive. In the case of the Grenoble program, changes in the site of the program and the level of commitment and cooperation from the new site, ESC Grenoble, have resulted in the feeling that a resident director is no longer necessary to meet the students' needs or to oversee the interests of the consortium. This is most unfortunate as it virtually guarantees a certain indifference on the part of our faculty as they are deprived of the chance for a first-hand on-site experience with its inevitable resulting "conversion" to the benefits of study abroad.

Details of the Consortium Organization

The University of Connecticut's Study Abroad Office was asked to finalize the organizational details of the program and was designated as the program manager on behalf of the Consortium. It wrote a master Consortium agreement which required the signatures of the partner universities' academic officers. It also developed a program budget, course descriptions, and other program materials. The first group of students set off for Grenoble in January of 1985.

1. Financial Arrangements
There is no cost to the partner universities for membership in the Consortium, but the Grenoble semester program budget includes a $200 per participant management fee that is passed along directly to the student. The University of Connecticut's Study Abroad Office is responsible for determining the overall budget and sharing it with other consortium members. Air transportation and other local travel arrangements are also negotiated and included in the budget. Each consortium school collects money from its students and forwards it to the University of Connecticut. Finally, it is important to stress once again that one of the benefits of being a consortium member is that the students are enrolled through their home school so any student financial packages continue uninterrupted.

2. Host Contact
It is the responsibility of the University of Connecticut Study Abroad Office to negotiate all contracts and arrangements with the host institution, dispense payments to the host institution, and to monitor activities throughout the term of the program. This includes fiscal, academic, and student life issues. Faculty teaching in the programs and course content need to be reviewed by all Consortium representatives each semester and it is up to the lead institution to see that the host institution supplies relevant information so that proper assessments may be made.

Here is another point where the value of being a consortium comes into play. Should changes need to be made, the voice of a consortium of schools, rather than an individual school, has a greater impact. With the proper choice of a host program and the consortium's willingness to maintain good relations with the host institution, the consortium members can exercise a good deal of influence over the program design and quality.

3. Grades and Grade Distribution

Perhaps grades and grading policies are among the most sensitive issues in higher education. The University of Connecticut's Study Abroad Office is responsible for receiving all the grades from the host institution and then distributing them to consortium members. The consortium framework allows each consortium school to process the courses and grades in the manner approved for their institution. In some instances, courses are processed as transfer work and, while a minimum grade must be achieved to earn credit, no letter grade is attached to the course. At the University of Connecticut, the courses are assigned an actual course equivalent number, the earned grade is posted and calculated into the grade point average, and the course may count toward graduation requirements. There are several advantages to this latter method of processing:

(1) it clearly complies with the federal guidelines that must be met for students to maintain financial aid;
(2) students take the courses more seriously when they know the grades will impact their GPA;
(3) faculty can better assess the academic level of the program by seeing the posted grades listed on the transcript with the student's other grades.

An established consortium program has several advantages for faculty concerned about quality. The faculty have decision-making power over the program and the courses that make up the consortium offerings, as well as input into the instruction of the courses. The advantage to the students is that they know prior to going abroad that their courses will be accepted by their home institution and exactly how their courses and grades will be posted on their transcripts.

4. "Nurturing" of Participants

As the lead school, the University of Connecticut is responsible for creating an environment that encourages student participation. This includes a range of activities from the designing of the recruitment brochure to the designing and processing of the evaluation instrument students complete upon their return. While each Consortium member school promotes the program on its campus and makes the admission decisions for its students, all informational packets regarding travel, VISAs and passports, the nature of living abroad, international student ID's, and personal travel pointers, are furnished by the University of Connecticut. The member campus coordinators are responsible for organizing an orientation session for program participants before they leave campus, and for providing their students abroad with updated information throughout the semester on issues such registration and return travel arrangements.

5. Resident Director

Depending on the program, it is sometimes beneficial to have a faculty member, known as a Resident Director, go with the students on the study abroad program to direct the program on-site. This can be particularly helpful during the initial semesters of the program, especially if there is not an office at the host institution dedicated to assisting international students. Consortia at the University of Connecticut have worked both with and without Resident Directors. The Grenoble program had a Resident Director for approximately 10 years until the host school instituted a very helpful and competent liaison office and expanded its course offerings so that an additional instructor was not needed. A Resident Director still accompanies the students of the New England Consortium program in Granada. The responsibility for providing the Resident Director rotates among the consortium schools, thereby not burdening one school with the absence of a faculty member every year. As lead school, the University of Connecticut is responsible for presenting orientation workshops for the Resident Directors and for monitoring the expenditures of the Resident Director – which is especially important in a public institution where state regulations and budgeting restrictions are carefully scrutinized.

The main advantages of providing faculty with the opportunity of spending a semester or year abroad are:

(1) a first-hand look at the overseas academic program;
(2) the kindling of a vested interest in promoting the program at home; and
(3) faculty are usually impacted by the same life-altering revelations that our students experience.

6. Other Issues

Anytime you are working with several independent units, you need to be prepared for differing perspectives. Each consortium member may be working under a different policy structure and a different academic calendar. Coordination of issues (such as fee payments) needs to be carefully structured to recognize the autonomy of each consortium partner while still being mindful of the overall consortium needs. We believe that an annual meeting of all the Consortium campus representatives is critical for the success of the joint effort. In addition to the essential continuing assessment of the academic program, the annual meeting provides the Consortium members with the opportunity to work together as a group for a single purpose. Ideas and concerns are shared. Over the years our working relationships have become friendships that greatly contribute to the success of this Consortium.

Faculty at each institution must be kept appraised of the procedures in place for quality control and feel that they have input to that process. Understandably, faculty take their role as arbitrators of academic quality very seriously and nothing will do more damage to a program than the perception that it fails to meet the academic standards of the home institution. Students, on the other hand, may find that they are unprepared for the educational style they find abroad. Often there is far more reliance on independent study, fewer tests and quizzes, and more self-directed work. Many education systems abroad rarely offer A's and students find that their Grade Point Averages (GPA's) may decrease. Creating good working relationships and trust among all constituents is critical so that the proper balance between academic quality and student preparation can be maintained and expectations will be both clearly defined and met.

FUTURE INVESTIGATIONS

While there are advantages for business schools to join together to create study abroad program opportunities, a pilot survey of business schools indicates that most schools are running individual programs for their students.

A survey was e-mailed to twenty-two AACSB accredited undergraduate business programs randomly selected from schools the University of Connecticut would consider using in a benchmarking study. A copy of the survey is included in the appendix. With three delivery failures, there was a 42% response rate. Results, while positive about the availability of study abroad programs for business students, do not indicate that consortia membership is prevalent:

- all respondents indicated offering Study Abroad programs that included business courses;
- five programs responded that they offered 10+ programs, one responded offering 6–10 programs and two responded offering 1–5 programs;
- all respondents indicated that some programs were available in English in countries where English was not the heritage language;
- administration appears to be split on campuses, with three schools indicating that programs were run through a university/college-wide centralized office while the remaining schools indicated that their system was some type of combination: "We have multi division, divisional and individually run programs."; "We run our own. The rest of the University is centralized."; "Most programs are administered

by a campus-wide office, however, recently that office refused to administer programs that are designed exclusively for business students;"
- in all but one instance, grades were transferred along with credits and the courses were allowed to count toward meeting requirements;
- only two of the schools surveyed indicated membership in a consortium. One did not specify the consortium but the one that did indicated University participation in CIEE and IES (International Education Service);
- of the remaining schools that were not members of a consortium, two indicated that they made a conscious decision not to join a consortium while four indicated that the idea was never discussed. One of those indicating never discussed did note that if they were to consider a consortium, AACSB accreditation of other programs in the consortium would be an important factor.

Considering that consortia for business study abroad programs can be cost effective, increase student options, and strengthen the negotiating position with the host institution, it is interesting not only that there are not many business schools joining consortia, but the majority of schools in this survey have not even considered being part of a consortium. Assuming these schools are a representative sample of business programs, there appears to be opportunities both to develop consortia to offer new programs and to invite partners to share and enhance existing programs. Further research as to why the consortium model is not used more widely by business schools should also be conducted.

SUMMARY

Participation in consortia for business programs has been beneficial for the University of Connecticut Study Abroad Office and the School of Business. Not only have the students had the opportunity to partake in programs that give them an international experience, but they have also shared this experience with students from other parts of the United States. The joint strength of the consortium members has added to the ability to design programs that achieve the quality standards desired. Additionally, it has brought business programs together and created a network that can be tapped for other purposes.

Each consortium group will find that there are individual needs, philosophies and practices that are unique to their situation and structure. Sometimes it may require give-and-take to make aspects of the program work, but at least for the University of Connecticut the value of having the consortia agreements far outweighs any negatives. The authors hope that the information included in this paper will be helpful to schools considering developing their own consortium for study abroad.

NOTES

1. 1998 Amendments to the Higher Education Act of 1965-International Education. http://www.ed.gov/legislation/HEA/sec601.html April 2001.

2. NAFSA: National International Education Policy **President Clinton Issues Executive Memorandum on International Education**
http://www.nafsa.org/content/PublicPolicy/USIntlEdPolicy/alliancepaper.htm April 2001.

3. NAFSA: Association of International Educators, *Important Data on International Educational Exchange*.
http://www.nafsa.org/content/PublicPolicy/DataonInternational Education/FactSheet.htm April 2001.

4. NAFSA: Association of International Educators, *Toward an International Education Policy for the United States*.
http://www.nafsa.org/content/PublicPolicy/USIntlEdPolicy/alliancepaper.htm April 2001.

5. NAFSA: Senators Kerry, Lugar Introduce Resolution on International Education Policy for the United States.
http://www.nafsa.org/content/PublicPolicy/USIntlEdPolicy/alliancepaper.htm April 2001.

6. NAFSA: Important Data on International Education Exchange To and From the United States.
http://www.nafsa.org/content/PublicPolicy/USIntlEdPolicy/alliancepaper.htm April 2001.

7. NAFSA
http://www.nafsa.org//content/InsideNAFSA/EthicsandStandards/PrinciplesStudyAbroad.htm April 2001.

8. CIEE: Council on International Educational Exchange.
http://www.ciee.org/about/index.htm April 2001.

THE STRUCTURE AND PROCESS OF CURRICULUM INTEGRATION IN STUDY ABROAD PROGRAMS: THE UNIVERSITY OF AKRON INTERNATIONAL BUSINESS MODEL

Bruce D. Keillor and James R. Emore

INTRODUCTION

The continuing globalization of business and recent world events underscore the importance of educating students to develop a broad world view. Internationalizing the undergraduate curriculum has moved to the forefront of higher education in business. And international travel and study has become a core part in the curriculum. However, creating and coordinating a meaningful study abroad experience is perhaps the most challenging issue faced by academics and administrators involved in international business education. While the concept of incorporating a practical or "real world" component into a university degree program is not unique, particularly in business education, the structural obstacles and other difficulties associated with bringing about truly international learning experiences tend to be very different. On the one hand, the student(s) involved generally are highly motivated for such an experience. The challenge on the student side is one of channeling this excitement through the proper process in order to ensure they receive maximum transfer credit. This means, from the institutional side, it is necessary to fit the experience, whose characteristics sometimes fall outside the conventional

Study Abroad: Perspectives and Experiences from Business Schools
Advances in International Marketing, Volume 13, 227–245.
ISSN: 1474-7979/PII: S1474797902130146

institutional structure, into an individual's degree program and still meet administrative criteria as they relate to content, rigor, accreditation requirements, etc.

As educators, one of the things we desire, perhaps above all else, is being able to work with motivated students. By and large, students endeavoring to participate in some type of study abroad experience are characterized by their high level of motivation. Typically, this is true due to one, or both, of the following reasons. First, the degree programs in which study abroad courses can be incorporated for credit tend to be more rigorous, such as business, foreign languages, etc. and generally only a reasonably motivated individual can succeed in such a program. Second, the excitement of traveling, studying, and perhaps even working in another country is also a powerful motivator for potential study abroad participants.

Unfortunately, this motivation to participate, and other characteristics which make these individuals especially interesting to work with, frequently does not also extend to numerous planning and organizational details which must be addressed in order to minimize the potential problems associated with study abroad experiences. This lack of forward thinking often starts with fundamental issues, such as identifying a destination institution, and extends to a lack of planning related to academic credit transfer, costs related to tuition fee payments, financial aid, medical insurance, and travel and living expenses, as well as general expectations related to living and studying in a foreign environment.

The importance of gaining some type of overseas experience in their degree programs is essential both to the quality of the students' international business education as well as to enhancing their competitiveness upon graduation, whether in terms of career-related opportunities or graduate school application. The underlying issue from an institutional and program perspective is to provide students with a process which assists them with their preparation while integrating the study abroad experience into the home institution's degree structure so that it is educationally meaningful and constructive and does not place a substantial burden on the student's ability to complete their degree program in the expected time. This requires the institution to address both philosophical as well as procedural issues and create a flexible structure and process which meets the needs of both the student and the institution. The fundamental key to success is implementation flexibility. But before the program is implemented, curricular integration as it relates to structure and process must be considered.

CURRICULAR INTEGRATION – PROCESS AND PROCEDURAL ISSUES

The International Business program at The University of Akron is an example for developing and implementing a study abroad program at the undergraduate level.

Clearly, there are a number of established recognized programs in existence and this chapter does not presume that the structure, policies, or process employed by The University of Akron is ideal. However, it does provide a good working model for newer International Business programs faced with rapid growth, a diverse student body, and/or limited resources. As anyone involved in IB education knows, international business courses and programs have tremendous appeal to students. The greater career opportunities generally available to business students and the allure of the international aspect of study and travel abroad can easily draw students away from other degree programs. In addition, international business has quickly become one of the most popular undergraduate majors and attracts sizable numbers of new students. This is particularly true once the new IB program is functioning with a solid core of high achieving, highly motivated students. Quality attracts quality. And international business is an area where you can build a reputable program at the undergraduate level in a fairly short period of time. At the same time, the resources (e.g. administrative, travel, etc.) required to operate a study and travel abroad programs within a College of Business can be substantial.

The University of Akron model described here is one which has shown itself to be reasonably effective in conditions of tremendous enrollment growth and restricted resources. In the five years between 1996 and 2001, the enrollment of undergraduate students majoring in International Business at the university has grown from less than 10 to over 200. Adding the MBA students with a declared international business concentration and those undergraduates pursuing another major and a minor in international business the Akron program has quickly emerged as one of the largest in the country. In addition to the challenge of managing such rapid growth, the College of Business faces both an opportunity and a challenge associated with the makeup of its undergraduate student body. The University of Akron is a large metropolitan university with a diverse mix of traditional and non-traditional students, the majority of whom attend full-time but a significant minority (approximately 30%) who work full-time and attend school part-time in the evenings. The opportunity with our working students is that their work experiences make the class discussions so much richer than they otherwise would be. The challenge with our working students is that most of them are not able to benefit from study abroad opportunities because of family and work commitments, but they may be able to participate in travel abroad programs.

We have attempted to make study abroad or travel abroad a core part of the international business curriculum. For the non-traditional student, we attempt to create a study or travel experience that can provide a meaningful international business activity while meeting the spirit of the IB curriculum.

One of the primary reasons for this tremendous growth is the innovativeness of the curriculum, both in terms of course offerings and in incorporating a study abroad or travel abroad experience into the degree program. From the perspective of coursework, The University of Akron program includes the typical IB offerings as well as a number of more advanced courses, some required such as International Financial Reporting, International Business Practices, and Multinational Corporations, while others are elective such as International Banking and International Business Law. Additionally, all students are required to complete either a traditional international internship or an international business practicum in order to ensure some level of "real-world" international experience as part of the international business degree requirements. Although not necessarily new in concept (other schools require international experience), in practice The University of Akron approach is designed to be highly flexible in order to achieve our objective of providing every international business major with a meaningful international activity or experience.

Students who study abroad do not want to feel penalized or "waste" an entire semester or year as a result of enrolling in courses at a foreign university. Most of the uncertainty regarding how much academic credit will transfer and what course-by-course articulations will be accepted should be eliminated before the student leaves their home institution. The one uncertainty, a rather significant one at that, which cannot be removed is schedule uncertainty. It is common for students to arrive at the host institution only to find that one or more courses they thought they could schedule will not be offered. Usually, with only a day or two before school starts, students tend to panic unless they are prepared for such contingencies. First, students should not leave home without having more courses approved to take than they intend to register for. International universities don't always have the commitment to a planned schedule of classes that students have been used to at their home institution. Expect the unexpected and prepare accordingly. Second, e-mail has made resolution of this and most other obstructions to a smooth start much simpler and much less expensive (i.e. there is no need to incur costly long-distance telephone calls at odd hours) than in the past. Just be sure that all parties are prepared to respond to e-mails within 24 hours of a student sending their SOS. Time is not a luxury students on study abroad have.

The practicum component was specifically designed to accommodate a number of international activities or experiences and allow students to gain academic credit for an international experience which might otherwise fall outside of the typical degree structure. Any academic who has attempted to develop course-by-course articulations with other U.S. universities can appreciate the challenge of trying to match up specific courses with international universities. Academics can be very protective of their curriculum and course content. A "not-invented-here" syndrome is still quite prevalent among academics at accredited institutions, in basic core business courses let alone more advanced courses in the major. Flexibility had better be the watchword; otherwise, international business students will be very disappointed when they find out that "yes" their study abroad credits will transfer, they just might not count for many, if any, course requirements in their degree program. However, in order to achieve this curricular requirement a number of procedural issues had to be addressed and a process developed in order to create a structure capable of dealing with a large number of students as efficiently and consistently as possible.

On the surface, the basics of creating a study abroad program seem simple enough. Experience has shown, however, that without a functioning, coordinated process the amount of time consumed, both by faculty and staff, can rise at an alarming rate. Even with an efficient process in place, any student who wishes to study at an international university with whom there is not an explicit course-by-course articulation sets into motion a very labor-intensive process of collecting course descriptions and course syllabi, and evaluating courses for course content. Once completed, then courses are usually re-evaluated on a three-year cycle. While it is impossible to address all possible issues and scenarios in a limited space, it is possible to outline a working model which should, with minimal adaptation, be applicable for most institutions. The process model is shown in Fig. 1, while the procedural flow through the organization is shown in Fig. 2.

Student Eligibility

As stated earlier, international business students are very often some of the most highly motivated and highest achieving students. Unfortunately, while they are highly motivated as students, typically they are not encouraged to enroll in introductory business courses until they have completed a year of general education requirements. The notion being that students will be more academically mature and ready for more rigorous business subjects like accounting, finance, and statistics. However, through early involvement in active international business student organizations, students become aware of the opportunities to travel and study abroad. Also, international business student organizations have many undergraduate and graduate international student members who discuss the culture, politics, and business climate of their native countries with other members or make presentations to the entire student group. In this way, we try to stimulate international business majors interest in travel and study abroad early in their academic careers and to get new freshmen and sophomore students to begin thinking about and preparing for study abroad as part of their curriculum in their junior year. This leads students to seek out opportunities to connect with their international business "identities" and the subject of study abroad is frequently broached by freshman and sophomores.

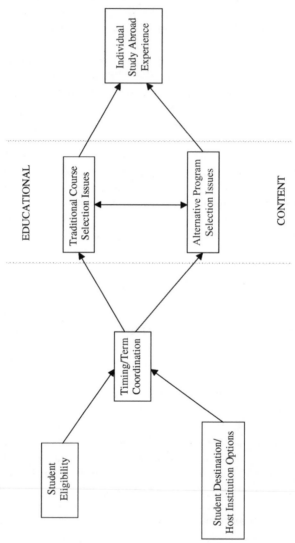

Fig. 1. The University of Akron International Business Study Abroad Program: The Process Model.

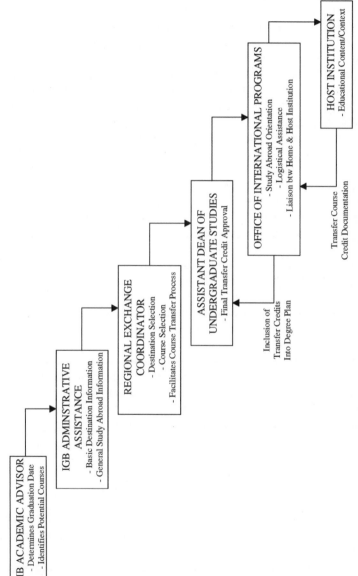

Fig. 2.   The University of Akron International Business Study Abroad Program: The Procedural Model.

At this point two basic approaches can be adopted. On one hand, it could be argued that sending students early in their program (i.e. as freshman and sophomores) might be advisable given the maximum course transfer possibilities as these individuals are typically in the process of completing a wide-range of general education requirements. However, while it may be tempting to allow so-called "early" majors to engage in a study abroad experience, it is important to revisit the educational purpose of such an experience in the context of an international business program. Clearly, international experience is valuable to such students at any time. Yet, it is not uncommon for students, for a variety of reasons (e.g. financial) to plan for only one such trip.

Thus, having the ability to include at least some business courses in the student's overseas program would seem appropriate. Under these circumstances, The University of Akron has determined the most suitable time for international business students to participate in study abroad would be during their junior year. It is at this time in their degree program students will be beginning their basic business core courses as well as completing their general education requirements. Clearly, seniors, or even freshman or sophomores, are not prohibited from study abroad.

However, seniors usually have advanced level courses in their majors remaining to complete and such highly specialized courses may not have similar counterparts at many foreign universities. While freshmen and sophomores may not have completed the prerequisites necessary to enroll in many core business courses or more advanced liberal arts courses dealing with cultural diversity and different world civilizations, to say nothing of the social and academic maturity required for study abroad. So their options are also limited. But undergraduates in their junior year are in a unique position to have a variety of core business courses, courses in their major area, and higher-level general education courses from which to choose. So the opportunities to study aspects of business from the perspective of another culture and country and to maximize the number of transfer credits which fulfill specific degree requirements are generally at their greatest in the junior year.

Student Destination/Host Institution

Closely tied to when students engage in a study abroad program is the issue of "where" (i.e. host institution). Sometimes students will have a particular institution pre-selected for their experience. Although such initiative is not necessarily to be discouraged, a study abroad program whose foundation is based on the notion that students should generate destination choice, risk student selection of universities for which no close partnership arrangements exist, and which will quickly become a resource drain. At the front end, faculty and staff spend considerable time with individual students working through destination options with which neither may have any knowledge or experience. And, on the back end, administrators must to some extent constantly "re-invent the wheel" in determining course-by-course articulations and transfer credit. To say the least, this is neither a very efficient, nor a very effective process.

Without eliminating the opportunity for a particular student to study at a host institution toward which they feel particularly drawn, the destination component of the model which reduces resource drain, and helps focus students in their selection process, is one where the home institution forms partnership ties, directly through the business school, with a limited number of host institutions. For example, The University of Akron, at the university-level, has exchange agreements with over two dozen universities around the globe. Currently, however, only about eight of these, located in Korea (2), Mexico (1), Great Britain (2), France (2) and Denmark (1) are actively and regularly used by business students. Organizationally, international business faculty members serve as Regional Exchange Coordinators (i.e. there is a coordinator designated for Asia, Latin America, and Europe) and assist students in selecting an institution from the list of partner schools depending upon the student's basic location preference.

There are several reasons for the selection of these particular host locations. Perhaps the overriding reason is that all of these institutions offer coursework in English. International business majors at The University of Akron have the choice of taking either a foreign language or a cultural or interdisciplinary track, with the majority opting for the latter. In the past, many international business programs distinguished themselves from a traditional business education through a required language component. However, as the marketplace becomes increasingly globalized, English is emerging as the "language of business." Further, requiring students to focus on one language tends to overly specialize their education, which may not serve them well over the course of a career which may require them to operate in numerous countries.

In establishing the program direction, the overwhelming feedback from the corporate world was that individuals were increasingly expected to move around various regions during their career and that specialization, particularly to the limited extent to which undergraduates could be expected to achieve, generally did not enhance those students' attractiveness as job candidates. This approach is somewhat supported given recent moves away from so-called "area studies" by established institutions, most notably Thunderbird. That is not to say students are discouraged from language studies. In fact, many of our international business majors who select the foreign language option, choose that option because of their passion for a particular foreign language or country. Rather the approach is to create a program where students can be effectively equipped to be successful internationally using a broader educational model.

A second reason for the choice of these schools is the course selection offered and its content. Each institution offers more than just one or two business courses per term which are accessible to Akron students. They provide a regular offering of business courses as well as non-business courses, particularly those related to local culture, history, politics, and economics, for which a student might receive general education credit. In addition, the fact that the course materials are in English greatly facilitates the ability to monitor course content and rigor as it removes the language barrier for University of Akron faculty and staff involved in the course articulation process. This wide-range of accessible course possibilities is essential to ensure students will be able to enroll as full-time students, fulfill reciprocity requirements in the exchange agreement, and allow them to complete their degree program in a timely fashion.

Third, each institution has the willingness and expertise to provide study abroad students with real-world work experiences including internships, cooperative education programs, practicums, and independent study opportunities which not only enhance their education but also make them much more competitive in the job market upon graduation. Very few U.S. universities are capable of securing access to international work experience for their students, particularly at the undergraduate level. One way to address this problem is through grants or other government and non-profit organizations (e.g. The Fund for the Improvement of Post Secondary Education). However, at The University of Akron experience has shown one of the real attributes, which often goes unnoticed by U.S. universities, is the ability of their overseas partners to secure substantial numbers of internships and other practical work-related experiences for U.S. students. Being able to secure such positions on a reasonably large scale can easily position the U.S. program with a distinct competitive advantage.

However, one note of caution here: Making arrangements for an internship in the student's major field through a foreign university is perhaps the most complicated part of the entire approval process and presents some unique challenges. To summarize, we look for resolution of the majority of the following issues when developing internship positions:

- A demonstrated commitment from top management in hosting the internship student;
- A detailed job description listing the intern's duties and responsibilities that are related to the student's academic major with the goal of developing relevant transferable skills;
- A person willing to serve as a designated supervisor and mentor for the intern;

- A list of available projects in which to engage the student for the duration of their internship;
- Demonstrated support for the internship student by supervisor(s) and co-workers (availability to address questions and concerns on an on-going basis); and
- Enough work for the student to complete 300 hours on the job if that student is taking the internship class for three credit hours (100 field hours per credit hour) – Co-op students receive no academic credit but also need to complete approximately 300 field hours as well.

Timing/Term Coordination

The problem of term coordination remains one of the biggest challenges in integrating the study abroad experience without adding to degree completion time. Many host institutions, particularly in Europe, start their fall semester around late September (with several weeks of classes and exams in January) and spring semester runs roughly from mid-February to mid-June. A U.S. student choosing to study abroad in the fall frequently is faced with the prospect of a Christmas holiday alone and a return date several weeks after classes have started back home.

The University of Akron has found that spring term is generally more suitable for students to study overseas for several reasons. First, the fact that the end of the spring term overlaps into the summer, rather than a regular academic year makes it much easier to manage from the perspective of the home institution. Further, the weeks between completing the fall term at home, and the beginning of the spring term overseas, provides students with time to prepare for the experience. Finally, by ending in the summer, the student has the opportunity to extend their time abroad in order to travel, or in some cases, work.

An alternative which is becoming increasingly viable is study abroad during the summer. Traditionally, summer terms were not generally offered overseas. However, due to demand from local students and the recognition that U.S. students represent tremendous revenue opportunities, more host institutions are offering summer programs particularly in business. Again, one note of caution is warranted here. Some foreign universities do not waive foreign students' tuition fees during summer terms; that is, reciprocity agreements do not necessarily apply in the summer. Check before committing.

One of the places where the Akron program has been able to achieve substantial enrollment growth is through so-called nontraditional students. Having an IB program which is flexible enough to accommodate the needs of individuals who are working full-time and attending school part-time has initially proven to be a strong competitive advantage. These offerings, which allow students to gain international experience without spending an entire term abroad, plays an important role in the flexibility of the Akron program. An example of one of these shorter programs is provided under the "Travel Abroad" section later in the chapter.

Educational Content

Another issue which must be addressed is the actual educational experience itself and the awarding of transfer credits. If a student chooses the traditional full-term study abroad option, courses must be selected and content evaluated. Similarly, if some type of alternative model is being considered, the program must also be evaluated for content and rigor.

Course Selection Issues

Obviously, prior to making any determination as to the courses in which the student will register, the courses which will actually be offered must be determined. This is a somewhat deceptively simple statement. As is the case at many U.S. universities, the host institution course catalog is frequently not an accurate reflection of the courses which are regularly offered. Additionally, it is not uncommon for courses to be cancelled, or the schedule to be altered, with little or no warning. The approach that seems to work best is one where students arrive with a selection of host institution courses pre-approved by their home faculty advisor, designed to fit into their degree plan, from which they can construct their schedule. Experience has shown that students who only have a limited number of courses pre-selected frequently have to make alterations "in-country" which can easily put their credit transfers at risk.

It is during the course selection period that course content must be evaluated, unless the course has already been evaluated recently as part of another student's program. As discussed earlier, host institutions who offer courses in English make this process much easier. In such cases, the syllabus, textbooks, and course materials used can be compared with home courses faculty who teach in that particular area. It is here that the philosophical purpose for the study abroad experience must be weighed heavily against the desire for one-to-one content equivalence. Occasionally, faculty and administrators involved in the evaluation of course content will lose sight of the underlying purpose of a study abroad experience and its importance in international business education. But such a proprietary view on the part of a faculty member of the content of a course is not anywhere near as rigid as it was in years past. In fact, at Akron, the entire transfer course evaluation process for both domestic and international courses is very student-friendly. That was not the case five years ago.

Rather than seeking exact course content and rigor, a standard of "underlying intent" might be more appropriate. Just as course content and rigor varies by instructor and term within the home institution, it should not be surprising that obtaining exact coverage equivalence becomes difficult to determine. Provided a given course at a host institution demonstrates a reasonable level of consistency when compared to the home course, it would seem appropriate to approve the transfer. In making a study abroad program function, it is always vital to remember the educational value of studying in another culture and country and the means by which the *context* in which the course is offered enhances the *content* of the course.

Program Selection Issues

For those students with family or work obligations or limited finances, shorter-term programs may be a more viable option than a semester or year of study abroad. These may include study tours, short (i.e. 1–3 weeks) classroom based courses, or experiential/work-based activities. The host institution, home institution, or a variety of third-party providers may offer such programs. The short-term programs should not be discounted; they have distinct advantages for both students and faculty. For students, the advantages include the ability to take part with a virtual guarantee of no disruption in their degree plan completion, less time commitment, and potentially greatly reduced cost. On the faculty side, because of the shorter time involved, the awarding of credits frequently means the student is required to complete an additional assignment such as a research paper submitted to a member, or group, of the home faculty. This enables home faculty to better control the educational quality of the experience.

One example of a short-term study program is the London study program offered by The University of Akron's Institute for Global Business in conjunction with a local partner institution. Offered during the 4-week summer intersession, the program enables 25–30 students the chance to earn six credits. Using an Akron faculty member, students earn three credits in international marketing in a traditional class held from 8 a.m.–noon three days/week. They then earn an additional three credits in their required international business practicum by completing a pre-arranged group (approximately 4 students/group) marketing project with a London-based organization. The courses are also open to the host institution students who comprise about one-third of the enrollment. Under this model students can complete a substantial number of required credits in a compressed period of time which matches Akron's schedule for an affordable price. In addition, they receive real-world international business experience and references. The University of Akron also has the ability to control the entire educational experience as it is organized and staffed through the Institute for Global Business with faculty assistance from the host partner for the project-based course.

Study tours, on the other hand, usually last from two to five weeks duration and focus more on traveling to a number of cities, historic sites, and countries, giving participants exposure to the different customs, history, viewpoints, and business practices of the people and countries within that region. However, great care must be taken to organize the trip to ensure that the travel is a worthwhile learning experience and much more than simply a sightseeing tour of several countries.

While less formal than study abroad, shorter travel-abroad programs have the potential to provide a unique learning experience which can't be duplicated in any other venue. With study abroad, students usually reside near a single university and spend most of their time studying or interacting with other students and faculty from the host university. Travel abroad can expose students to a broader view of a foreign culture(s) and a more realistic view of our own.

Since such trips involve studying the history, culture, politics, and business environment of the host countries, the travel could fulfill a requirement in several different areas. For example, such a trip could satisfy a general education requirement (e.g. a world civilization and cultural diversity requirement), a foreign language requirement (e.g. study of the culture, civilization, and language of a particular country) or an international business requirement (e.g. the international business practicum or a global interdisciplinary requirement such as the study of Asian culture).

One of the benefits of such course-equivalency flexibility is the rich interdisciplinary mix of business, history, foreign language, and many other majors who sign up for these trips. With so much time spent traveling, students have long periods when they can exchange ideas and differing viewpoints with other students from their home university as well as with their international hosts. How often do you hear of such exchanges among different disciplines on the campus of the home university? Also, each student may be assigned a fellow student from the host country who acts as interpreter. Most students report that they frequently engaged in lengthy discussions and exchanges of ideas with other students and professors about the country's history, politics, and local traditions and customs. Certainly, recent events have established international understanding and cooperation as critical to our economic well-being and safety.

International study tours tend to be focused in a certain geographic area (e.g. China and Korea), with travel to selected cities and sites, many of which are cultural or natural treasures (e.g. Kyong-Joo, Korea's old capital, The Great Wall of China, and The Forbidden City), and offer insight into a particular country's rich history. Many of these sites may be designated as World Heritage sites by the United Nations Educational, Scientific, and Cultural Organization (UNESCO). Students return home with a much better understanding of, and appreciation for, the culture, history, social customs, economics, and industry of a particular country. Exposure to different overseas communities will likely result in fewer cultural stereotypes for all parties involved.

Visits to international cities may involve trips to local firms (e.g. Daewoo Shipbuilding, Pohan Steel, Hyundai Motor Company) or financial markets (e.g. Shanghai Stock Market). These trips can include plant tours and presentations regarding a firm's global competition and strategy. In addition, arrangements can be made for presentations at universities in the host country, where professors discuss how business practices in the host country differ from those in the U.S.

One residual benefit of shorter programs is that they may spark the interest of some students who may want to spend a semester or more studying in one of the host countries. And with e-mail, friendships forged abroad can easily become lifelong friends.

Other than the substantial time needed to organize such trips, establishing international connections is another key factor in the success of study and travel abroad programs. A high quality international learning experience will not take place without preparation and relationship-building, usually on the part of faculty, administrators, and staff from the office of international programs at the home institution in conjunction with alumni and friends at universities and businesses in the host country who may be able to open doors that would otherwise be inaccessible. These international connections may result from faculty whose native country is the host country, faculty exchanges where the host country's faculty may teach a class in the U.S. and our faculty may teach courses at the host university, collaborative research projects, friendships developed at conferences, or other interactions which have developed over time.

Also, for universities and colleges which do not have many student exchange agreements with international universities or who may not have the human resources to organize travel abroad or study abroad programs, there are hundreds, if not thousands, of programs available through other universities nationally. So startup may simply be a matter of surfing the web.

Credit Transfer

All of the discussion thus far points toward the most crucial issue of all: actual credit transfer. Provided the model has been followed this should be the most straight-forward and quickest piece of the process. Under The University of Akron model, the credit transfer simply requires the student to complete a transient (guest student) permission form on which all the proposed courses to be taken are listed, along with the approved University of Akron equivalents. This form is then signed by the Regional Exchange Coordinator, relevant department chair, and the office of the Assistant Dean for Undergraduate Studies in the College of Business Administration. Typically the list has more courses than the student plans to actually take in order to ensure maximum flexibility (see above). In order to maintain control it clearly:

(1) stipulates the maximum number of credits which can be transferred;
(2) prohibits the "double-counting" of courses;
(3) indicates the minimum grade required for the course to receive transfer credit; and
(4) requires pre-approval of transfer credits prior to departure to prevent students from attempting to make course transfer determinations outside of home faculty control.

Upon completion of the coursework, the student receives traditional transfer credit (i.e. both course credits and course grades appear on the student's transcript but the grades are not averaged into the student's GPA).

One approach to credit transfer which has been proposed, but shown not to work well in practice, is structured articulation. This involves developing a list of courses for each partner school with a pre-approved list of matching equivalent courses which would allow direct course credit that applies to the student's GPA. This would seem simple enough, however it is deceptively complex. Factoring in the number of partner schools, the number of courses offered, the various requirements and electives, and curricular revisions and changes, monitoring and maintaining these articulation lists can quickly turn into a full-time job. Additionally, some partner institutions utilize a grading system which does not articulate smoothly into the traditional "A-F" U.S. format.

An alternative is to use a precedent approach where previous student records are checked for approved courses and these are used to build a foundation based on actual activity. The University of Akron has found that if students engage in study abroad at the same time in their degree program, patterns emerge where over time students take the same courses at a particular host institution. This makes the credit transfer process much easier as it is not necessary to evaluate each course for every student. Grading philosophy can also vary tremendously by institution (e.g. grade distribution). By removing the issue of overseas credits being included in the student's GPA, it is possible to both produce a more uniformly comparable set of graduates and ensure a more positive experience for the students.

FLEXIBILITY: THE KEY TO SUCCESS

Once the program and the process are in place, the focus now turns to implementation. Over time, the success of any study abroad program needs two basic components:

(1) a defined structure and process; and
(2) the ability to be flexible.

It has been our experience at The University of Akron that flexibility in the following areas enables a program to grow rapidly and also provide a foundation for continued growth into the future:

Degree Plan Flexibility

As previously discussed, undergraduate students who are juniors, have the maximum flexibility in terms of their ability to enroll in both business-related and culture-based courses, either of which will count toward their degree requirements and give them an educational experience that has both "international" and "business" components.

Curriculum Flexibility

Building in some level of curriculum and credit-hour flexibility can also greatly facilitate a study abroad program. The University of Akron has incorporated an experiential component into the various requirements for international business majors. These include choices between special topics courses and independent study courses as well as international internships or practicums. These courses can easily be used for transfer credit whenever the student seeks to fit a suitable overseas experience into the Akron degree plan. Further, the experiential coursework has minimal pre-requisites so that any student admitted to the international business program can take the courses based on the best timing for themselves as individuals.

Content Flexibility

It is vital that some degree of flexibility also exist in the evaluation and approval of transfer credits. Clearly, it is not appropriate to award credits for what amounts to a principles course in place of a more advanced course (e.g. Principles of Marketing for International Marketing). However, at Akron the content evaluation process is based heavily on the underlying purpose of the experience rather than the need to re-construct Akron courses in another environment. To reach this point requires faculty buy-in, which did not exist at Akron several years ago and may not exist at another university. For example, it would be possible to transfer a host institution's Marketing Management course back to Akron as International Marketing on the basis that:

(1) both are essentially strategic level courses; and
(2) the intent of the International Marketing course is for students to consider marketing activities at the global, rather than the domestic, strategic level and studying marketing management in another culture and country more likely fulfills that purpose.

Transfer Flexibility

In addition, there needs to be a recognition that course offerings can change with little or no notice. Thus, students should arrive at the host institution with a list of approved courses (more than what they intend to enroll in) so that they are able to construct a practical schedule and are prepared for any possible last minute changes which might affect their status as full-time students, financial aid, course equivalency approvals, or expected degree completion time.

Participant Flexibility

The final piece in the entire puzzle, and one on which success also rests, is the attitude of the individual student participant. It is impossible to underestimate the value of pre-departure orientation which focuses on the participant's willingness to be flexible and recognize that no amount of preparation and structure can prevent some gap between expectations and reality from occurring at the most inopportune time. Students must be willing to alter plans and expectations regarding the entire experience on short notice in order to effectively assimilate and get the full value of the experience. E-mail addresses of key individuals in the approval process are critical to ensuring that "surprises" get resolved quickly and don't become unmanageable problems because they were not communicated in a timely fashion.

CONCLUSION

The structure and process described here is not intended to represent the ideal, or the only, means of creating and implementing a study or travel abroad program. Indeed, depending upon the individual institution's organizational structure and available resources, other models may be more effective. However, the underlying elements of The University of Akron approach to incorporating study abroad experiences into the international business education do provide a good foundation for any program and can be adapted to meet the requirements of each institution. Further, for schools just beginning, or seeking to substantially expand, international business study abroad programs, this model does provide a proven starting point which is flexible enough to be effectively adopted by a variety of institutions. Whatever model you choose to adopt, it is important to see study and travel abroad programs as part of a comprehensive strategy to incorporate internationalization into the curriculum for all majors, not just for international business majors.

INTERNATIONAL COMPARATIVE PERSPECTIVES ON STUDY ABROAD PROGRAMS IN BUSINESS SCHOOLS – GERMAN AND EUROPEAN PERSPECTIVES AS COMPARED TO AMERICAN PERSPECTIVES

Marion Festing

INTRODUCTION

Globalization is a key challenge at the beginning of 21st century. Countries, industries, firms and individuals have more cross-border interactions than ever. Important facilitators of these interactions include the following examples:

- The creation of free trade zones in different parts of the world: i.e. the North American Free Trade Association (NAFTA), or the European Union (EU).
- Further liberalization of world trade, partly enabled by the regulations of international organizations such as the World Trade Organization (WTO). Trade and investment barriers are falling and the world economy is moving towards a global marketplace.
- The increase in growth of foreign direct investment (FDI) and international trade.

Study Abroad: Perspectives and Experiences from Business Schools
Advances in International Marketing, Volume 13, 247–262.
© 2003 Published by Elsevier Science Ltd.
ISSN: 1474-7979/PII: S1474797902130158

- Important technological advances in information and communication technology. For example, the Internet provides not only a technological device for
  international trade but also facilitates quick information exchange and personal
  communication via e-mail etc.
- The decrease in the costs of transport and the increase in the speed of transport
  make imports and exports more attractive and thus, increase international trade.
  However, this trend also enables individuals to travel more than before – if it is
  for business reasons or for private purposes.

These are just some examples and we could continue this list. However, even from
this small number of examples it becomes clear that firms who are exposed to
global competition need to cope with the challenges of cross-border interactions.
They need to design appropriate strategies and processes, and intercultural settings
become an important part of business life. Inside the firm, intercultural interactions
may occur e.g. within intercultural teams. However, also negotiations with foreign
governments, suppliers and customers involve international interactions.

Consequently, a key success factor in the globalization of business is the
development of international experience and related to this, intercultural skills.
Thus, a question of crucial importance in a globalized world is: How can people
be prepared for globalization? How can international experience and intercultural
skills be developed?

These challenges of globalization can be best met through life-long learning
and ideally, a variety of institutions would be involved in the learning process.
In *school*, children may learn foreign languages at an early age. While learning
the language, they would also acquire first knowledge about foreign countries and
cultures. Then, at *higher education institutions*, students may be offered to spend
some time abroad and conduct parts of their studies at a foreign university. For
those students striving at working in the business sector, international business
topics can be offered, and students may be given the opportunity to do internships in foreign companies and countries. Once employed by a *firm*, learning by
doing, will increase the intercultural competence of the employees and managers.
Working in intercultural settings within the home country or sending employees on
expatriate assignments abroad are appropriate measures in this stage. The different
institutions involved in the development of international experience are outlined in
Fig. 1.

However, we would like to stress that the institutions may just offer incentives
and opportunities for developing international experience – it is the individual who
has to accept the challenge of improving and enriching his or her competence set.
As Fig. 1 shows, globalization does not only take place in a business environment

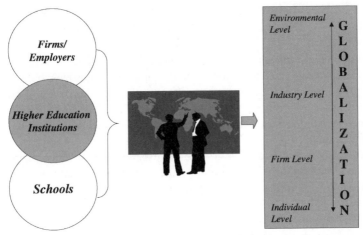

Fig. 1. Preparing People for Gobalization.

but more and more penetrates all facets of life. Consequently, the development of international experience should be an integral part of the personal development of a high number of people.

Within this paper, we will discuss the influence of higher education institutions on preparing people for globalization. The main focus is on higher international business education and within this context, primarily on study abroad programs.

As educational systems are strongly influenced by historical traditions we can observe differences not only in the educational systems in general but also with respect to internationalizing higher business education. These differences are in the center of consideration of this paper and will be outlined taking the example of Europe and America.

The paper is structured as follows: Within the next section, we will outline programs and experiences in study abroad programs from a European perspective. Then, differences between European and American perspectives are highlighted and discussed. The concluding remarks focus on lessons to be learned from the comparison of the different approaches. Examples of study abroad practices from different universities in Europe (ESCP-EAP European School of Management with campuses in Paris, Berlin, Oxford and Madrid; University of Paderborn/Germany) and the United States (Michigan State University) will complete our arguments. The selection of examples is not representative at all but draws on the experiences of the author.

INTERNATIONALIZING EDUCATION IN EUROPE – PROGRAMS AND EXPERIENCES

Since 1976, the *European Union* has initiated a range of activities to internation-alize education and training. Not only study abroad activities have been focused. This is just one part of the program to increase the international or European expe-rience of students within the Member States of the European Union. Besides this, there is a high emphasis on the internationalization of vocational training and on language training.

In 1995, these activities have lead to the establishment of three main educa-tional and vocational training programs: *Socrates, Leonardo da Vinci* and *Youth for Europe III*. Figure 2 gives an overview of the contents and objectives of these programs.

Furthermore, the *Tempus program* established in 1990 is designed to encour-age exchanges in the field of higher education between the *European Union* and the countries of central and eastern Europe, the former Soviet republics and Mongolia.

Although it is important to note that the *European Union* follows a strategy, which integrates the different facets of internationalizing education and training, within this paper we will concentrate on the *SOCRATES program*, which targets

Socrates
Main Objective: Encourages student mobility by
- Cooperation between universities (Erasmus program)
- Cooperation between schools (Comenius program)
- Language Learning (Lingua program)

Leonardo da Vinci
Main Objective: Promotes access to vocational training by
- Improving national vocational training systems and
- Encouraging innovation and life-long learning

Youth for Europe III
Main Objective: Facilitates the mobility of less privileged young people by
- Outside education structures
- Giving them access to local projects
- Complementing their training as citizens

Fig. 2. Education and Vocational Training in the EU.

higher education and thus, study abroad programs. The objectives of the *SOCRA-TES program* include the following (Gordon, Maiworm & Teichler, 2000, p. 401):

- Better knowledge of the EU languages.
- Cooperation among educational institutions for the enhancement of intellectual and teaching potential.
- Encouragement of teacher mobility, thus contributing to their skills and the European dimension in their studies.
- Encouragement of student mobility, again with the aim of contributing to the European dimensions of education.
- Encouragement of contacts among pupils.
- Encouragement of recognition of the period of study in another European country, and
- Encouragement of open and distance learning.

In the following, we will outline some experiences with respect to selected objectives. Information is mainly based on the SOCRATES 2000 evaluation study (Gordon, Maiworm & Teichler, 2000).

With respect to the first objective, *the better knowledge of European languages*, a survey has shown that in the academic year 1998/1999, 60% of the Erasmus students were exclusively taught in the host language, 25% followed partly courses in the host language, and 15% followed courses taught in their home language or in a third language. The teaching language in 42% of the courses was English, in 50% of the courses four other major European languages, and in 8% of the courses remaining languages. It is interesting to note that the use of the English language in teaching has not increased within the last decade.

However, students mainly followed courses in the host language in the United Kingdom, Italy, Ireland, France, Spain, Portugal, and Germany. Other countries such as Finland and the Netherlands were more successful in attracting foreign students when teaching in a third language, which has usually been English (Gordon, Maiworm & Teichler, 2000, p. 402). The small number of people speaking the languages of these relatively small countries may explain this phenomenon.

Another objective pursued by the *SOCRATES program* is *encouraging teacher mobility*. The most important means is providing more financial resources. As it is estimated that the number of mobile teachers increased from 1,400 in the early 1990s to about 7,000 within not even one decade the effects of the *SOCRATES program* are clearly visible. The duration of the foreign teaching activities is only eight days in average. However, these activities are part of the regular program of the host institution in most of the cases. Furthermore, a high number of the mobile teachers provide advice for their own students abroad or for the students at the host institution interested in going abroad (Gordon, Maiworm & Teichler, 2000,

p. 406). To sum up, it can be said that the encouragement of teacher mobility has been most effective in many ways.

Also the objective of increasing *student mobility* in Europe was successfully reached: The number of internationally mobile students doubled within a five-year period and amounts to 460,000 students during the academic years 1995/1996 through 1999/2000. This means that a yearly average of more than 80,000 students has spent a part of their studies abroad within the framework of the *Erasmus program*. The program now includes more than 1,600 universities in Europe, each sending around 50 students a year to other European countries. Among the total number of students, there is an average of 14,000 German students each year (Maiworm & Teichler, 2000, p. 62; BMBF, 1999). At the University of Paderborn/Germany the *SOCRATES program* accounts for nearly 75% of all students going abroad. In most of the cases, student mobility is supported by a scholarship from this program.

The average duration of the period abroad is almost seven months within the *SOCRATES program*. This can be confirmed when looking at the international mobile students from the University of Paderborn; in average they spend 7.5 months abroad. Within the SOCRATES evaluation, the academic quality of the host students has been assessed by the teachers as on par to home students on average, and the quality of the courses was assessed similarly independent from home or host country institution by the students (Gordon, Maiworm & Teichler, 2000, p. 408).

The *recognition of a temporary study abroad* as equivalent to the study at home is most important to the students. They choose study abroad programs, which are relevant to their final degree, and full academic recognition should ensure that they would not lose time in completing their degree by studying abroad. Taking into account these needs the European Commission has initiated the *European Credit Transfer System* (ECTS). In 2000, ECTS covers half of the students within the *Erasmus program* (Fig. 3).

ECTS provides a way of measuring and comparing learning achievements and enables the transfer from one education institution to another. Thus, insights into foreign curricula are facilitated and common procedures for academic recognition are established. Consequently, ECTS should have benefits for students as well as for the education institutions.

Credits are a value given to a course. They relate to the quantity of work required by the course. A year of studies would include 60 credits, a semester (usually 6 months) 30, and a trimester 20 credits. The ECTS grading scale provides information on the student's performance but does not replace the local grade. Usually, higher education institutions make their own decisions about how to apply the ECTS grading scale to their own system (Fig. 4).

ECTS benefits to the students

- ECTS guarantees academic recognition abroad.

- ECTS enables access to regular courses alongside local students, with the benefit of full participation in the academic life of the host institution. This characteristic of ECTS distinguishes it from many other student mobility programs.

- ECTS enables further studies abroad. A student may prefer not to go back to the home institution after the study period abroad, but rather to stay at the host institution – possibly to gain a degree – or to move to a third institution. The institutions themselves decide whether or not this is acceptable and what conditions the student must fulfill in order to get a diploma or transfer registration.

Fig. 3. ECTS Benefits to the Students (EC, 2000).

In summary, it can be said that the *SOCRATES program* and especially the *Erasmus program* have had positive effects on the Europeanization and internationalization of students and faculty members in many disciplines. However, the SOCRATES 2000 evaluation study also reports problems that need to be solved. Ranked according to their perceived importance they include the following issues (Maiworm & Teichler, 2000, p. 59):

(1) Insufficient individual grants for teacher mobility.
(2) Insufficient individual grants for students.
(3) Lack of internal personnel resources to handle administration and service functions related to SOCRATES.
(4) Lack of financial means to cover own institutional costs related to SOCRATES.
(5) Lack of interest of academic staff in teaching periods abroad.
(6) Lack of interest of the academic staff of home institutions in the curriculum-related domains of SOCRATES.

In summary, it can be said that the problems mainly relate to the financial resources available for the exchange programs. This underlines the fact that the internationalization of higher education is costly and must be supported by important financial resources.

ECTS benefits to higher education institutions
• ECTS creates curriculum transparency by providing detailed information on the curricula and their relevance towards a degree.
• ECTS helps academics to make academic recognition decisions based on prior agreement on the content of the study programs abroad between students and their home and host institutions.
• The use of ECTS can also be a catalyst for reflection on course curriculum structures, student workload and learning outcomes.
• With ECTS, higher education institutions preserve their autonomy and responsibility for all decisions concerning students' achievements, without amending existing course structures and assessment methods: all courses and assessments are those which are normally taken by regular students at the host institution.

Fig. 4. ECTS Benefits to Higher Education Institutions (EC, 2000).

However, there also seems to be a lack of interest on the side of some of the faculty members to individually engage in the internationalization of education. This last-mentioned problem may lose importance in the future when more and more faculty members will have acquired international experience within their studies themselves. This should lead to a higher interest in extending experiences in foreign countries when acting as a faculty member. Furthermore, engaging in study abroad activities could be an integral part of the career advancement of young academics supported by appropriate incentives. These are measures to be taken by governments and/or education institutions.

Besides the programs initiated by the *European Union* there are also examples of European business schools, which include study abroad as a basic element of their curriculum. These programs are not related to the *SOCRATES program*. Figure 5 will outline the example of ESCP-EAP European School of Management.

Objective and program of ESCP-EAP European School of Management

ESCP-EAP European School of Management exists to prepare multicultural business leaders for careers anywhere in the world. Through transnational research and teaching programs, we foster personal growth, expand management knowledge and contribute to the performance of some of the world's leading companies. ESCP-EAP has campuses in Paris / France, Oxford / United Kingdom, Madrid / Spain and Berlin / Germany.

For the foreseeable future the critical challenge is globalisation. Globalisation is not about uniform vision and practice. It is about doing business and managing assets in different countries with people holding different values, practising different work schedules and speaking different languages. This is a sea change for everyone. To prepare for this challenge, we at ESCP-EAP are developing a new type of business school. Because we believe that to meet the challenge of globalisation, business education must be different.

Uniquely ESCP-EAP has four campuses and a global network of academic partners. Multiple campuses and global alliances are the backbone of a transnational learning approach in management which enables students recruited worldwide to develop multicultural expertise and international exposure through first-hand experience.

In addition, to our cross-border infrastructure, at ESCP-EAP our 120 professors representing 15 nationalities define the school and its achievements. They work with colleagues around the world on cutting edge research projects and with leading companies on training and consulting assignments.

The ESCP-EAP Master's is an innovative, multi-country program delivered at the School's main campus in Paris and at its European campuses in Oxford, Madrid and Berlin. The European track includes three years of study in three countries and three languages (Paris - Oxford - Berlin or Oxford - Madrid - Paris). The international track includes study in Paris and the possibility to study at one of the 40 partner schools on an exchange program.

Fig. 5. The Example of ESCP-EAP (ESCP-EAP, 2000, pp. 2–3, 10).

KEY DIFFERENCES BETWEEN GERMAN/EUROPEAN AND AMERICAN STUDY ABROAD PROGRAMS

Within this section, we will identify differences between German and American approaches to study abroad programs. The decision to mainly compare a German and not a European perspective with the American perspective has several reasons. The author is German and thus, has more extensive experiences with the German system than with other European national systems. The distinction between German and European perspectives is important because educational systems in Europe differ to a great extent. They have country-specific historical traditions and these may also show in the approach to study abroad activities. However, taking a German perspective seems to be relevant as this is the country with the highest population in the *European Union* and a country with great economic strengths, which shows in the intensive exports activities and in the high amount of foreign direct investments of German firms (Festing, 2002).

Table 1 summarizes some of the key differences identified within the different discussions about American and European/German perspectives during the *International Roundtable on Study Abroad Programs in Business Schools,* held at Michigan State University in September 2001. Within the discussion of the most important differences, we will recur on the data presented within the section about the European Union in order to provide evidence for the differences not only from a German perspective but – whenever possible – also from a European perspective.

While American universities offer a variety of programs for undergraduate students this is not the case in Germany. In the European countries, it is difficult to get any funding for study abroad programs before the students have finished at least two years of studies and have completed a bachelor's degree or the *Vordiplom* in Germany. As funding is important for study abroad this may be a major reason why undergraduate study abroad programs do not exist on a regular basis in Germany.

During the discussions of the *Roundtable* it has been highlighted that the short-term programs are able to very well meet the requirements of the American undergraduate target group. At Michigan State University more than 75% of all study abroad participants in the academic year 2000–2001 were undergraduates. These students are – compared to German students – quite young and a short-term stay in a foreign country may encourage them to engage in a longer-term study abroad programs later within their graduate studies. Thus, a short-term program can be seen as waking the interest in international business, languages and in going abroad.

However, most of the European programs aim at longer term stays in the foreign countries. As mentioned above, the SOCRATES 2000 evaluation study has

Table 1. American and German Perspectives on Study Abroad.

	AMERICAN PERSPECTIVE	GERMAN PERSPECTIVE
TARGET GROUP	Undergraduates & graduate Students	Mainly graduate students
PERIOD OF TIME	Tendency towards short-term stays	Mainly long-term stays (one or two semesters)
LANGUAGE	High interest in programs taught in the mother language: English	Students follow courses in local languages to a high extent
INTEGRATION IN THE LOCAL EDUCATION SYSTEM & LOCAL CULTURE	Courses followed abroad must not be integrated in the local educational system. American students like summer schools.	Courses followed are often integrated in the local educational system. However, also German students like summer schools.
FUNDING	Scholarships are also available for short-term study abroad programs.	Scholarships are mainly available for graduate students who spend at least one semester abroad and gain credits for their studies in Germany.
CREDIT TRANSFER	Credit transfer needs to be organized in the bilateral relationship of the partner universities. The possibility of credit transfer is very important.	For inner-European study abroad programs credit transfer has been regulated by the *European Credit Transfer System*. The possibility of credit transfer is very important.
INVOLVEMENT OF HOME FACULTY IN THE PROGRAM ABROAD IN TERMS OF PRESENCE ABROAD	Presence of home faculty member during the study abroad program is common.	Presence of home faculty member during the study abroad program is not common.

reported an average stay of seven months in the foreign country. The average study abroad period of students from the University of Paderborn has been 7.5 months in the academic year 2000–2001. Also, most of the foreign students – the incomings – studying in study abroad programs at the University of Paderborn stayed for one semester. One third of the foreign students even stayed for a second semester. In contrast, the percentage of students going abroad for a semester e.g. at Michigan State University has been in the academic year 2000–2001 22.4%, those staying for a whole year represented 1.4% of all internationally mobile students.

While American students prefer programs taught in English, German and European students usually follow courses in the local language and are integrated in the local education system and culture. However, as German students learn foreign languages in school from the age of 8 they have a different language background than most of the Americans. This enables them – at least in traditional study abroad locations such as the English, French and Spanish speaking countries – to speak the language quite well from the beginning of their stay. Furthermore, in some universities one foreign language is compulsory for business students. For example, students studying business administration at the University of Paderborn in Germany have to take compulsory exams in *Business English*. If they study in the program of "International Business Studies" they even need to speak two foreign languages and study at least one semester abroad at one of the partner universities. The knowledge of at least two foreign languages is also required in most French business schools. The example of ESCP-EAP European School of Management has shown that these students even study in three languages in three different countries.

However, as has been shown by the SOCRATES 2000 evaluation study it has to be differentiated between the host countries the students go to. If they go to small countries such as the Netherlands or Finland, German and other European students more often follow English courses and do not follow courses in the local language. Figure 6 gives an overview on the countries targeted by study abroad programs of the University of Paderborn.

Credit transfer seems to be an important issue for all students independent from their national background. Only when credits from the host institution are recognized, the duration of their studies can be the same as if they had stayed in their home system. As has been outlined above, the *European Credit Transfer System* (ECTS) regulates credit transfer between European universities. So far, we miss such a system on an international basis. In the United States, we mainly find university-specific solutions for the organization of credit transfer. For example, Michigan State University has introduced an Academic Credit Transfer System (ACTS), which aims at facilitating credit transfer within the United States and with foreign partner universities. However, an internationally accepted credit transfer system including international standards would facilitate study abroad activities and would stimulate students to engage more in international programs.

The internationalization of faculty staff is an important issue in Europe as well as in America. However, the (timely) relationship between staff mobility and student mobility seems to be closer in American programs. In the United States, involvement of the home faculty members during the study abroad program is common. In contrast, in Europe international staff mobility may have a positive effect on consulting the students in the long run but it is not timely related to the student's stay abroad.

In conclusion, it can be said that there are important differences between German/European perspectives on study abroad. They mainly center around the period of time spent abroad and – an aspect which is related to this point – to the extent to which study abroad programs are integrated in the host country education system. In the following section we will discuss the effects of these differences on obtaining study abroad objectives in Europe and in the USA.

Country based analysis of study abroad activities of the University of Paderborn

The University of Paderborn has study abroad programs with 138 foreign universities, which are mainly located in Europe, the USA, Canada and East Asia. However, student exchange with Africa and South America is very limited. Table 2 gives an overview about the countries where business students from the University of Paderborn went to in the academic year 2000–01. It shows that 75% of the students have chosen to study in European countries while 25% get the chance to go to a university outside Europe. Study abroad programs outside Europe are very attractive to German students while places are limited. Consequently, competition for the places available is fierce.

Country	No. of Students	Country	No. of Students
Spain	29	Korea	3
United Kingdom	12	Ireland	3
France	9	Finnland	2
Sweden	8	Netherlands	2
USA	8	Greece	1
Canada	6	Japan	1
Australia	3	China	1

Table 2: Outgoing students from the University of Paderborn

Concerning the incoming students to Paderborn the result with respect to the countries of origin is different. While there is about the same number of students coming from European countries there is also an important proportion of students from Central and Eastern European countries such as Hungary, Poland, Bosnia, Kazakhstan, Russia, Slovenia and Latvia. Furthermore, there are also more students from East Asia.

Fig. 6. Country Based Analysis of Study Abroad Activities of the University of Paderborn.

EFFECTS OF THE DIFFERENT APPROACHES
ON STUDY ABROAD OBJECTIVES

A variety of study abroad objectives can be identified, which apply from a European as well as from an American perspective. Among the most important are the following:

* Personal growth;
* Development of intercultural skills;
* Development of language skills;
* Expansion of management knowledge;

The main difference in reaching these goals can be made when looking at the length of the stay abroad. While every stay abroad, even if it is only short-term, leads to more personal growth, to an improvement of the language skills and to an expansion of the management knowledge, a long-term stay may serve these objectives to a greater extent.

Furthermore, a long-term stay enables experiential learning to a greater extent, and this is one of the major preconditions to develop intercultural competence (Weber, Festing, Dowling & Schuler, 2001; Dowling, Schuler & Welch, 1999). From this discussion, it becomes clear that longer-term study abroad programs are better means to reach the objectives outlined above.

However, to motivate students to accept longer-term study abroad programs a variety of issues must be regulated and guaranteed. In Europe, study abroad – at least on an inner-European level – has experienced important growth due to the introduction of the *SOCRATES program*. Within the next section we will discuss, which facets of the European system may advance study abroad issues in America and which features of the American system may lead to a completion of the European or German approach.

LESSONS TO BE LEARNED FROM THE DIFFERENCES

At the beginning of this paper, we have outlined a trend toward globalization. As this is not a national phenomenon, the higher education institutions need to internationalize business education on a worldwide level in order to meet the requirements of the globalizing firms, the future employers of the business students.

To date, most large European companies expect a certain extent of international experience as well as the knowledge of at least one foreign language when recruiting their future managers. This seems to be more and more the case in American companies as well. While at this stage, the knowledge of foreign languages does not seem to be as essential to American companies as it is to European companies, international experience gained within the study abroad programs is considered as highly important in the U.S. as well. These different expectations of the future employers may represent one (demand-oriented) reason among others for the different approaches to study abroad in Europe and in the U.S. Others may, of course, include the very different geographical situation of Europe and the U.S.A. with an important difference in the number of national borders and different nationalities within the respective regions. In the following sections we will shortly discuss how European, American or even global study abroad practices can be extended.

Extending the European Perspective

As has been outlined above, in Germany study abroad at the undergraduate level is an exception. Thus, the German and maybe other European higher education institutions miss the opportunity to send students abroad in an early stage of their studies. If these programs existed this could lead to higher percentages of students acquiring international experience and initiate more students to participate in long-term study abroad programs later within their studies. Furthermore, exposure to a different business and educational environment could take place earlier within the career.

However, as the SOCRATES 2000 evaluation study has shown study abroad is costly. Thus, the trade-off between the (relatively) expensive short-term stays at a foreign university and long-term study abroad programs needs to be taken into account. Considering the contributions of short- and long-term programs to the attainment of the study abroad goals, an important shift in emphasis may be questionable as long as financial resources cannot be increased. Consequently, an important increase in short-term programs would require an increase in the financial resources attributed to study abroad by national governments or by the *European Union.*

Extending the Americans Perspective

While German/European study abroad programs lack short-term elements, American students do accept long-term study abroad programs only to a limited extent. One reason for this is that they do not want their studies to become longer due to a semester spent in a foreign country. To fully integrate the semester abroad, credit transfer between the home and the host institution needs to be organized.

Thus, the establishment of an international credit transfer system, which extends the borders of the *European Union* and is able to integrate experiences of individual American universities working with a university-specific credit transfer system, would be most helpful in encouraging American students to spend more time abroad. Furthermore, international or even global standards could facilitate student and credit transfer to a large extent on a worldwide basis.

In addition, an increase in language teaching in American schools as well as in management programs at higher education institutions could further motivate students to accept longer-term studies abroad. Integration into the respective local education system would be facilitated and the chances to develop intercultural competence would be enhanced. This aspect shows the importance of an integrative institutional perspective on the internationalization of our society in general and of business managers as a special case.

These short concluding remarks have made clear that the American and the European system can learn from each other in study abroad practices. Especially with respect to credit transfer, the wheel would not have to be invented again but the *European Credit Transfer System* could provide guidelines and experiences, which may in the long-run lead to an application not only in the United States but on a worldwide basis.

As has been stated at the beginning of this paper, globalization is a world-encompassing phenomenon. Consequently, study abroad programs, which are designed to meet the challenges of globalization in international business education, should allow to learn from best practices in other countries/regions. However, national differences due to historical traditions will never completely vanish.

REFERENCES

BMBF (2000). Das ERASMUS-Programm – Ergebnisse der Begleitforschung, Bonn, 1999.

Dowling, P. J., Welch, D. E., & Schuler, R. S. (1999). *International Human Resource Management. Managing People in a Multinational Context*. Cincinnati, OH.

EC (2000). ECTS – European Credit Transfer System, Brussels, 2000.

ESCP-EAP (2000). The ESCP-EAP *Master's in Management. Learn everywhere. Manage anywhere*. Paris, 2000.

Festing, M. (2002). The globalization process. An interdisciplinary perspective. Habilitation Thesis. Paderborn, Germany.

Gordon, J., Maiworm, F., & Teichler, U. (2000). Overall Summary and Recommendations, SOCRATES 2000 Evaluation Study.

Maiworm, F., & Teichler, U. (2000). ERASMUS and the Policies of Higher Education Institutions, SOCRATES 2000 Evaluation Study.

Weber, W., Festing, M., Dowling, P. J., & Schuler, R. S. (2001). *Internationales Personalmanagement* (2nd ed.). Wiesbaden, 2001.